PHILOSOPHY AND CIVILIZATION

John Dewey

PHILOSOPHY
AND
CIVILIZATION

CAPRICORN BOOKS

NEW YORK

INTRODUCTORY NOTE

I AM indebted to the editors of the *Philosophical Review*, the *Monist*, the *Psychological Review*, and the *Journal of Philosophy* for permission to reprint various essays included in this volume. I wish also to thank the officers of the Third International Congress of Philosophy for permission to use the essay which gives the volume its title. Special acknowledgments are due Longmans, Green & Co. the publishers, and Dr. Dickinson Miller the editor for their generosity in allowing me to use the essay on "The Practical Character of Reality" which appeared originally in the volume of essays in honor of William James; to Coward-McCann and Company, and Dr. Horace M. Kallen, publishers and editors respectively, for permission to reprint the essay on *Philosophies of Freedom* which appeared in the volume, *Freedom in the Modern World;* to publishers of *Psychologies of 1930,* Clark University Press, and Dr. Carl Murchison, editor, for permission to use the essay called *Experience and Conduct*. The final essay on *Science and Society* has not appeared in print before.

J. D.

CONTENTS

PHILOSOPHY AND CIVILIZATION

Philosophy and Civilization

VOLUMES have been written about each term of our theme.
What *is* civilization? philosophy? Yet time passes, and
ambiguities and complexities cannot be eliminated by
definition; we can only circumvent them by begging questions.
But as to one of the terms at least, namely, philosophy, we
shall frankly make what is begged explicit. A statement of the
relations of philosophy to civilization will, after all,
only expound, in some indirect manner, the view of philosophy to which one is already committed. Unless this fact is
faced, we shall not only beg the issue, but we shall deceive
ourselves into thinking that we are setting forth the conclusions of an original inquiry, undertaken and executed independently of our own philosophical conceptions.

As for myself, then, the discussion is approached with the
antecedent idea that philosophy, like politics, literature and
the plastic arts, is itself a phenomenon of human culture. Its
connection with social history, with civilization, is intrinsic.
There is current among those who philosophize the conviction
that, while past thinkers have reflected in their systems the
conditions and perplexities of their own day, present-day
philosophy in general, and one's own philosophy in particular,
is emancipated from the influence of that complex of institutions which forms culture. Bacon, Descartes, Kant each
thought with fervor that he was founding philosophy anew
because he was placing it securely upon an exclusive intellectual basis, exclusive, that is, of everything but intellect. The
movement of time has revealed the illusion; it exhibits as
the work of philosophy the old and ever new undertaking of
adjusting that body of traditions which constitute the actual
mind of man to scientific tendencies and political aspirations

which are novel and incompatible with received authorities. Philosophers are parts of history, caught in its movement; creators perhaps in some measure of its future, but also assuredly creatures of its past.

Those who assert in the abstract definition of philosophy that it deals with eternal truth or reality, untouched by local time and place, are forced to admit that philosophy as a concrete existence is historical, having temporal passage and a diversity of local habitations. Open your histories of philosophy, and you find written throughout them the same periods of time and the same geographical distributions which provide the intellectual scheme of histories of politics, industry or the fine arts. I cannot imagine a history of philosophy which did not partition its material between the occident and the orient; which did not find the former falling into ancient, medieval and modern epochs; which, in setting forth Greek thought, did not specify Asiatic and Italian colonies and Athens. On the other hand, those who express contempt for the enterprise of philosophy as a sterile and monotonous preoccupation with unsolvable or unreal problems, cannot, without convicting themselves of Philistinism, deny that, however it may stand with philosophy as a revelation of eternal truths, it is tremendously significant as a revelation of the predicaments, protests and aspirations of humanity.

The two views of the history of thought are usually proffered as irreconcilable opposites. According to one, it is the record of the most profound dealings of the reason with ultimate being; according to the other, it is a scene of pretentious claims and ridiculous failures. Nevertheless, there is a point of view from which there is something common to the two notions, and this common denominator is more significant than the oppositions. Meaning is wider in scope as well as more precious in value than is truth, and philosophy is occupied with meaning rather than with truth. Making such a statement is dangerous; it is easily misconceived to signify that truth is of no great importance under any circumstances; while the fact is that truth is so infinitely important when it is important at all, namely, in records of events and descriptions of existences, that we extend its claims to regions where it has no jurisdiction. But even as respects truths, meaning is the wider category; truths are but one class of meanings, namely, those in which a claim to verifiability by their consequences is an intrinsic part of their meaning. Beyond this island of meanings which in their own nature are true or false lies the ocean of meanings to which truth and falsity are irrelevant. We do not inquire whether Greek civilization was true or false, but we are immensely concerned to penetrate its meaning. We may indeed ask for the truth of Shakespeare's *Hamlet* or Shelley's *Skylark,* but by truth we now signify something quite different from that of scientific statement and historical record.

In philosophy we are dealing with something comparable to the meaning of Athenian civilization or of a drama or a lyric. Significant history is lived in the imagination of man, and philosophy is a further excursion of the imagination into its own prior achievements. All that is distinctive of man, marking him off from the clay he walks upon or the potatoes he eats, occurs in his thought and emotions, in what we have agreed to call consciousness. Knowledge of the structure of sticks and stones, an enterprise in which, of course, truth is essential, apart from whatever added control it may yield, marks in the end but an enrichment of consciousness, of the area of meanings. Thus scientific thought itself is finally but a function of the imagination in enriching life with the significance of things; it is of its peculiar essence that it must also submit to certain tests of application and control. Were significance identical with existence, were values the same as events, idealism would be the only possible philosophy.

[5]

It is commonplace that physically and existentially man can but make a superficial and transient scratch upon the outermost rind of the world. It has become a cheap intellectual pastime to contrast the infinitesimal pettiness of man with the vastnesses of the stellar universes. Yet all such comparisons are illicit. We cannot compare existence and meaning; they are disparate. The characteristic life of man is itself the meaning of vast stretches of existences, and without it the latter have no value or significance. There is no common measure of physical existence and conscious experience because the latter is the only measure there is for the former. The significance of being, though not its existence, is the emotion it stirs, the thought it sustains.

It follows that there is no specifiable difference between philosophy and its rôle in the history of civilization. Discover and define the right characteristic and unique function in civilization, and you have defined philosophy itself. To try to define philosophy in any other way is to search for a will-of-the-wisp; the conceptions which result are of purely private interpretation, for they only exemplify the particular philosophies of their authorship and interpretation. Take the history of philosophy from whatever angle and in whatever cross-section you please, Indian, Chinese, Athenian, the Europe of the twelfth or the twentieth century, and you find a load of traditions proceeding from an immemorial past. You find certain preoccupying interests that appear hypnotic in their rigid hold upon imagination and you also find certain resistances, certain dawning rebellions, struggles to escape and to express some fresh value of life. The preoccupations may be political and artistic as in Athens; they may be economic and scientific as today. But in any case, there is a certain intellectual work to be done; the dominant interest working throughout the minds of masses of men has to be clarified, a result which can be accomplished only by selection, elimination, reduction and formulation; the interest has to be intellectually forced, exaggerated in order to be focused. Otherwise it is not intellectually in consciousness, since all clear consciousness by its very nature marks a wrenching of something from its subordinate place to confer upon it a centrality which is existentially absurd. Where there is sufficient depth and range of meanings for consciousness to arise at all, there is a function of adjustment, of reconciliation of the ruling interest of the period with preoccupations which had a different origin and an irrelevant meaning. Consider, for example, the uneasy, restless effort of Plato to adapt his new mathematical insights and his political aspirations to the traditional habits of Athens; the almost humorously complacent union of Christian supernaturalism in the middle ages with the naturalism of pagan Greece; the still fermenting effort of the recent age to unite the new science of nature with inherited classic and medieval institutions. The life of all thought is to effect a junction at some point of the new and the old, of deep-sunk customs and unconscious dispositions, that are brought to the light of attention by some conflict with newly emerging directions of activity. Philosophies which emerge at distinctive periods define the larger patterns of continuity which are woven in effecting the enduring junctions of a stubborn past and an insistent future.

Philosophy thus sustains the closest connection with the history of culture, with the succession of changes in civilization. It is fed by the streams of tradition, traced at critical moments to their sources in order that the current may receive a new direction; it is fertilized by the ferment of new inventions in industry, new explorations of the globe, new discoveries in science. But philosophy is not just a passive reflex of civilization that persists through changes, and that changes while persisting. It is itself a change; the patterns formed in this junction of the new and the old are prophecies rather than

[7]

records; they are policies, attempts to forestall subsequent developments. The intellectual registrations which constitute a philosophy are generative just because they are selective and eliminative exaggerations. While purporting to say that such and such is and always *has* been the purport of the record of nature, in effect they proclaim that such and such *should* be the significant value to which mankind should loyally attach itself. Without evidence adduced in its behalf such a statement may seem groundless. But I invite you to examine for yourselves any philosophical idea which has had for any long period a significant career, and find therein your own evidence. Take, for example, the Platonic patterns of cosmic design and harmony; the Aristotelian perpetually recurrent ends and grooved potentialities; the Kantian fixed forms of intellectual synthesis; the conception of nature itself as it figured in seventeenth and eighteenth century thought. Discuss them as revelations of eternal truth, and something almost childlike or something beyond possibility of decision enters in; discuss them as selections from existing culture by means of which to articulate forces which the author believed should and would dominate the future, and they become preciously significant aspects of human history.

Thus philosophy marks a change of culture. In forming patterns to be conformed to in future thought and action, it is additive and transforming in its rôle in the history of civilization. Man states anything at his peril; once stated, it occupies a place in a new perspective; it attains a permanence which does not belong to its existence; it enters provokingly into wont and use; it points in a troubling way to need of new endeavors. I do not mean that the creative element in the rôle of philosophy is necessarily the dominant one; obviously its formulations have been often chiefly conservative, justificatory of selected elements of traditions and received institutions. But even these preservative systems have had a transforming if not exactly a creative effect; they have lent the factors which were selected a power over later human imagination and sentiment which they would otherwise have lacked. And there are other periods, such as those of the seventeenth and eighteenth centuries in Europe, when philosophy is overtly revolutionary in attitude. To their authors, the turn was just from complete error to complete truth; to later generations looking back, the alteration in strictly factual content does not compare with that in desire and direction of effort.

Of the many objections which may be brought against the conception that philosophy not only *has* a rôle, but that it *is* a specifiable rôle in the development of human culture, there are two misconceptions which I wish to touch upon. What has been said, taken without qualifying additions, might suggest a picture of a dominant system of philosophy at each historic period. In fact there are diverse currents and aspirations in almost every historic epoch; the divergence of philosophic systems instead of being a reproach (as of course it is from the standpoint of philosophy as a revelation of truth) is evidence of sincerity and vitality. If the ruling and the oppressed elements in a population, if those who wish to maintain the *status quo* and those concerned to make changes, had, when they became articulate, the same philosophy, one might well be skeptical of its intellectual integrity. The other point is much more important. In making a distinction between meaning and truth and asserting that the latter is but one type of meaning, important under definite conditions, I have expressed the idea as if there might be in the processes of human life meanings which are wholly cut off from the actual course of events. Such is not the intent; meanings are generated and in some degree sustained by existence. Hence they cannot be wholly irrelevant to the world of existence; they all have some revelatory office which should be apprehended as correctly as possible. This is true of politics, religion and art as well as of

[9]

philosophy. They all tell something of the realm of existence. But in all of them there is an exuberance and fertility of meanings and values in comparison with which correctness of telling is a secondary affair, while in the function termed science accuracy of telling is the chief matter.

In the historic rôle of philosophy, the scientific factor, the element of correctness, of verifiable applicability, has a place, but it is a negative one. The meanings delivered by confirmed observation, experimentation and calculation, scientific facts and principles, serve as tests of the values which tradition transmits and of those which emotion suggests. Whatever is not compatible with them must be eliminated in any sincere philosophizing. This fact confers upon scientific knowledge an incalculably important office in philosophy. But the criterion is negative; the exclusion of the inconsistent is far from being identical with a positive test which demands that only what has been scientifically verifiable shall provide the entire content of philosophy. It is the difference between an imagination that acknowledges its responsibility to meet the logical demands of ascertained facts, and a complete abdication of all imagination in behalf of a prosy literalism.

Finally, it results from what has been said that the presence and absence of native born philosophies is a severe test of the depth of unconscious tradition and rooted institutions among any people, and of the productive force of their culture. For sake of brevity, I may be allowed to take our own case, the case of civilization in the United States. Philosophy, we have been saying, is a conversion of such culture as exists into consciousness, into an imagination which is logically coherent and is not incompatible with what is factually known. But this conversion is itself a further movement of civilization; it is not something performed upon the body of habits and tendencies from without, that is, miraculously. If American civilization does not eventuate in an imaginative formulation of itself, if it merely rearranges the figures already named and placed—in playing an inherited European game—that fact is itself the measure of the culture which we have achieved. A deliberate striving for an American Philosophy as such would be only another evidence of the same emptiness and impotency. There is energy and activity, among us, enough and to spare. Not an inconsiderable part of the vigor that once went into industrial accomplishment now finds its way into science; our scientific "plant" is coming in its way to rival our industrial plants. Especially in psychology and the social sciences an amount of effort is putting forth which is hardly equaled in any one other part of the world. He would be a shameless braggart who claimed that the result is as yet adequate to the activity. What is the matter? It lies, I think, with our lack of imagination in generating leading ideas. Because we are afraid of speculative ideas, we do, and do over and over again, an immense amount of dead, specialized work in the region of "facts." We forget that such facts are only data; that is, are only fragmentary, uncompleted meanings, and unless they are rounded out into complete ideas—a work which can only be done by hypotheses, by a free imagination of intellectual possibilities—they are as helpless as are all maimed things and as repellent as are needlessly thwarted ones.

Please do not imagine that this is a plea in disguise for any particular type of philosophizing. On the contrary, any philosophy which is a sincere outgrowth and expression of our own civilization is better than none, provided it speaks the authentic idiom of an enduring and dominating corporate experience. If we are really, for instance, a materialistic people, we are at least materialistic in a new fashion and on a new scale. I should welcome then a consistent materialistic philosophy, if only it were sufficiently bold. For in the degree in which, despite attendant esthetic repulsiveness, it marked the coming to consciousness of a group of ideas, it would formulate a coming to self-consciousness of our civilization. Thereby it would furnish ideas, supply an intellectual polity, direct further observations and experiments, and organize their results on a grand scale. As long as we worship science and are afraid of philosophy we shall have no great science; we shall have a lagging and halting continuation of what is thought and said elsewhere. As far as any plea is implicit in what has been said, it is, then, a plea for the casting off of that intellectual timidity which hampers the wings of imagination, a plea for speculative audacity, for more faith in ideas, sloughing off a cowardly reliance upon those partial ideas to which we are wont to give the name of facts. I have given to philosophy a more humble function than that which is often assigned it. But modesty as to its final place is not incompatible with boldness in the maintenance of that function, humble as it may be. A combination of such modesty and courage affords the only way I know of in which the philosopher can look his fellowman in the face with frankness and with humanity.

The Development of American Pragmatism

THE purpose of this article is to define the principal theories of the philosophical movements known under the names of Pragmatism, Instrumentalism, or Experimentalism. To do this we must trace their historical development; for this method seems to present the simplest way of comprehending these movements, and at the same time avoiding certain current misunderstandings of their doctrines and their aims.

The origin of Pragmatism goes back to Charles Sanders Peirce, the son of one of the most celebrated mathematicians of the United States, and himself very proficient in the science of mathematics; he is one of the founders of the modern symbolic logic of relations. Unfortunately Peirce was not at all a systematic writer and never expounded his ideas in a single system. The pragmatic method which he developed applies only to a very narrow and limited universe of discourse. After William James had extended the scope of the method, Peirce wrote an exposition of the origin of pragmatism as he had first conceived it; it is from this exposition that we take the following passages.

The term "pragmatic," contrary to the opinion of those who regard pragmatism as an exclusively American conception, was suggested to him by the study of Kant. In the *Metaphysic of Morals* Kant established a distinction between *pragmatic* and *practical*. The latter term applies to moral laws which Kant regards as *a priori*, whereas the former term applies to the rules of art and technique which are based on experience and are applicable to experience. Peirce, who was an empiricist, with the habits of mind, as he put it, of the laboratory, consequently refused to call his system "practical-ism," as some of his friends suggested. As a logician he was interested in the art and technique of real thinking, and espe-cially interested, as far as pragmatic method is concerned, in the art of making concepts clear, or of construing adequate and effective definitions in accord with the spirit of scientific method.

Following his own words, for a person "who still thought in Kantian terms most readily, *"praktisch"* and *"pragmatisch"* were as far apart as the two poles; the former belonging in a region of thought where no mind of the experimental type can ever make sure of solid ground under his feet, the latter ex-pressing relation to some definite human purpose. Now quite the most striking feature of the new theory was its recognition of an inseparable connection between rational cognition and rational purpose." [1]

In alluding to the experimental type of mind, we are brought to the exact meaning given by Peirce to the word "pragmatic." In speaking of an experimentalist as a man whose intelligence is formed in the laboratory, he said: "Whatever assertion you may make to him, he will either understand as meaning that if a given prescription for an experiment ever can be and ever is carried out in act, an experience of a given description will result, or else he will see no sense at all in what you say." And thus Peirce developed the theory that "the rational purport of a word or other ex-pression, lies exclusively in its conceivable bearing upon the conduct of life; so that, since obviously nothing that might not result from experiment can have any direct bearing upon con-duct, if one can define accurately all the conceivable experi-mental phenomena which the affirmation or denial of a con-cept could imply, one will have therein a complete definition of the concept. [2]

[1] *Monist*, vol. 15, p. 163.   [2] *Ibid.*, p. 162.

The essay in which Peirce developed his theory bears the title: *How to Make Our Ideas Clear.* [1] There is a remarkable similarity here to Kant's doctrine. Peirce's effort was to interpret the universality of concepts in the domain of *experience* in the same way in which Kant established the law of practical reason in the domain of the *a priori.* "The rational meaning of every proposition lies in the future. . . . But of the myriads of forms into which a proposition may be translated, what is that one which is to be called its very meaning? It is, according to the pragmatist, that form in which the proposition becomes applicable to human conduct, not in these or those special circumstances, nor when one entertains this or that special design, but that form which is most directly applicable to self-control under every situation, and to every purpose." [2] So also, "the pragmatist does not make the *summum bonum* to consist in action, but makes it to consist in that process of evolution whereby the existent comes more and more to embody generals . . ." [3] — in other words — the process whereby the existent becomes, with the aid of action, a body of rational tendencies or of habits generalized as much as possible. These statements of Peirce are quite conclusive with respect to two errors which are commonly committed in regard to the ideas of the founder of pragmatism. It is often said of pragmatism that it makes action the end of life. It is also said of pragmatism that it subordinates thought and rational activity to particular ends of interest and profit. It is true that the theory according to Peirce's conception implies essentially a certain relation to action, to human conduct. But the rôle of action is that of an intermediary. In order to be able to attribute a meaning to concepts, one must be able to apply them to existence. Now it is by means of action that this application is made possible. And the modification of exist-

[1] *Popular Science Monthly*, 1878.
[2] *Monist*, vol. 15, pp. 173–4.   [3] *Ibid.*, p. 178.

ence which results from this application constitutes the true meaning of concepts. Pragmatism is, therefore, far from being that glorification of action for its own sake which is regarded as the peculiar characteristic of American life.

It is also to be noted that there is a scale of possible applications of concepts to existence, and hence a diversity of meanings. The greater the extension of the concepts, the more they are freed from the restrictions which limit them to particular cases, the more is it possible for us to attribute the greatest generality of meaning to a term. Thus the theory of Peirce is opposed to every restriction of the meaning of a concept to the achievement of a particular end, and still more to a personal aim. It is still more strongly opposed to the idea that reason or thought should be reduced to being a servant of any interest which is pecuniary or narrow. This theory was American in its origin in so far as it insisted on the necessity of human conduct and the fulfillment of some aim in order to clarify thought. But at the same time, it disapproves of those aspects of American life which make action an end in itself, and which conceive ends too narrowly and too "practically." In considering a system of philosophy in its relation to national factors it is necessary to keep in mind not only the aspects of life which are incorporated in the system, but also the aspects against which the system is a protest. There never was a philosopher who has merited the name for the simple reason that he glorified the tendencies and characteristics of his social environment; just as it is also true that there never has been a philosopher who has not seized upon certain aspects of the life of his time and idealized them.

The work commenced by Peirce was continued by William James. In one sense James narrowed the application of Peirce's pragmatic method, but at the same time he extended it. The articles which Peirce wrote in 1878 commanded almost no attention from philosophical circles, which were then under the dominating influence of the neo-kantian idealism of Green, of Caird, and of the Oxford School, excepting those circles in which the Scottish philosophy of common sense maintained its supremacy. In 1898 James inaugurated the new pragmatic movement in an address entitled, "Philosophical Conceptions and Practical Results," later reprinted in the volume, *Collected Essays and Reviews.* Even in this early study one can easily notice the presence of those two tendencies to restrict and at the same time to extend early pragmatism. After having quoted the psychological remark of Peirce that "beliefs are really rules for action, and the whole function of thinking is but one step in the production of habits of action," and that every idea which we frame for ourselves of an object is really an idea of the possible effects of that object, he expressed the opinion that all these principles could be expressed more broadly than Peirce expressed them. "The ultimate test for us of what a truth means is indeed the conduct it dictates or inspires. But it inspires that conduct because it first foretells some particular turn to our experience which shall call for just that conduct from us. And I should prefer to express Peirce's principle by saying that the effective meaning of any philosophic proposition can always be brought down to some particular consequence, in our future practical experience, whether active or passive; the point lying rather in the fact that the experience must be particular, than in the fact that it must be active." [1] In an essay written in 1908 James repeats this statement and states that whenever he employs the term "the practical," he means by it, "the distinctively concrete, the individual, the particular and effective as opposed to the abstract, general and inert—'Pragmata' are things in their plurality—particular consequences can perfectly well be of a theoretic nature." [2] [3]

[1] *Collected Essays and Reviews*, p. 412.   [2] *The Meaning of Truth*, pp. 209-210.
[3] In a footnote James gave an example of the errors which are committed in con-

William James alluded to the development which he gave to Peirce's expression of the principle. In one sense, one can say that he enlarged the bearing of the principle by the substitution of particular consequences for the general rule or method applicable to future experience. But in another sense this substitution limited the application of the principle, since it destroyed the importance attached by Peirce to the greatest possible application of the rule, or the habit of conduct—its extension to universality. That is to say, William James was much more of a nominalist than Peirce.

One can notice an extension of pragmatism in the above passage. James there alludes to the use of a method of determining the meaning of truth. Since truth is a term and has consequently a meaning, this extension is a legitimate application of pragmatic method. But it should be remarked that here this method serves only to make clear the meaning of the term "truth," and has nothing to do with the truth of a particular judgment. The principal reason which led James to give a new color to pragmatic method was that he was preoccupied with applying the method to determine the meaning of philosophical problems and questions, and that moreover, he chose to submit to examination philosophical notions of a theological or religious nature. He wished to establish a criterion which would enable one to determine whether a given philosophical question has an authentic and vital meaning or whether, on the contrary, it is trivial and purely verbal; and

---

nection with the term "Practical," quoting M. Bourdeau who had written that "Pragmatism is an Anglo Saxon reaction against the intellectualism and rationalism of the Latin mind. . . . It is a philosophy without words, a philosophy of gestures and of facts, which abandons what is general and holds only to what is particular." In his lecture at California, James brought out the idea that his pragmatism was inspired to a considerable extent by the thought of the British philosophers, Locke, Berkeley, Hume, Mill, Bain, and Shadworth Hodgson. But he contrasted this method with German transcendentalism, and particularly with that of Kant. It is especially interesting to notice this difference between Peirce and James: the former attempted to give an experimental, not an *a priori* interpretation of Kant, whereas James tried to develop the point of view of the British thinkers.

in the former case, what interests are at stake when one accepts and affirms one or the other of two theses in dispute. Peirce was above all a logician; whereas James was an educator and humanist and wished to force the general public to realize that certain problems, certain philosophical debates, have a real importance for mankind, because the beliefs which they bring into play lead to very different modes of conduct. If this important distinction is not grasped, it is impossible to understand the majority of the ambiguities and errors which belong to the later period of the pragmatic movement.

James took as an example the controversy between theism and materialism. It follows from this principle that if the course of the world is considered as completed, it is equally legitimate to assert that God or matter is its cause. Whether one way or the other, the facts are what they are, and it is they which determine whatever meaning is to be given to their cause. Consequently the name which we can give to this cause is entirely arbitrary. It is entirely different if we take the future into account. God then has the meaning of a power concerned with assuring the final triumph of ideal and spiritual values, and matter becomes a power indifferent to the triumph or defeat of these values. And our life takes a different direction according as we adopt one or the other of these alternatives. In the lectures on pragmatism published in 1907, he applies the same criticism to the philosophical problem of the One and the Many, that is to say of Monism and Pluralism, as well as to other questions. Thus he shows that Monism is equivalent to a rigid universe where everything is fixed and immutably united to others, where indetermination, free choice, novelty, and the unforeseen in experience have no place; a universe which demands the sacrifice of the concrete and complex diversity of things to the simplicity and nobility of an architectural structure. In what concerns our beliefs, Monism demands a rationalistic temperament leading to a

[19]

fixed and dogmatic attitude. Pluralism, on the other hand, leaves room for contingence, liberty, novelty, and gives complete liberty of action to the empirical method, which can be indefinitely extended. It accepts unity where it finds it, but it does not attempt to force the vast diversity of events and things into a single rational mold.

From the point of view of an educator or of a student or, if you will, of those who are thoroughly interested in these problems, in philosophical discussions and controversies, there is no reason for contesting the value of this application of pragmatic method, but it is no less important to determine the nature of this application. It affords a means of discovering the implications for human life of philosophical conceptions which are often treated as of no importance and of a purely dialectical nature. It furnishes a criterion for determining the vital implications of beliefs which present themselves as alternatives in any theory. Thus as he himself said, "the whole function of philosophy ought to be to find the characteristic influences which you and I would undergo at a determinate moment of our lives, if one or the other formula of the universe were true." However, in saying that the whole function of philosophy has this aim, it seems that he is referring rather to the teaching than to the construction of philosophy. For such a statement implies that the world formulas have already all been made, and that the necessary work of producing them has already been finished, so that there remains only to define the consequences which are reflected in life by the acceptance of one or the other of these formulas as true.

From the point of view of Peirce, the object of philosophy would be rather to give a fixed meaning to the universe by formulas which correspond to our attitudes or our most general habits of response to the environment; and this generality depends on the extension of the applicability of these formulas to specific future events. The *meaning* of concepts of "matter" and of "God" must be fixed before we can even attempt to reach an understanding concerning the *value* of our belief in these concepts. Materialism would signify that the world demands on our part a single kind of constant and general habits; and God would signify the demand for another type of habits; the difference between materialism and theism would be tantamount to the difference in the habits required to face all the detailed facts of the universe. The world would be one in so far as it would be possible for us to form a single habit of action which would take account of all future existences and would be applicable to them. It would be many in so far as it is necessary for us to form several habits, differing from each other and irreducible to each other, in order to be able to meet the events in the world and control them. In short, Peirce wrote as a logician and James as a humanist.

William James accomplished a new advance in Pragmatism by his theory of the will to believe, or as he himself later called it, the right to believe. The discovery of the fundamental consequences of one or another belief has without fail a certain influence on that belief itself. If a man cherishes novelty, risk, opportunity and a variegated esthetic reality, he will certainly reject any belief in Monism, when he clearly perceives the import of this system. But if, from the very start, he is attracted by esthetic harmony, classic proportions, fixity even to the extent of absolute security, and logical coherence, it is quite natural that he should put faith in Monism. Thus William James took into account those motives of instinctive sympathy which play a greater rôle in our choice of a philosophic system than do formal reasonings; and he thought that we should be rendering a service to the cause of philosophical sincerity if we would openly recognize the motives which inspire us. He also maintained the thesis that the greater part of philosophic problems and especially those which touch on

religious fields are of such a nature that they are not susceptible of decisive evidence one way or the other. Consequently
he claimed the right of a man to choose his beliefs not only in
the presence of proofs or conclusive facts, but also in the absence of all such proof. Above all when he is forced to choose
between one meaning or another, or when by refusing to
choose he has a right to assume the risks of faith, his refusal is
itself equivalent to a choice. The theory of the will to believe
gives rise to misunderstandings and even to ridicule; and
therefore it is necessary to understand clearly in what way
James used it. We are always obliged to act in any case; our
actions and with them their consequences actually change
according to the beliefs which we have chosen. Moreover it
may be that, in order to discover the proofs which will ultimately be the intellectual justification of certain beliefs—the
belief in freedom, for example, or the belief in God—it is
necessary to begin to act in accordance with this belief.

In his lectures on pragmatism, and in his volume of essays
bearing the title *The Meaning of Truth,* which appeared
in 1909, James extended the use of the pragmatic method to
the problem of the nature of truth. So far we have considered
the pragmatic method as an instrument in determining the
meaning of words and the vital importance of philosophic
beliefs. Now and then we have made allusion to the future
consequences which are implied. James showed, among other
things, that in certain philosophic conceptions, the affirmation
of certain beliefs could be justified by means of the nature of
their consequences, or by the differences which these beliefs
make in existence. But then why not push the argument to the
point of maintaining that the meaning of truth in general is
determined by its consequences? We must not forget here that
James was an empiricist before he was a pragmatist, and
repeatedly stated that pragmatism is merely empiricism
pushed to its legitimate conclusions. From a general point of

view, the pragmatic attitude consists in "looking away from first things, principles, 'categories,' supposed necessities; and of looking towards last things, fruits, consequences, facts." It is only one step further to apply the pragmatic method to the problem of truth. In the natural sciences there is a tendency to identify truth in any particular case with a verification. The verification of a theory, or of a concept, is carried on by the observation of particular facts. Even the most scientific and harmonious physical theory is merely an hypothesis until its implications, deduced by mathematical reasoning or by any other kind of inference, are verified by observed facts. What direction, therefore, must an empirical philosopher take who wishes to arrive at a definition of truth by means of an empirical method? He must, if he wants to apply this method, and without bringing in for the present the pragmatic formula, first find particular cases from which he then generalizes. It is therefore in submitting conceptions to the control of experience, in the process of verifying them, that one finds examples of what is called truth. Therefore any philosopher who applies this empirical method without the least prejudice in favor of pragmatic doctrine, can be led to conclude that truth "means" verification, or if one prefers, that verification, either actual or possible, is the definition of truth.

In combining this conception of empirical method with the theory of pragmatism, we come upon other important philosophical results. The classic theories of truth in terms of the coherence or compatibility of terms, and of the correspondence of an idea with a thing, hereby receive a new interpretation. A merely mental coherence without experimental verification does not enable us to get beyond the realm of hypothesis. If a notion or a theory makes pretense of corresponding to reality or to the facts, this pretense cannot be put to the test and confirmed or refuted except by causing it to pass over into the realm of action and by noting the results which it yields in the form of the concrete observable facts to which this notion or theory leads. If, in acting upon this notion, we are brought to the fact which it implies or which it demands, then this notion is true. A theory corresponds to the facts when it leads to the facts which are its consequences, by the intermediary of experience. And from this consideration the pragmatic generalization is drawn that all knowledge is prospective in its results, except in the case where notions and theories after having been first prospective in their application, have already been tried out and verified. Theoretically, however, even such verifications or truths could not be absolute. They would be based upon practical or moral certainty, but they are always subject to being corrected by unforeseen future consequences or by observed facts which had been disregarded. Every proposition concerning truths is really in the last analysis hypothetical and provisional, although a large number of these propositions have been so frequently verified without failure that we are justified in using them as if they were absolutely true. But, logically, absolute truth is an ideal which cannot be realized, at least not until all the facts have been registered, or as James says "bagged," and until it is no longer possible to make other observations and other experiences.

Pragmatism, thus, presents itself as an extension of historical empiricism, but with this fundamental difference, that it does not insist upon antecedent phenomena but upon consequent phenomena; not upon the precedents but upon the possibilities of action. And this change in point of view is almost revolutionary in its consequences. An empiricism which is content with repeating facts already past has no place for possibility and for liberty. It cannot find room for general conceptions or ideas, at least no more than to consider them as summaries or records. But when we take the point of view of pragmatism we see that general ideas have a very different rôle to play than that of reporting and registering past experiences. They are the bases for organizing future observations and experiences. Whereas, for empiricism, in a world already constructed and determined, reason or general thought has no other meaning than that of summing up particular cases, in a world where the future is not a mere word, where theories, general notions, rational ideas have consequences for action, reason necessarily has a constructive function. Nevertheless the conceptions of reasoning have only a secondary interest in comparison with the reality of facts, since they must be confronted with concrete observations.[1]

Pragmatism thus has a metaphysical implication. The doctrine of the value of consequences leads us to take the future into consideration. And this taking into consideration of the future takes us to the conception of a universe whose evolution is not finished, of a universe which is still, in James' term, "in the making," "in the process of becoming," of a universe up to a certain point still plastic.

Consequently reason, or thought, in its more general sense, has a real, though limited, function, a creative, constructive function. If we form general ideas and if we put them in action, consequences are produced which could not be produced otherwise. Under these conditions the world will be different from what it would have been if thought had not intervened. This consideration confirms the human and moral importance of thought and of its reflective operation in experience. It is therefore not true to say that James treated reason, thought, and knowledge with contempt, or that he regarded them as mere means of gaining personal or even social profits. For him reason has a creative function, limited because

[1] William James said in a happy metaphor, that they must be "cashed in," by producing specific consequences. This expression means that they must be able to lead to concrete facts. But for those who are not familiar with American idioms, James' formula was taken to mean that the consequences themselves of our rational conceptions must be narrowly limited by their pecuniary value. Thus Mr. Bertrand Russell wrote recently that pragmatism is merely a manifestation of American commercialism.

specific, which helps to make the world other than it would have been without it. It makes the world really more reasonable; it gives to it an intrinsic value. One will understand the philosophy of James better if one considers it in its totality as a revision of English empiricism, a revision which replaces the value of past experience, of what is already given, by the future, by that which is as yet mere possibility.

These considerations naturally bring us to the movement called instrumentalism. The survey which we have just made of James' philosophy shows that he regarded conceptions and theories purely as instruments which can serve to constitute future facts in a specific manner. But James devoted himself primarily to the moral aspects of this theory, to the support which it gave to "meliorism" and moral idealism, and to the consequences which followed from it concerning the sentimental value and the bearing of various philosophical systems, particularly to its destructive implications for monistic rationalism and for absolutism in all its forms. He never attempted to develop a complete theory of the forms or "structures" and of the logical operations which are founded on this conception. Instrumentalism is an attempt to establish a precise logical theory of concepts, of judgments and inferences in their various forms, by considering primarily how thought functions in the experimental determinations of future consequences. That is to say, it attempts to establish universally recognized distinctions and rules of logic by deriving them from the reconstructive or mediative function ascribed to reason. It aims to constitute a theory of the general forms of conception and reasoning, and not of this or that particular judgment or concept related to its own content, or to its particular implications.

As far as the historical antecedents of instrumentalism are concerned, two factors are particularly important, over and above this matter of experimental verification which we have already mentioned in connection with James. The first of these two factors is psychological, and the second is a critique of the theory of knowledge and of logic which has resulted from the theory proposed by neo-kantian idealism and expounded in the logical writings of such philosophers as Lotze, Bosanquet, and F. H. Bradley. As we have already said, neo-kantian influence was very marked in the United States during the last decade of the nineteenth century. I myself, and those who have collaborated with me in the exposition of instrumentalism, began by being neo-kantians, in the same way that Peirce's point of departure was kantianism and that of James was the empiricism of the British School.

The psychological tendencies which have exerted an influence on instrumentalism are of a biological rather than a physiological nature. They are, more or less, closely related to the important movement whose promoter in psychology has been Doctor John Watson and to which he has given the name of Behaviorism. Briefly, the point of departure of this theory is the conception of the brain as an organ for the co-ordination of sense stimuli (to which one should add modifications caused by habit, unconscious memory, or what are called today "conditioned reflexes") for the purpose of effecting appropriate motor responses. On the basis of the theory of organic evolution it is maintained that the analysis of intelligence and of its operations should be compatible with the order of known biological facts, concerning the intermediate position occupied by the central nervous system in making possible responses to the environment adequate to the needs of the living organism. It is particularly interesting to note that in the *Studies in Logical Theory* (1903), which was their first declaration, the instrumentalists recognized how much they owed to William James for having forged the instruments which they used, while at the same time, in the course of the studies, the authors constantly declared their belief in a close union of the "normative" principles of logic and the real processes of thought, in so far as these are determined by an objective or biological psychology and not by an introspective psychology of states of consciousness. But it is curious to note that the "instruments" to which allusion is made, are not the considerations which were of the greatest service to James. They precede his pragmatism and it is among some of the pages of his *Principles of Psychology* that one must look for them. This important work (1890) really developed two distinct theses.

The one is a re-interpretation of introspective psychology, in which James denies that sensations, images and ideas are discrete and in which he replaces them by a continuous stream which he calls "the stream of consciousness." This conception necessitates a consideration of relations as an immediate part of the field of consciousness, having the same status as qualities. And throughout his *Psychology* James gives a philosophical tinge to this conception by using it in criticizing the atomism of Locke and of Hume as well as the *a-priorism* of the synthesis of rational principles by Kant and his successors, among whom should be mentioned in England, Thomas Hill Green, who was then at the height of his influence.

The other aspect of his *Principles of Psychology* is of a biological nature. It shows itself in its full force in the criterion which James established for discovering the existence of mind. "The pursuance of future ends and the choice of means for their attainment are thus the mark and criterion of the presence of mentality in a phenomenon." [1] The force of this criterion is plainly shown in the chapter on Attention, and its relation to Interest considered as the force which controls it, and its teleological function of selection and integration; in the chapter on Discrimination and Comparison (Analysis and Abstraction), where he discusses the way in

[1] *Psychology,* vol. I, p. 8.

which ends to be attained and the means for attaining them evoke and control intellectual analysis; and in the chapter on Conception, where he shows that a general idea is a mode of signifying particular things and not merely an abstraction from particular cases or a super-empirical function,—that it is a teleological instrument. James then develops this idea in the chapter on reasoning where he says that "the only meaning of essence is teleological, and that classification and conception are purely teleological weapons of mind."

One might complete this brief enumeration by mentioning also the chapter of James' book in which he discusses the Nature of Necessary Truths and the Rôle of Experience, and affirms in opposition to Herbert Spencer, that many of our most important modes of perception and conception of the world of sensible objects are not the cumulative products of particular experience, but rather original biological sports, spontaneous variations, which are maintained because of their applicability to concrete experiences after once having been created. Number, space, time, resemblance and other important "categories" could have been brought into existence, he says, as a consequence of some particular cerebral instability, but they could by no means have been registered on the mind by outside influence. Many significant and useless concepts also arise in the same manner. But the fundamental categories have been cumulatively extended and reinforced because of their value when applied to concrete instances and things of experience. It is therefore not the origin of a concept, it is its application which becomes the criterion of its value; and here we have the whole of pragmatism in embryo. A phrase of James' very well summarizes its import: "the popular notion that 'Science' is forced on the mind *ab extra*, and that our interests have nothing to do with its constructions, is utterly absurd."

Given the point of view which we have just specified, and

the interest attaching to a logical theory of conception and judgment, and there results a theory of the following description. The adaptations made by inferior organisms, for example their effective and co-ordinated responses to stimuli, become teleological in man and therefore give occasion to thought. Reflection is an indirect response to the environment, and the element of indirection can itself become great and very complicated. But it has its origin in biological adaptive behavior and the ultimate function of its cognitive aspect is a prospective control of the conditions of the environment. The function of intelligence is therefore not that of copying the objects of the environment, but rather of taking account of the way in which more effective and more profitable relations with these objects may be established in the future.

How this point of view has been applied to the theory of judgment is too long a story to be told here. We shall confine ourselves here to saying that, in general, the "subject" of a judgment represents that portion of the environment to which a reaction must be made; the predicate represents the possible response or habit or manner in which one should behave towards the environment; the copula represents the organic and concrete act by which the connection is made between the fact and its signification; and finally the conclusion, or the definitive object of judgment, is simply the original situation transformed, a situation which implies a change as well in the original subject (including its mind) as in the environment itself. The new and harmonious unity thus attained verifies the bearing of the data which were at first chosen to serve as subject and of the concepts introduced into the situation during the process as teleological instruments for its elaboration. Until this final unification is attained the perceptual data and the conceptual principles, theories, are merely hypotheses from a logical point of view. Moreover, affirmation and negation are intrinsically a-logical: they are acts.

Such a summary survey can hardly pretend to be either convincing or suggestive. However, in noting the points of resemblance and difference between this phase of pragmatism and the logic of neo-hegelian idealism, we are bringing out a point of great importance. According to the latter logic, thought constitutes in the last analysis its object and even the universe. It is necessary to affirm the existence of a series of forms of judgment, because our first judgments, which are nearest to sense, succeed in constituting objects in only a partial and fragmentary fashion, even to the extent of involving in their nature an element of contradiction. There results a dialectic which permits each inferior and partial type of judgment to pass into a more complete form until we finally arrive at the total judgment, where the thought which comprehends the entire object or the universe is an organic whole of interrelated mental distinctions. It is evident that this theory magnifies the rôle of thought beyond all proportion. It is an objective and rational idealism which is opposed to and distinct from the subjective and perceptual idealism of Berkeley's school. Instrumentalism, however, assigns a positive function to thought, that of *re*constituting the present stage of things instead of merely knowing it. As a consequence, there cannot be intrinsic degrees, or a hierarchy of forms of judgment. Each type has its own end, and its validity is entirely determined by its efficacy in the pursuit of its end. A limited perceptual judgment, adapted to the situation which has given it birth, is as true in its place as is the most complete and significant philosophic or scientific judgment. Logic, therefore, leads to a realistic metaphysics in so far as it accepts things and events for what they are independently of thought, and to an idealistic metaphysics in so far as it contends that thought gives birth to distinctive acts which modify future facts and events in such a way as to render them more reasonable, that is to say, more adequate to the ends which we propose for ourselves. This ideal element is more and more accentuated by the inclusion progressively of social factors in human environment over and above natural factors; so that the needs which are fulfilled, the ends which are attained are no longer of a merely biological or particular character, but include also the ends and activities of other members of society.

It is natural that continental thinkers should be interested in American philosophy as it reflects, in a certain sense, American life. Thus it should be clear after this rapid survey of the history of pragmatism that American thought continues European thought. We have imported our language, our laws, our institutions, our morals, and our religion from Europe, and we have adapted them to the new conditions of our life. The same is true of our ideas. For long years our philosophical thought was merely an echo of European thought. The pragmatic movement which we have traced in the present essay, as well as neo-realism, behaviorism, the absolute idealism of Royce, the naturalistic idealism of Santayana, are all attempts at re-adaptation; but they are not creations *de novo*. They have their roots in British and European thought. Since these systems are re-adaptations they take into consideration the distinctive traits of the environment of American life. But as has already been said, they are not limited to reproducing what is worn and imperfect in this environment. They do not aim to glorify the energy and the love of action which the new conditions of American life exaggerated. They do not reflect the excessive mercantilism of American life. Without doubt all these traits of the environment have not been without a certain influence on American philosophical thought; our philosophy would not be national or spontaneous if it were not subject to this influence. But the fundamental idea which the movements of which we have just spoken have attempted to express, is the idea that action and opportunity justify themselves only to the degree in which they render life more reasonable and increase its value. Instrumentalism maintains in opposition to many contrary tendencies in the American environment, that action should be intelligent and reflective, and that thought should occupy a central position in life. That is the reason for our insistence on the teleological phase of thought and knowledge. If it must be teleological in particular and not merely true in the abstract, that is probably due to the practical element which is found in all the phases of American life. However that may be, what we insist upon above all else is that intelligence be regarded as the only source and sole guarantee of a desirable and happy future. It is beyond doubt that the progressive and unstable character of American life and civilization has facilitated the birth of a philosophy which regards the world as being in continuous formation, where there is still place for indeterminism, for the new, and for a real future. But this idea is not exclusively American, although the conditions of American life have aided this idea in becoming self-conscious. It is also true that Americans tend to underestimate the value of tradition and of rationality considered as an achievement of the past. But the world has also given proof of irrationality in the past and this irrationality is incorporated in our beliefs and our institutions. There are bad traditions as there are good ones: it is always important to distinguish. Our neglect of the traditions of the past, with whatever this negligence implies in the way of spiritual impoverishment of our life, has its compensation in the idea that the world is recommencing and being remade under our eyes. The future as well as the past can be a source of interest and consolation and give meaning to the present. Pragmatism and instrumental experimentalism bring into prominence the importance of the individual. It is he who is the carrier of creative thought, the author of action, and of its application. Subjectivism is an old story in philosophy; a story which began in Europe and not in America. But American philosophy, in the systems which we have expounded, has given to the subject, to the individual mind, a practical rather than an epistemological function. The individual mind is important because only the individual mind is the organ of modifications in traditions and institutions, the vehicle of experimental creation. One-sided and egoistic individualism in American life has left its imprint on our practices. For better or for worse, depending on the point of view, it has transformed the esthetic and fixed individualism of the old European culture into an active individualism. But the idea of a society of individuals is not foreign to American thought; it penetrates even our current individualism which is unreflective and brutal. And the individual which American thought idealizes is not an individual *per se,* an individual fixed in isolation and set up for himself, but an individual who evolves and develops in a natural and human environment, an individual who can be educated.

If I were asked to give an historical parallel to this movement in American thought I would remind my reader of the French philosophy of the enlightenment. Every one knows that the thinkers who made that movement illustrious were inspired by Bacon, Locke, and Newton; what interested them was the application of scientific method and the conclusions of an experimental theory of knowledge to human affairs, the critique and reconstruction of beliefs and institutions. As Höffding writes, they were animated "by a fervent faith in intelligence, progress, and humanity." And certainly they are not accused to-day, just because of their educational and social significance, of having sought to subordinate intelligence and science to ordinary utilitarian aims. They merely sought to free intelligence from its impurities and to render it sovereign. One can scarcely say that those who glorify intelligence and reason in the abstract, because of their value for those who find personal satisfaction in their possession, estimate intelligence more truly than those who wish to make it the indispensable guide of intellectual and social life. When an American critic says of instrumentalism that it regards ideas as mere servants which make for success in life, he only reacts, without reflection, to the ordinary verbal associations of the word "instrumental," as many others have reacted in the same manner to the use of the word "practical." Similarly a recent Italian writer, after having said that pragmatism and instrumentalism are characteristic products of American thought, adds that these systems "regard intelligence as a mere mechanism of belief, and consequently attempt to re-establish the dignity of reason by making of it a machine for the production of beliefs useful to morals and society." This criticism does not hold. It is by no means the production of beliefs useful to morals and society which these systems pursue. It is the formation of a faith in intelligence, as the one and indispensable belief necessary to moral and social life. The more one appreciates the intrinsic esthetic, immediate value of thought and of science, the more one takes into account what intelligence itself adds to the joy and dignity of life, the more one should feel grieved at a situation in which the exercise and joy of reason are limited to a narrow, closed and technical social group and the more one should ask how it is possible to make all men participators in this inestimable wealth.

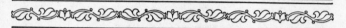

The Practical Character of Reality

I

RECENTLY I have had an experience which, insignificant in itself, seems to mean something as an index-figure of the present philosophic situation. In a criticism of the neokantian conception that *a priori* functions of thought are necessary to constitute knowledge, it became relevant to deny its underlying postulates: viz., the existence of anything properly called mental states or subjective impressions precedent to all objective recognitions, and which accordingly needed some transcendental function to order them into a world of stable and consistent reference. It was argued that such so-called original mental data are in truth turning points of the readjustment, or making over, through a state of incompatibility and shock, of objective affairs. This doctrine was met by the cry of "Subjectivism!" It had seemed to its author to be a criticism, on ground at once naturalistic and ethical, of the ground proposition of subjectivism. Why this diversity of interpretations? So far as the writer can judge, it is due to the fact that certain things characteristic of practical life, such things as lack and need, conflict and clash, desire and effort, loss and satisfaction, had been frankly referred to reality; and to the further fact that the function and structure of knowing had been systematically connected with these practical features. These conceptions are doubtless radical enough; the latter was perhaps more or less revolutionary. The probability, the antecedent probability, was that hostile critics would have easy work in pointing out specific errors of fact and interpretation. But no: the simpler, the more effective method, was to dismiss the whole thing as anarchic subjectivism.

[36]

This was and remains food for thought. I have been able to find but one explanation: In current philosophy, everything of a practical nature is regarded as "merely" personal, and the "merely" has the force of denying legitimate standing in the court of cosmic jurisdiction. This conception seems to me the great and the ignored assumption in contemporary philosophy; many who might shrink from the doctrine were it expressly formulated hang desperately to its implications. Yet as an underlying assumption, it is surely sheer prejudice, a culture-survival. If we suppose the traditions of philosophic discussion wiped out and philosophy starting afresh from the most active tendencies of to-day,—those striving in social life, in science, in literature, and art,—one can hardly imagine any philosophic view springing up and gaining credence, which did not give large place, in its scheme of things, to the practical and personal, and to them without employing disparaging terms, such as phenomenal, merely subjective, and so on. Why, putting it mildly, should what gives tragedy, comedy, and poignancy to life, be excluded from things? Doubtless, what we call life, what we take to be genuinely vital, is not all of things. But it is a part of things; and is that part which counts most with the philosopher—unless he has quite parted with his ancient dignity of lover of wisdom. What becomes of philosophy as far as humane and liberal interests are concerned, if, in an age when the person and the personal loom large in politics, industry, religion, art, and science is led by the idea of evolution to introduce into the nalism, whenever the personal comes into view? When science is led by the idea of evolution to introduce into the world the principles of initiative, variation, struggle, and selection; and when social forces have driven into bankruptcy absolutistic and static dogmas as authorities for the conduct of life, it is trifling for philosophy to decline to look the situation in the face. The relegation, as matter of course, of need, of stress and strain, strife and satisfaction, to the merely personal and the merely personal to the limbo of something which is neither flesh, fowl, nor good red herring, seems the thoughtless rehearsal of ancestral prejudice.

When we get beyond the echoing of tradition, the sticking point seems to be the relation of knowledge to the practical function of things. Let reality be in itself as "practical" as you please, but let not this practical character lay profane hands on the ark of truth! Every new mode of interpreting life—every new gospel—is met with the charge of antinomianism. Imagination when bound by custom apprehends the restrictions that are relaxed and the checks that are removed, but not the inevitable responsibilities and tests that the new idea brings in. And so the conception that knowledge makes a difference in and to things looks licentious to those who fail to see that the necessity of doing this business well, of making the *right* difference, puts intelligence under bonds it never yet has known: most of all in philosophy, the most gayly irresponsible of the procedures, and the most irresponsively sullen, of the historic fruits of intelligence.

Why should the idea that knowledge makes a difference to and in things be antecedently objectionable? If one is already committed to a belief that Reality is neatly and finally tied up in a packet without loose ends, unfinished issues or new departures, one would object to knowledge making a difference just as one would object to any other impertinent obtruder. But if one believes that the world itself is in transformation, why should the notion that knowledge is the most important mode of its modification and the only organ of its guidance be *a priori* obnoxious?

There is, I think, no answer save that the theory of knowledge has been systematically built up on the notion of a static universe, so that even those perfectly free to feel the lessons of physics and biology concerning moving energy and evolution, and of history concerning the constant transformation of man's affairs (science included), retain an unquestioning belief in a theory of knowledge which is out of any possible harmony with their own theory of the matters to be known. Modern epistemology, having created the idea that the way to frame right conceptions is to analyze knowledge, has strengthened this view. For it at once leads to the view that realities must themselves have a theoretic and intellectual complexion—not a practical one. This view is naturally congenial to idealists; but that realists should so readily play into the hands of idealists by asserting what, on the basis of a formal theory of knowledge, realities must be, instead of accepting the guidance of things in divining what knowledge *is,* is an anomaly so striking as to support the view that the notion of static reality has taken its last stand in ideas about knowledge. Take, for example, the most striking, because the extreme case—knowledge of a past event. It is absurd to suppose that knowledge makes a difference to the final or appropriate content of knowledge: to the subject-matter which fulfils the requirements of knowing. In this case, it would get in its own way and trip itself up in endless regress. But it seems the very superstition of intellectualism to suppose that this fact about knowledge can decide what is the nature of that reference to the past which, when rightly made, is final. No doctrine about knowledge can hinder the belief—if there be sufficient specific evidence for it—that what we know as past may be something which has *irretrievably* undergone just the difference which knowledge makes.

Now arguments against pragmatism—by which I mean the doctrine that reality possesses practical character and that this character is most efficaciously expressed in the function of intelligence [1]—seem to fall blandly into this fallacy. They assume that to hold that knowledge makes a difference in existences is equivalent to holding that it makes a difference in the object *to be* known, thus defeating its own purpose; witless that the reality which is the appropriate object of knowledge in a given case may be precisely a reality in which knowing has succeeded in making the needed difference. This question is not one to be settled by manipulation of the concept of knowledge, nor by dialectic discussion of its essence or nature. It is a question of facts, a question of what knowing exists as in the scheme of existence. If things undergo change without thereby ceasing to be real, there can be no *formal* bar to knowing being one specific kind of change in things, nor to its test being found in the successful carrying into effect of the kind of change intended. If knowing be a change in a reality, then the more knowing reveals this change, the more transparent, the more adequate, it is. And if all existences are in transition, then the knowledge which treats them as if they were something of which knowledge is a kodak fixation is just the kind of knowledge which refracts and perverts them. And by the same token a knowing which actively participates in a change in the way to effect it in the needed fashion would be the type of knowing which is valid. If reality be itself in transition—and this doctrine originated not with the objectionable pragmatist but with the physicist and naturalist and historian—then the doctrine that knowledge *is* reality making a particular and specified sort of change in itself seems to have the best chance at maintaining a theory of knowing which is in wholesome touch with the genuine and valid.

[1] This definition, in the present state of discussion, is an arbitrary or personal one. The text does not mean that "pragmatism" is currently used exclusively in this sense; obviously there are other senses. It does not mean it is the sense in which it *ought* to be used. I have no wish to legislate either for language or for philosophy. But it marks the sense in which *is* is used in this paper; and the pragmatic movement is still so loose and variable that I judge one has a right to fix his own meaning, provided he serves notice and adheres to it.

II

If the ground be cleared of *a priori* objections, and if it be evident that pragmatism cannot be disposed of by any formal or dialectic manipulations of "knowledge" or "truth," but only by showing that some specific things are not of the sort claimed, we may consider some common sense affiliations of pragmatism. Common sense regards intelligence as having a purpose, and knowledge as amounting to something. I once heard a physicist, quite innocent of the pragmatic controversy, remark that the knowledge of a mechanic or farmer was what the Yankee calls gumption—acknowledgment of things in their belongings and uses, and that to his mind natural science was gumption on a larger scale: the convenient cataloguing and arranging of a whole lot of things with reference to their most efficacious services. Popularly, good judgment is judgment as to the relative values of things: good sense is horse sense, ability to take hold of things right end up, to fit an instrument to an obstacle, to select resources apt for a task. To be reasonable is to recognize things in their office as obstacles and as resources. Intelligence, in its ordinary use, is a practical term; ability to size up matters with respect to the needs and possibilities of the various situations in which one is called to do something; capacity to envisage things in terms of the adjustments and adaptations they make possible or hinder. One objective test of the presence or absence of intelligence is influence upon behavior. No capacity to make adjustments means no intelligence; conduct evincing management of complex and novel conditions means a high degree of reason. Such conditions at least suggest that a reality-to-be-known, a reality which is the appropriate subject-matter of knowledge is reality-of-use-and-in-use, direct or indirect, and that a reality which is not in any sort of use, or bearing upon use, may go hang, *so far as knowledge is concerned.*

No one, I suppose, would deny that knowledge *issues* in some action which changes things to some extent—be the action only a more deliberate maintenance of a course of conduct already instinctively entered upon. When I see a sign on the street corner I can turn or go on, knowing what I am about. The perceptions of the scientist need have no such overt or "utilitarian" uses, but surely after them he behaves differently, as an inquirer if in no other way; and the cumulative effect of such changes finally modifies the overt action of the ordinary man. That knowing, *after the event,* makes a difference of this sort, few I suppose would deny: if that were all pragmatism means, it would perhaps be accepted as a harmless truism. But there is a further question of fact: just how is the "consequent" action related to the "precedent" knowledge? When *is* "after the event"? What degree of continuity exists? Is the difference between knowing and acting intelligently one of kind or simply one of dominant quality? How does a thing, if it is not already in change in the knowing, manage to issue at its term in action? Moreover, do not the changes actively effected constitute the whole *import* of the knowledge, and hence its final measure and test of validity? If it merely *happens* that knowing when it is done with passes into some action, by what miracle is the subsequent action so pat to the situation? Is it not rather true that the "knowledge" is instituted and framed in anticipation of the consequent issue, and, in the degree in which it is wise and prudent, is held open to revision during it? Certainly the moralist (one might quote, for example, Goethe, Carlyle, and Mazzini) and the common man often agree that full knowledge, adequate assurance of reality is found only in the issue which fulfills ideas; that we have to do a doctrine to *know* its truth; otherwise it is only dogma or doctrinaire program. Experimental science is a recognition that no idea is entitled to be termed knowledge till it has passed into such overt manipulation of physical conditions as constructs the object to which the idea refers. If one could get rid of one's traditional logical theories and set to work afresh to frame a theory of knowledge on the basis of the procedure of the common man, the moralist, and the experimentalist, would it be the forced or the natural procedure to say that the realities which we *know,* which we are sure of, are precisely those realities that have taken shape in and through the active procedures of knowing?

I turn to another type of consideration. Certainly one of the most genuine problems of modern life is the reconciliation of the scientific view of the universe with the claims of the moral life. Are judgments in terms of the redistribution of matter in motion (or some other closed formula) alone valid? Or are accounts of the universe in terms of possibility and desirability, of initiative and responsibility, also valid? There is no occasion to expatiate on the importance of the moral life, nor upon the supreme importance of intelligence within the moral life. But there does seem to be occasion for asking how moral judgments—judgments of the would and should—relate themselves to the world of scientific knowledge. To frame a theory of knowledge which makes it necessary to deny the validity of moral ideas, or else to refer them to some other and separate kind of universe from that of common sense and science, is both provincial and arbitrary. The pragmatist has at least tried to face, and not to dodge, the question of how it is that moral and scientific "knowledge" can both hold of one and the same world. And whatever the difficulties in his proffered solution, the conception that scientific judgments are to be assimilated to moral is closer to common sense than is the theory that validity is to be denied to moral judgments because they do not square with a preconceived theory of the nature of the world to which scientific judgments must refer. And all moral judgments are about changes to be made.

III

I turn to one affiliation of the pragmatic theory with the results of recent science. The necessity, for the occurrence of an event in the way of knowledge, of an organism which reacts or behaves in a specific way, would seem to be as well established as any specific proposition. It is a peculiar fact, a fact fit to stir curiosity, that the rational function seems to be intercalated in a scheme of practical adjustments. The parts and members of the organism are certainly not there primarily for pure intellection or for theoretic contemplation. The brain, the last physical organ of thought, is a part of the same practical machinery for bringing about adaptation of the environment to the life requirements of the organism, to which belong legs and hand and eye. That the brain frees organic behavior from complete servitude to immediate physical conditions, that it makes possible the liberation of energy for remote and ever expanding ends is, indeed, a precious fact, but not one which removes the brain from the category of organic devices of behavior.[1] That the organ of thinking, of knowledge, was at least originally an organ of conduct, few, I imagine, will deny. And even if we try to believe that the cognitive function has supervened as a different operation, it is difficult to believe that the transfiguration has been so radical that knowing has lost all traces of its connection with vital impulse. But unless we so assume, have we any alternatives except to hold that this continual presence of vital impulse is a disturbing and refracting factor, which forever prevents knowledge from reaching its own aim; or else that a certain promoting, a certain carrying forward of the

---

[1] It is interesting to note how the metaphysical puzzles regarding "parallelism," "interaction," "automatism," the relation of "consciousness" to "body," evaporate when one ceases isolating the brain into a peculiar physical substrate of mind at large, and treats it simply as one portion of the body which is the instrumentality of adaptive behavior.

vital impulse, importing certain differences in things, *is* the aim of knowledge?

The problem cannot be evaded—save ostrich wise—by saying that such considerations are "merely genetic," or "psychological," having to do only with the origin and natural history of knowing. For the point is that the organic reaction, the behavior of the organism, affects the *content* of awareness. The subject-matter of all awareness is thing-related-to-organism—related as stimulus direct or indirect or as material of response, present or remote, ulterior or achieved.

No one—so far as I know—denies this with respect to the perceptual field of awareness. Pains, pleasures, hunger, and thirst, all "secondary" qualities, involve inextricably the "interaction" of organism and environment. The perceptual field is distributed and arranged as the possible field of selective reactions of the organism at its center. Up and down, far and near, before and behind, right and left, hard and soft (as well as white and black, bass and alto), involve reference to a center of behavior.

This material has so long been the stock in trade of both idealistic arguments and proclamations of the agnostic "relativity" of knowledge that philosophers have grown aweary of listening. But even this lethargy might be quickened by a moderate hospitality to the pragmatic interpretation. That red, or far and near, or hard and soft, or big and little, involves a relation between organism and environment, is no more an argument for idealism than is the fact that water involves a relation between hydrogen and oxygen.[1] It is, however, an argument for the ultimately practical value of these distinctions—that they are *differences* made in what things would have been without organic behavior—differences made not by "consciousness" or "mind," but by the organism as the active center of a system of activities. Moreover, the whole agnostic

[1] I owe this illustration to my colleague, Dr. Montague.

sting of the doctrine of "relativity" lies in the assumption that the ideal or aim of knowledge is to repeat or copy a prior existence—in which case, of course, the making of contemporaneous differences by the organism in the very fact of awareness would get in the way and forever hinder the knowledge function from the fulfillment of its proper end. Knowledge, awareness, in this case suffers from an impediment which no surgery can better. But if the aim of knowing be precisely to make *certain* differences in an environment, to carry on to *favorable issue,* by the readjustment of the organism, certain changes going on indifferently in the environment, then the fact that the changes of the organism enter pervasively into the subject-matter of awareness is no restriction or perversion of knowledge, but part of the fulfillment of its office.

The only question would then be whether *proper* reactions take place. The whole agnostic, positivistic controversy is flanked by a single move. The issue is no longer an ideally necessary but actually impossible copying, *versus* an improper but unavoidable modification of reality through organic inhibitions and stimulations: but it is the right, the economical, the effective, and, if one may venture, the useful and satisfactory reaction *versus* the wasteful, the enslaving, the misleading, and the confusing reaction. The presence of organic responses, influencing and modifying every content, every subject-matter of awareness, is the undoubted fact. But the significant thing is the *way* organic behavior enters in— the *way* it influences and modifies. We assign very different values to different types of "knowledge,"—or subject-matters involving organic attitudes and operations. Some are only guesses, opinions, suspicious characters; others are "knowledge" in the honorific and eulogistic sense—science; some turn out mistakes, blunders, errors. Whence and how this discrimination of quality in what is taken at its own time to be good knowledge? Why and how is the content of some "knowledge" genuine-knowing and of other mis-knowing? Awareness is itself a blanket term, covering, in the same bed, delusion, doubt, confusion, ambiguity, and definition, organization, logical conclusiveness assured by evidence and reason. Any naturalistic or realistic theory is committed to the idea that all of these terms bear impartially the same relation to things considered as sheer existence. What we must have in any case is the same existences—the same in kind—only differently arranged or linked up. But why then the tremendous difference in value? And if the un-naturalist, the non-realist, says the difference is one of existential kind, made by the working here malign, there benign, of "consciousness," "psychical" operations and states, upon the existences which are the direct subject-matter of knowledge, there is still the problem of discriminating the conditions and nature of the respective beneficent and malicious interventions of the peculiar "existence" labeled consciousness.[1] The realness of error, ambiguity, doubt and guess poses a problem. It is a problem which has perplexed philosophy so long and has led to so many speculative adventures, that it would seem worth while, were it only for the sake of variety, to listen to the pragmatic solution according to which it is the business of the organic adaptation involved in all knowing to make a *certain* difference in reality, but *not* to make any old or casual difference. The right, the true and good, difference is that which carries out satisfactorily the specific purpose for the sake of which knowing occurs. All manufactures are the product of an activity, but it does not follow that all manufactures are equally good. And so all "knowledges" are differences made in things by knowing, but some differences are not calculated or wanted in the

[1] Of course on the theory I am interested in expounding, the so-called action of "consciousness" means simply the organic releases in the way of behavior which are the conditions of awareness, and which also modify its content.

knowing, and hence are disturbers and interlopers when they come—while others fulfill the intent of the knowing, being in harmony with the consistent behavior of the organism and re-inforcing and enlarging its function. A mistake is literally a mishandling; a doubt is a temporary suspense and vacillation of reactions; an ambiguity is the tension of alternative but incompatible mode of responsive treatment; an inquiry is a tentative and retrievable (because intra-organic) mode of activity, entered upon prior to launching upon a knowledge which is public, ineluctable—without anchors to windward— since it has taken physical effect through overt action.

It is practically all one to say that the norm of honorable knowing is to make no difference in *its* object, and that its aim is to attain and buttress a specific kind of difference in reality. Knowing fails in its business if it makes a change in its *own* object—that is a mistake; but its own object is none the less a prior existence changed in a certain way. Nor is this a play upon the two senses—end and subject-matter—of "object." The organism has its appropriate functions. To maintain, to expand, adequate functioning is its business. This functioning does not occur *in vacuo*. It involves co-operative and readjusted changes in the cosmic medium. Hence the appropriate subject-matter of awareness is not reality at large, a metaphysical heaven to be mimeographed at many removes upon a badly constructed mental carbon paper which yields at best only fragmentary, blurred, and erroneous copies. Its proper and legitimate object is that relationship of organism and environment in which functioning is most amply and effectively attained; or by which, in case of obstruction and consequent needed experimentation, its later eventual free course is most facilitated. As for the other reality, metaphysical reality *at large,* it may, so far as awareness is concerned, go to its own place.

For ordinary purposes, that is for practical purposes, the

truth and the realness of things are synonymous. We are all children who say "really and truly." A reality which is taken in organic response so as to lead to subsequent reactions that are off the track and aside from the mark, while it is, existentially speaking, perfectly real, is not *good* reality. It lacks the hallmark of value. Since it is a certain *kind* of object which we want, one which will be as favorable as possible to a consistent and liberal or growing functioning, it is this kind, the *true* kind, which for us monopolizes the title of reality. Pragmatically, teleologically, this identification of truth and "reality" is sound and reasonable: rationalistically, it leads to the notion of the duplicate versions of reality, one absolute and static because exhausted; the other phenomenal and kept continually on the jump because otherwise its own inherent nothingness would lead to its total annihilation. Since it is only genuine or sincere things, things which are good for what they lay claim to in the way of consequences, which we want or are after, *morally* they alone are "real."

IV

So far we have been dealing with awareness as a fact—a fact there like any fact—and have been concerned to show that the subject-matter of awareness is, in any case, things in process of change; and in such change that the knowing function takes a hand in trying to guide it or steer it, so that *some* (and *not* other) consequences accrue. But what about the awareness itself? What happens when it is made the subject-matter of awareness? What sort of a thing is it? It is, I submit, mere sophistication (futile at that), to argue either that we cannot become aware of awareness without involving ourselves in an endless regress, or that whenever we are aware of anything we are thereby necessarily aware of awareness once for all, so that it has no character save a purely formal and empty one. Taken concretely, awareness is an event with certain specifiable conditions. We may indeed be aware of it formally, as a bare fact, just as we may be cognizant of an explosion without knowing anything of its nature. But we may also be aware of it in a curious and analytic spirit, undertaking to study it in detail. This inquiry, like any other inquiry, proceeds by determining conditions and consequences. Here awareness is a characteristic fact, presenting to inquiry its own characteristic ear-marks, and a valid knowledge of awareness is the same sort of thing as valid knowledge of the spectrum or of a trotting horse; it proceeds generically in the same way and must satisfy the same generic tests.

What, then, is awareness found to be? The following answer, dogmatically summary in form, involves positive difficulties, and glides over many points where our ignorance is still too great. But it represents a general trend of scientific inquiry, carried on, I hardly need say, on its own merits without respect to the pragmatic controversy. Awareness means *attention,* and attention means a crisis of some sort in an existent situation; a forking of the roads of some material, a tendency to go this way and that. It represents something the matter, something out of gear, or in some way menaced, insecure, problematical and strained. This state of tension, of ambiguous indications, projects and tendencies, is not merely in the "mind," it is nothing merely emotional. It is in the facts of the situation as transitive facts; the emotional or "subjective" disturbance is just a part of the larger disturbance. And if, employing the *language* of psychology, we say that attention is a phenomenon of conflicting habits, being the process of resolving this conflict by finding an act which functions all the factors concerned, this language does not make the facts "merely psychological"—whatever that means.[1] The

---

[1] What does it mean? Does the objectivity of fact disappear when the biologist gives it a biological statement? Why not object to his conclusions on the ground that they are "merely" biological?

habits are as biologic as they are "personal," and as cosmic as they are biologic. They are the total order of things expressed in one way; just as a physical or chemical phenomenon is the same order expressed in another way. The statement in terms of conflict and readjustment of habits is at most one way of locating the disturbance in *things;* it furnishes no substitute for, or rival of, reality, and no "psychical" duplication.

If this be true, then awareness, even in its most perplexed and confused state, that of maximum doubt and precariousness of subject-matter, means things entering, *via* the particular thing known as organism, into a peculiar condition of differential—or additive—change. How can we refuse to raise and consider the question of how things in this condition are related to the prior state which emerges into it, and to the subsequent state of things into which it issues? [1]

Suppose the case to be awareness of a chair. Suppose that this awareness comes only when there is some problematic affair with which the chair is in some way—in whatever degree of remoteness—concerned. It may be a wonder whether it is a chair at all; or whether it is strong enough to stand on; or where I shall put it; or whether it is worth what I paid for it; or, as not infrequently happens, the situation involved in uncertainty may be some philosophic matter in which the perception of the chair is cited as evidence or illustration. (Humorously enough, awareness of it may even be cited in the course of a philosophic argument intended to show that awareness has nothing to do with situations of incompleteness and ambiguity.) Now what of the change the chair undergoes in entering this way into a situation of perplexed inquiry?

[1] It is this question *of the relation to one another of different successive states of things* which the pragmatic method substitutes for the epistemological inquiry of how one sort of existence, purely mental, temporal but not spatial, immaterial, made up of sublimated gaseous consciousness, can get beyond itself and have valid reference to a totally different kind of existence—spatial and extended; and how it can receive impressions from the latter, etc.,—all the questions which constitute that species of confirmed intellectual lock-jaw called epistemology.

Is this any part of the genuineness of that chair with which we are concerned? If not, where is the change found? In something totally different called "consciousness"? In that case how can the operations of inquiry, of observation and memory and reflection, ever have any assurance of getting referred back to the *right* object? Positively the presumption is that the *chair-of-which-we-are-speaking is* the chair *of-which-we-are-speaking;* it is the *same* thing that is out there which is also involved in the doubtful situation. Moreover, the reference to "consciousness" as the exclusive locus of the doubt only repeats the problem, for "consciousness," by the theory under consideration, means, after all, only the chair *as* concerned in the problematical situation. The *physical* chair remains unchanged, you say. Surely, if, as is altogether likely, what is *meant by* physical is precisely *that part* of the chair as object of total awareness which remains unaffected, for certain possible purposes, by entering for certain other actual purposes into the situation of awareness. But how can we segregate, *antecedently* to experimental inquiry, the "physical" chair from the chair which is now the object to be known; into what contradictions do we fall when we attempt to define the object of one awareness not in its own terms, but in terms of a selected type of object which is the appropriate subject-matter of some other cognizance!

But awareness means inquiry as well as doubt—there are the negative and positive, the retrospective and the prospective relationships of the thing. This means a genuinely *additive* quality—one of readjustment in prior things.[1] I know the dialectic argument that nothing can assume a new relation, because in order to do so it must already be completely related— when it comes from an absolutist I can understand why he holds it, even if I cannot understand the idea itself. But apart

[1] We have arrived here, upon a more analytic platform, at the point made earlier concerning the fact that knowing *issues* in action which changes things.

from this conceptual reasoning we must follow the lead of our subject-matter; and when we find a thing assuming new relations in the process of inquiry, must accept the fact, and frame our theory of things and of knowing to include it, not assert that it is impossible because we already have a theory of knowledge which precludes it. In inquiry, the existence which has become doubtful always undergoes experimental reconstruction. This may be largely imaginative or "speculative." We may view certain things *as if* placed under varying conditions, and consider what then happens to them. But such differences are really transformative as far as they go,—and besides, such inquiries never reach conclusions finally justifiable. In important and persistent inquiry, we insist upon something in the way of actual physical making—be it only a diagram. In other words, *science,* or knowing in its honorific sense, is experimental, involving physical construction. We insist upon something being *done about* it, that we may see how the idea when carried into effect comports with the other things through which our activities are hedged in and released. To avoid this conclusion by saying that knowing makes no difference in the "truth," but merely is the preliminary exercise which discovers it, is that old friend whose acquaintance we have repeatedly made in this discussion: the fallacy of confusing an existence anteceding knowing with the object which terminates and fulfills it. For knowing to make a difference in its own final term is gross self-stultification; it is none the less so when the aim of knowing is precisely to guide things straight up to this term. When "truth" means the accomplished introduction of certain new differences into conditions, why be foolish enough to introduce other differences, which are not wanted since they are irrelevant and misleading?

Were it not for the teachings of sad experience, it would not be necessary to add that the change in environment made by knowing is not a total or miraculous change. Transformation, readjustment, reconstruction, all imply prior existences: existences which have characters and behaviors of their own which must be accepted, consulted, humored, manipulated or made light of, in all kinds of differing ways in the different contexts of different problems. Making a difference in reality does not mean making any more difference than we find by experimentation can be made under the given conditions—even though we may still hope for different fortune another time under other circumstances. Still less does it mean making a thing into an unreality, though the pragmatist is sometimes criticized as if any change in reality must be a change into non-reality. There are difficulties, indeed, both dialectic, and real or practical, in the fact of change—in the fact that only a permanent can change and that change is alteration of a permanent. But till we enjoin botanists and chemists from referring to changes and transformations in their subject-matter on the ground that for anything to change means for it to part with its reality, we may as well permit the logician to make similar references.

V

Sub specie æternitatis? or *sub specie generationis?* I am susceptible to the esthetic charm of the former ideal—who is not? There are moments of relaxation: there are moments when the demand for peace, to be let alone and relieved from the continual claim of the world in which we live that we be up and doing something about it, seems irresistible; when the responsibilities imposed by living in a moving universe seem intolerable. We contemplate with equal mind the thought of the eternal sleep. But, after all, this is a matter in which reality and not the philosopher is the court of final jurisdiction. Outside of philosophy, the question seems fairly settled; in science, in poetry, in social organization, in religion—wherever religion is not hopelessly at the mercy of a Frankenstein philosophy which it originally called into being to be its own slave. Under such circumstances there is danger that the philosophy which tries to escape the form of generation by taking refuge under the form of eternity will only come under the form of a bygone generation. To try to escape from the snares and pitfalls of time by recourse to traditional problems and interests: —rather than that let the dead bury their own dead. Better it is for philosophy to err in active participation in the living struggles and issues of its own age and times than to maintain an immune monastic impeccability, without relevancy and bearing in the generating ideas of its contemporary present. In the one case, it will be respected, as we respect all virtue that attests its sincerity by sharing in the perplexities and failures, as well as in the joys and triumphs, of endeavor. In the other case, it bids fair to share the fate of whatever preserves its gentility, but not its activity, in descent from better days; namely, to be snugly ensconced in the consciousness of its own respectability.

Appearing and Appearance

THE idea of appearance has played a large and varied rôle in philosophic thought. In ancient philosophy, it was ontological in character, being used to denote a realm of being which was infected with defect or non-being and hence expressed itself in instability and change. In modern thinking, it has been chiefly an epistemic idea. Ontologically, there is but one kind of being; but this, as it affects the senses, or is itself affected by the faculties and conditions of knowing, becomes subjectivistically altered from its real estate. In both cases the distinction of appearance from reality is, of course, invidious. To an empiricist the distinction, however invalid he may consider it to be metaphysically or epistemologically, must have an empirical basis and origin which are misinterpreted in the traditional doctrines. It is accordingly incumbent upon him to give an analytic account of the origin and rôle of the meaning of appearance such as will acknowledge the empirical facts while eliminating historic misconstructions.

In its simplest and basic form, "appearance" denotes the fact that some things are at a particular time evident, patent, overt, open, outstanding, conspicuous, in contrast with·others which are hidden, concealed, latent, covered up, remote. One of the things which itself soon "appears" or becomes obvious is that there is a connection between what is apparent and what is covert, such that what appears has a representative function. It is a revelation, manifestation, exhibition. It can be understood only as a culminating eventuation of something beside itself which may be otherwise hidden—as prophets reveal the will of God—or may be overt in another connection —as trophies exhibit a victory won in war. A further specification of this function is so significant and so common as to deserve a class to itself. We take in the third place something which appears—in the first sense—as the clew to something hidden or unapparent, and as the basis of search for it: as sign, indication, evidence.

I

The primary, innocent neutral meaning of appearance may best be expressed participially, by the word "appearing." The world is so constituted that things appear and disappear; the opposite to appearance is not reality but disappearance. Owing to rotation, the light of a beacon on the seas appears and disappears every so often. Similarly, owing to the rotation of the earth, the sun appears in the morning and disappears at night. In the springtime leaves appear on the trees; they disappear in winter. Land disappears after a ship has got a distance at sea; another land appears after an interval of days. What is indicated by the term "appearance" is coming into view, sensibly or intellectually—as when the meaning of an obscure passage "dawns" on the mind, or the clew to a desired invention presents itself to an Edison. Appearance signifies conspicuousness, outstandingness, obviousness, being patent, evident in plain view. Its contrast is being obscured, hidden, concealed, absent, remote. A book appears on publication, a king appears once in a while to his subjects, an actor appears daily on the stage. An eclipse of the moon appears at calculable intervals.

If there is a metaphysical problem in the "world of appearances" there must also be one in a "world of disappearances." This correlativity of appearing and disappearing is in reality highly significant; it indicates the existence of a temporal process having phases. The fundamental importance of this temporal characteristic can be better dealt with at a later stage of our own account. At this point, I only want to emphasize that any existential question which arises can only concern stages in some temporal process that includes a cycle of phases. When a thing appears, its hereness and nowness are emphatically realized. If the Aristotelian categories of potentiality and actuality were in vogue, we could well say that appearing marks an actualization of a potential here-now. From any point of view, we must say that it marks a stage in the history of some object having different phases, owing to varied relations to other things. Thus the different appearances of the moon, as it waxes and wanes, are not matters of some unfolding from within any more than they are marks of degrees of reality; they are functions of its movement in relation to the movement of the earth.

It may, however, be objected that the epistemological aspect of the matter can not be so easily disposed of. It will be contended that since an appearance is always to somebody it involves dependence upon the mind or consciousness in or to which a thing appears; for this reason, I suppose, appearances are often called presentations, and presentations are then either identified with states of mind or at least with things modified by mind. But appearance does not denote a total or pervasive character, an intrinsic quality, but a relation which is additive. A lad appears in school; he answers present when the roll is called. No one thinks of supposing that this presence abrogates his being or reduces his reality. It marks a phase of his biography determined by his relations to school, class, and teachers, just as his absence marks a phase determined by other relations, vacation, illness, playing hookey, etc. So a presentation marks the existence of a thing in relation to an organism; the table before me is in view. If I close my eyes, it disappears from view:—a particular relationship ceases, namely, that with a certain part of my organism.

This relation is physical, existential, not epistemic. Its establishment is, indeed, a necessary condition of knowing, but it does not constitute knowledge, in either of its two senses:

either as something actually known or as something *to be* known:—a theme for inquiry, a subject of an investigation which shall terminate in knowledge. The sun is efficaciously present to the soil it warms, the plants whose growth it effects. Or, taking the case of the organism, its appearance may, just like the sounding of an alarm clock, operate as a signal to begin the round of daily duties. It may, indeed, be known, identified, for just what it is, or it may be present as an occasion of inquiry in order to discover what it is. But knowing in both these senses denotes that something in addition to the original appearance is taking place; that the thing appearing is entering into more complex relationships. In short, while the appearance is a condition of knowing, it is not a case of knowing. Furthermore, we must note that the relation which determines a thing to appear is definite, specifiable, not wholesale. A table disappears—not absolutely but with respect to sight; when the eyes close, it may still be present to the hand. Failure to bear in mind the definite character of the organic relation that conditions an appearance is largely responsible for treating it as if it involved a unique problem.

II

The second sense of "appearance" is display, exhibition, manifestation, revelation. In some instances this meaning is but an intensification of that just dealt with. A vivid, spectacular appearance of something is a "show" in an emphatic sense, just as an unusual ball-player or child musician is popularly called a "phenomenon." But in many cases the idea of showing, manifesting, implies something other than the merely striking character of the appearance in question. It calls attention explicitly to the connection between the whole temporal cycle and the phase of it prominent at a particular time in a particular context. This connection is implied in the first sense of appearing. But the idea of manifestation does something more than make the implicit explicit. It designates the appearance as a member of an inclusive *whole*. A display of fireworks may be only a striking appearance. But it may also be a commemoration of a notable event. A procession may be only a vivid pageant; but it may also be a celebration. The presentation is now a representation; it calls to mind a total situation such that *reference* to it gives the appearing object its meaning. It is the appearance *of* something in the sense of expression. Thus a particular act of ill-temper reveals a standing disposition; it is a transient ebullition of something enduring; similarly with a manifestation of greed, a display of courage. An actor appears, but not just in the sense that a man who has been absent is present. Appearance *as* an actor signifies the assumption of a rôle or part, and this implies the whole, the drama, in which the rôle is a contributing member. The subject-matter of the rôle would be, relatively, non-sense by itself and the drama would be defective without the part. A similar context is exemplified when a lawyer appears in behalf of a client. His presence is wholly representative, but it is a necessary phase in the realization of that which is represented. He takes a part in legal proceedings which exhibit a controversy in process of solution. There is thus explicit in appearance as manifestation an added relation. The sun appears and its appearance is a phase of the sun's career. But it does not realize its special status by means of appearing on behalf of anything else, such that its representative office makes a definitive contribution to the whole. If, however, we take the rising of the sun in relation to the constitution of the entire system, the particular event may *then* be said to be a manifestation. On the one hand, it is seen to be a necessary part of the whole, and on the other hand, it can be understood only when it is placed in its relations within the organized system as a whole.

This second meaning leads to a third, the distinctively intellectual one, determining the logical import of "appearance." A representative exhibition may be more or less adequate or perfect—as in the case of lawyer, diplomat, and actor. We say they are or are not true, faithful, to their function. They may *mis*represent. Moreover, in the case of a delegate, a diplomat, credentials are demanded and offered. The question of claim and *right* enters in. When an appearance is taken as a manifestation, an organized whole is presupposed. The whole is known and the special place and rôle of the part is taken for granted. Suppose, however, a doubt arises as to whether the thing appearing is *entitled* to act in behalf of another; a claim is involved which must be investigated before "manifestation" may be predicated. Representative capacity instead of being assumed presents a problem, an inquiry to be undertaken. Yet we must not confuse the nature of the problem. We may assert that it is *false* that a man is an agent or representative of those whom he pretends to appear in behalf of. This does not mean that the "appearance" is false or unreal, but that the objective relations required to confer upon it the rôle which is claimed are lacking. Are the delegate's credentials in order? What is the nature of the body by whom he was chosen? There is an epistemic relation in the sense of knowledge of the relations which obtain to other objective things, but not an epistemological problem in the usual meaning of epistemology, namely, a direct and unique relation of a thing known to a knower.

A typical case of "appearance" wherein the exact objective reference which constitutes a representative office (as a contribution in an inclusive whole) is at issue, is found when there is a question of legal liability in certain transactions. Did or did not a certain person "hold himself out" as agent for a certain principal? Or was a man who claimed to be an agent of another in making a certain agreement authorized to do so? Or, putting the two questions together, did he claim a repre-

sentative character, and if so was he so authorized to act in
that manner so that certain obligations are incumbent on a
principal? In any such case, there is a question of whether a
certain *allegation* was made or implied, and if so whether the
relations to other things constituting the whole in question
bear out the assertion. There is a problem, and there is inquiry.
The solution of the problem one way or another depends upon
what relations are discovered to exist to other things. If these
objective relations are ignored, then "appearance" is taken to
denote a relation to something behind or underneath which is
wholly different in *kind* from what appears. The relation is
taken in a lump, statically and in a co-existential cross-section.
Hence the "reality" of what appears lies in a different realm
of being. But in truth what is behind and covert is other
things of the same kind but which have to be searched for in
order to determine the genuineness of the representative office
claimed. What is "back" is homogenous with what appears.

When there is doubt as to an alleged representative relation and it has to be settled by inquiry into connections with
other things, we are obviously in a realm where "appearance"
has an intellectual significance. What does the appearing
thing *signify?* Is the claimed signifying capacity valid? Truth
and falsity are involved. In this meaning there are further
relations involved than in the second case where manifestation or exhibition is taken as an *undoubted* part of the situation. As the second sense of appearance makes explicit a connection with an inclusive whole, whose various manifestations
are determined by the nature of the whole to be a serial order,
so the third sense makes explicit the necessity of determining
a *right* to inclusion within this whole; or, stated more generally, makes necessary the determination of the interrelated
whole of which it is actually a constituent. This determination
involves a complex set of relations. In the proposition "The
sun appears" there is implied the relation of the event termed

"rising" to the sun as an enduring object which passes through a cycle of changes. When we say "The rising of the sun is a manifestation of the structure of the solar system" the relation is to the whole system of which the appearance of the sun at a determinate place and time is a function. The same is true in the proposition "Booth appears in the part of Hamlet," where the drama of Hamlet—or perhaps the entire Shakesperian system—is implied as the inclusive whole; so also in the proposition "Coolidge is the legal president of the United States." But in the last proposition "legal" introduces a relationship which is not explicit in the second sense, as is evident if we imagine the proposition denied. The question of validity, or right, enters in. The system is no longer taken for granted as including the part which "manifests" it in a particular phase but must be sought for. It is also necessary to determine the exact nature of the appearing object which is alleged to be a representative part of the whole.

III

There is involved in the latter determination a triadic set of relations. First, there is the relation which the man in his primary qualities sustains to himself as "holding himself out" as agent or as purporting to be an official. This is a reflexive relation. Secondly, as necessary for the *conclusive* determination of this relation there is the relation of the person claiming the office, rôle, or part to the principal or those represented. In the third place, depending upon this determination, there is a relation to those with whom he has dealings in virtue of the office. This third relationship constitutes the differential feature of the significance of appearance which is now before us. It is the consequences which follow when the claim to a certain office is legitimate and which do not follow when it is not justified which make it necessary in case of doubt to ascertain the rightfulness of the claim. In virtue of being an officer

of the law a man has distinctive dealings with other persons;
he has effective connections with them which he does not have
as a human being apart from the representative capacity.
There is an obvious difference between Booth playing a certain rôle and a man *claiming* to be Booth taking the same part.
In the first instance, those concerned, those affected by the
playing of the part, either like it or do not like it. But if the
claim is proved invalid, they have redress; they can exercise
claims in return.

We have selected as typical illustrations instances of persons who put forth a representative claim. The purpose of the
illustrative instances is to prepare the way for an examination
of cases where an appearing object is *taken* to have a particular representative capacity and office, that of being a sign or
evidence of other things: cases where the assertion is not made
by a person on his own account, but is made by the one who
takes the thing as evidence or sign of something else. The same
triad of relations is found in both cases. Hence analysis of
the cases in which the claim is self-asserted instead of depending upon some one's taking or using the appearing object as
representative is relevant. When something is *taken* to be
smoke and smoke is taken to be a sign of fire, there is also
found the added and differential trait of relation to consequences, which consequences differ according as the representative rôle is or is not justified. When one takes the appearing object as a sign of fire, there are reactions and consequences
appropriate to fire. Otherwise one merely reacts just to the
appearing object in its own appearing or presented qualities
and not as a sign. There is the same difference of treatment
and consequences found in responding just to a sound and to a
sound which is also a word, that is, to which a meaning is assigned, standing for something beyond itself. It is one and the
same whether we say we deal with the whole which includes
the manifestation or with the manifesting object as a member

of the whole; the difference is purely verbal. But in the case of an appearance as sign or evidence of something else, there is the need of determining how justified or valid is the claimed sign relationship, since responsive dealing and consequences depend upon the answer obtained to this question.

IV

The nub of the whole matter turns upon the nature of the reflexive relationship, the relation which an appearing object in its intrinsic qualities bears to the properties that capacitate it to be a sign of something else. That the appearing object is *in* evidence is a truism; the statement is tautologous. But *of* what is it evidence? The latter question introduces a distinction *within* the thing used as sign, a reflexive relation. That the relation to something else involved in being a sign of it is reflected into the appearing object itself is obvious from the fact that we take things as signs when we do not know *of* what they are signs. This happens in every inquiry, since inquiry implies first that some appearing object is a sign, and secondly that we do not as yet know of what it is a sign or evidence. This mode of taking would be impossible unless there were a distinction and relation set up within the appearing object between itself in its primary qualities and itself in its signifying office: just as a sheriff can neither identify his office as sheriff with all his personal peculiarities, needs, and capacities, nor yet wholly sink the latter in his official capacity. He must distinguish within himself characteristics which belong to him *qua* human being from characteristics belonging to him as officer, and at the same time relate them to each other. Unless he does the latter, his office becomes a purely disembodied function; it can become operative only through traits which belong to him as a human being, his hands, legs, tongue, and wits.

We may take as illustrative evidence the case of a sound

used as a sign of something else—as a word in language. A child reacts first to a sound as a sound—as the adult reacts to sounds in a language he does not understand as gibberish or as quasi-musical. Taking it as a sign depends upon not treating it merely as a sound and also upon *not identifying* it with the thing meant. This is the same as saying that one must distinguish it as sound from its properties as signifying. The result is both a degradation and an enhancement. The former affects the sound in its primary existential qualities; the latter the sound as a sign. Mere sound is reduced to a vehicle or carrier; the latter gives the sound dignity and status. A good example is found in mathematical symbols where the direct quality of the appearing object is reduced as near a minimum as is consistent with having any appearance at all in order that there may be gain in effective representative import. Relationships react into the thing used as symbol to redetermine its *prior* estate.

This effect of the reflexive relation is of great importance. It is the clew to understanding the traditional misconstruction of the nature of appearances. The essence of this misinterpretation is that it notes and retains in mind the degradation of immediate existential quality, while it fails to note that this reduction is due to and for the sake of the performance of an office as sign of something else—as in our monetary system a bullion value is reduced existentially to a piece of paper while the paper at the same time gains value as a token of indebtedness. The degradation is taken to be something intrinsic, belonging to an existence as such. The appearing object certainly exists, but lacks self-justifying existence. It is therefore said to be only fragmentary, inherently defective, a puzzling anomaly in the order of being. There inevitably ensues the derogatory valuation of "appearance."

This analysis applies also to the "epistemological" misconstruction of the nature of appearance, though now with especial reference to the second of the triad of relations, that of the relation of the appearing thing as sign of some doubtful object to that of which it is a sign. The *legitimacy* of a case of "holding out" as agent does not depend upon a direct and unique relation of a man to those to whom he holds himself out but upon his antecedent relations to others. So the validity of using a thing as sign of this or that inferred object depends not on its direct relation to the knower, but upon its specific relations to other things. As long as these remain in question, we say that "apparently" it signifies this or that. "It *seems* to do so." "Apparently" and "seeming" have nothing to do with its direct and co-existential relation to the knower, nor with its intrinsic quality as affected by this relation. They designate the doubtful state of an inferred object. Whenever final judgment in inference is suspended an appearing object gains a distinctive intellectual status, such as is conveyed in propositions like: "The bill seems to be counterfeit"; "the patient appears to have typhoid," etc.

Instead of denoting an intrinsic distortion of reality due to relation to a knower, "appearance" here marks a safeguard and precaution characteristic of all careful inferential inquiry. By use of "appears," "seems," attention is called to the as yet uncertain status of the inferred object, while at the same time a record is made of the fact that the thing which appears (in the first sense) has a certain amount of evidential force attached to it. Permit this distinctive phase of partial, inconclusive, representative capacity to be ignored, and "seeming" is inevitably taken to be a quality of what appears, due to relation of the thing in itself to a knower.

V

It is submitted that in the foregoing considerations is found the explanation of the category of "phenomena" as opposed to true realities that is found in Greek thought. Men are

[67]

now in possession of methods of inquiry which have proved their efficacy to unravel the knots which come along with frustrated inference. There are still, of course, many cases in which we can not complete an attempted inference; when, that is, we can not tell just *what* some thing means although it is undoubted in its existential manifestation. But our technique of inquiry has succeeded in so many cases (and in so many cases we have managed to improve a defective technique until it has proved adequate) that in practice we recognize such cases as instances of blocked inference, and lay the subject-matter aside for further investigation. We employ the subject-matter to define a *problem* for research. But when the distinction between phenomena and noumena as two orders of Being was formulated, there was no technique of experimental analysis. The mechanical and the mathematical instruments of intellectual resolution were both lacking. Consequently, the world was full of anomalies—things which undoubtedly existed, but which could not be understood or duly connected with other things. It was an easy and not unnatural generalization to say that they constituted a realm on their own account. All that could be done, in the absence of methods which would link them into members of a course of events, thereby explaining them, was to *classify* them with one another as "phenomena."

This account is confirmed by the fact that the higher and contrasting realm of being was antithetically conceived to be noumena. Things which appear are present in sense-perception; the eye, ear, hand are the media of their determinate presence. Inferred objects that define their meaning and also constitute their full reality are, on the other hand, *qua* inferred, objects of *thought*. This statement is a truism, inference and thought being synonymous. Now at present our scientific technique is such that we can, speaking generally, experimentally control conditions so that an inferred object may itself be rendered perceptible, if not in its entirety, at least in respect to some of its defining features. The existential subject-matter arrived at by calculation is at least a candidate for observation. When the technique of observational analysis is not adequate to bring the calculated objects into view or render them apparent, they are treated as hypothetical. But Greek methods of inquiry made no provision for the "category" of the hypothetically existent any more than it did for the temporarily problematic. Hence the intelligible object which furnished meaning and stability to the perceptible object was treated as final, not as intermediate. It was intrinsically and wholly the object of thought, the noumenon, while in inference conducted by physical and mathematical methods there is no break in kind between the object which appears and the inferred object. For such inference proceeds by insertion of intermediaries which are sufficiently numerous and compact to be members of a temporal continuum. For lack of such methods, Greek speculation made a single jump from the apparent object to the object of thought; the absence of intermediary connecting links necessarily shoved the latter into a non-temporal realm.

The hard and fast distinction between the perceptible object as mere appearance and the intelligible object as ultimate reality is thus a projection, from a period when methods of inferential inquiry were deficient, into a period when methods actually practiced leave no place for the distinction. The important thing to bear in mind is that when an ulterior object of inquiry is constituted, the perceptible or apparent object no longer stands over against what is inferred, but is included along with it in a comprehensive series or an inclusive whole. Any case of physical investigation illustrates what is here asserted. When, for example, the appearances or phenomena termed malaria are satisfactorily understood, they present themselves as part of the life-history of anopheles in connection with the life-history of the creature who is their host. When the inference is completed in the categorical assertion of an object, both the appearing (perceived) thing which has been employed as sign and the inferred (intelligible) object lose the isolation they possess during the process of inquiry and delayed inference. They both become members of an interrelated inclusive whole, so that the category of "manifestation" becomes applicable. A one-to-one relation in isolation between the appearing thing and what it means is characteristic only of the period of doubt and inquiry. The reason why our focal awareness fastens so exclusively upon the perceived or appearing object and the definite inferred or intelligible object is obvious. They are terms in a literal sense, defining terminals of the inclusive whole; nothing is gained by giving attention to the latter. The case is similar to the presence of a locked door and search for its key. The reality is the whole operation of opening the locked door. But the sought-for key is literally the key to this operation, just as the lock defines the problem. As soon as the key which fits, is found, the operation takes place as a matter of course. It is passed over in explicit consciousness just because it is taken for granted as that which gives meaning to the key and to the search for it.

VI

We have, however, temporarily turned aside from the explanation of the epistemological misconstruction. Deferred inference, or relation to a missing but signified object, is expressed in such propositions as "This seems to be pure milk (but perhaps it is skimmed milk)." But such propositions as "It looks blue or chalky" have a distinctly different intellectual force. "The man down on the street looks very small from here"—the top of a high building. "That distant mountain appears blue." "The rails seem to converge; the stick

appears bent; the coin seems elliptical." Such propositions
(which have been made of late the object of much puzzled
speculation) have a ready interpretation when taken in their
logical status, that is, as involved in the use of appearing
things as signs of something else. In the cases previously
analyzed it was the inferred object which is merely "apparent," that is apparently but not surely signified. The propositions just stated refer to the way in which the object used as
evidence presents itself. They state the appearing object as it
appears—in our first neutral sense. But they state it with a
purpose—that of defining the exact nature of the evidence at
hand. "The stick seems bent in water" does not mean that the
appearing object *seems* bent. It means that what appears *is*
something bent, though not necessarily the stick; perhaps it is
light.

The first step is to put ourselves on guard against depending upon the vague term "seems," "appears." We must specify
the respect in which it appears, to eye, ear, touch, smell. If I
say that a straight stick rising out of water *looks* bent (implying relation to the eye) I but state an objective fact, verified
by a camera, and explained by well-known physical principles.
In exactly the same way when I say that a moving whistle
sounds higher or lower in pitch as it approaches or recedes,
I state a fact of relationship to the ear. Incredible as it may
appear, a serious problem has been made out of the fact that
a fire feels colder as we move away from it. The process of
creating the "problem" is as follows. The fire has really but
one temperature. How is that fact to be reconciled with the
fact that at different distances it *seems* to be of many different temperatures? Of course, it cannot; but the statement is
so mixed as to be absurd; the problem, not the solution, is at
fault. The temperature of the air affected by the fire changes
with distance; this is a physical fact, and what is *felt* is the
temperature of the air. Thus to say that the fire *feels* colder

as we recede is to state an incontrovertible fact; there would be a problem only if it were not so.

It may seem like a trick to do away with this "problem" by substituting specific terms, "looks," "sounds," "feels," for the general term "appears," "seems." But the force of the substitution is to call attention to a specific relation to that particular part of the nervous organism which is involved as a condition, a physical or causal condition, of the appearance of the thing which is to serve as sign. The propositions under discussion make explicit the exact nature of the thing to be used as evidence, before it is used.

This becomes evident if, instead of stating a definitive or concluded judgment such as "The straight stick looks bent in the water," we say merely, "There is present a form which to the eye looks bent," a statement of fact, but of fact about the appearing object irrespective of any inferential use made of it. If we say "The round coin looks elliptical seen from this angle" we again state a correct judgment. If we say "There is present to the eye an elliptical form" we describe the nature of the appearance (in our first sense) preliminary to making inferential use of it. It may be said, however, that we have unduly simplified the situation in getting rid of the alleged problem. It may be objected that the real problem lies in the fact that there are many appearances, and that the question to be answered is which of these, if any, is or corresponds to the real object, a stick or penny. Why, for example, should the circular form, the thing appearing in perpendicular vision, be assigned any superiority over other appearances to the eye? The reply is that it is *not;* the superiority assigned to it is that of being a *better sign.* And that it is such is something learned by experience in making use of various appearing objects as bases of inferring other things.

A man sights with his eye along the edge of a board he has been planing and says "it *looks* straight." This is simply a statement of fact, of the same kind as when he says "it is a board." If he said "it *is* straight," he would have made an inference from what appears to his eye, perhaps a wrong one. When he confined himself to saying "it looks straight" he limits himself to a statement of the nature of what appears, and suspends inferential judgment; it is just as if a geologist were to confine his report to saying that there are certain marks on the rock which *suggest* a trilobite, while he refrains from asserting that they *are* a fossil trilobite. In any such case, the one who makes the judgment recognizes in effect that the conditions of the appearing object are complex; they include both the edge of the board and his sensori-cerebral apparatus. Both conditions are involved in the temporal series of which the last term is the appearing object. No epistemic import is assigned to vision, but the visual apparatus is taken for what it is, one of the physically causal conditions of what appears or is present. Distrusting the adequacy of this appearance as sign or evidence, one then resorts to production of another appearance, the process being identical with any physical experiment where conditions are intentionally varied. One runs a finger over the edge and says "It feels uneven here and there." The implication is not that a tactile appearance is more real than a visual, but that for certain purposes it affords a better sign of a sought-for object. If one is still in doubt one may fall back upon mechanical appliances—upon relations to other things instead of relations to the organism —in order to determine that appearance which shall serve as a sign. As actual existence all "appearances" stand on the same level; as signs some are better than others, just as what one witness says is better evidence than what another says, although the utterances of each are equally actual occurrences.

VII

We conclude with a summary. The original and neutral

sense of appearance is just that something previously remote, covert or obscure *appears*—comes into view, into actualized presence. When the thing appearing is referred without question to a whole of which it is a related member, it is termed an exhibition, manifestation, display, expression. But often this reference can not be made directly; what it belongs to has to be searched for. The evident object is now treated as evidence; it gains the rôle of sign or index of something or other. In its reflexive relation it sets a problem to be inquired into. The appearance is now an appearance *of* something whose nature is to be determined by inference from the appearing objects and from others which may be aligned with it. Appearing now takes temporarily the form of seeming rather than of showing. But "seeming" does not signify that something seems to exist, but that a certain *object* seems to be *pointed* to: "seeming" denotes an essayed, but temporarily blocked, inference. Finally, it is often necessary in the interest of control of inference to state the causal conditions of that appearing thing which is used as sign. In this operation, organic conditions of touch, sight, hearing, smell, or taste are specified and "appears" is specified into feels, looks, sounds, smells, tastes thus and so. The process is no different from when a scientist specifies the physical apparatus which he has employed in producing the phenomena which are used as evidence in drawing an inference.

This point is worth dwelling upon. It has been implied throughout that the relation to organic apparatus involved in such terms as "looks," "sounds," "feels," "tastes" is a reference to a causal condition of the production of the particular object which appears, not a reference to a knower, an epistemological reference, and that this relation is specified as a safeguard of the use to be made of it in inference from it. The statement is thus precisely analogous to the pains which a scientific experimenter takes to specify exactly the apparatus through which he obtains the subject-matter from which he infers certain conclusions. If a man uses a microscope in obtaining his evidential subject-matter he tells of its nature and manner of employment so that another can decide *how* the objects were made to appear. The statement that a thing "looks thus and so" is of precisely the same sort; the difference being, on the one hand, the greater degree of refinement of causal condition in the case of the microscope, and on the other hand, the presence of an *organic* mechanism as a condition of the appearance of anything whatever. A similar principle applies to the use of a sense-organ under different conditions and to recourse to various sense organs: not because the appearance conditioned by one is more real existentially than that of any other, or less real than that of the thing inferred, but because in this way subject-matter better for purposes of inference is secured. So, in the laboratory, conditions are intentionally varied and precisely for the same reason: to obtain a fuller amount of evidential material and to use its various phases as means of checking the use of other portions.

The general notion of "appearance" we have broken up into a number of meanings each distinctive in a particular contextual situation. The elimination of traditional misconstruction is procured when we keep these meanings definite, each in its proper place, and do not transfer and mix traits of one with those of another. Four distinctive situations are stated in such propositions as the following: (I) The sun appears (rises, or emerges from a cloud)—the primitive and neutral meaning. (II) The sun's appearing at this place and time is a manifestation of certain characteristics of the structure of the system to which sun and earth belong; a type of proposition which states the conclusion of any completed inquiry accepted as valid knowledge. (III) The sun seems to move (apparently moves) from east to west across a stationary earth; the statement of an inferred object with an intimation

of suspense and doubt concerning its correctness, or as preliminary to its rejection and the statement of another inferred
total object such as "In reality, the earth rotates and its rotation, while the sun remains stationary with reference to the
earth, accounts for the appearing objects which were used
(wrongly) as the basis of the other inference." And finally
(IV) The sun looks to the eye about the size of a twenty-
five cent piece—a statement of a fact which is to serve as part
of the matter of an inference as to its actual size, or in inference about its distance, etc.

In denying the metaphysical interpretation of appearance
as an inferior order of being, it is not meant, of course, to deny
all metaphysical implications in a certain sense of "metaphysical." On the contrary, the argument rests throughout on
the fact that existential subject-matter in each of the four types
of propositions is a series or temporal order of interrelated elements forming an inclusive whole of which the appearances
are members. If this existential fact be denied, some form of
bad metaphysics is bound to result. Nor is it implied that no
general theory of knowledge is involved. On the contrary, the
analysis points to the fact that knowledge requires as its precondition an appearing object which results from an integrated interaction of all factors, the organism included, and
that the completed object of knowledge is precisely such an
interrelated and self-manifesting whole as includes an appearance.

The Inclusive Philosophic Idea

THERE are at the present time a considerable number of persons who habitually employ the social as a principle of philosophic reflection and who assign it a force equal and even superior to that ascribed to the physical, vital and mental. There are others, probably a greater number, who decline to take "social" seriously as a category of description and interpretation for purposes of philosophy, and who conceive any attempt so to take it as involving a confusion of anthropology and sociology with metaphysics. The most they would concede is that cultural material may throw light on the genesis and history of human beliefs about ultimate subject-matter. Then it is asserted that it is but a case of the familiar genetic fallacy, the confusion of the history of belief with the nature of that believed, to assign to such an account a place anywhere except within the history of human culture. Such a situation solicits attention; and I desire to state as far as space permits what is the intent of those who attribute genuine philosophic import to the idea of the social.

A start may be conveniently made by noting that associated or conjoint behavior is a universal characteristic of all existences. Knowledge is in terms of related objects and unless it is supposed that relations are a subjective intrusion, or that, *à la* Hume, only *ideas* are associated, relation as the nerve of science correlates with association among things. This fact being noted, we observe that the qualities of things associated are displayed only in association, since in interactions alone are potentialities released and actualized. Furthermore, the manifestation of potentialities varies with the manner and range of association. This statement is only a formal way of calling attention to the fact that we characterize an element, say hydrogen, not only, as the name implies, in terms of its water-forming potentiality but ultimately in terms of consequences effected in a whole range of modes of conjoint behavior.[1]

These considerations being premised, attention fastens upon the fact that the more numerous and varied the forms of association into which anything enters, the better basis we have for describing and understanding it, for the more complex is an association the more fully are potentialities released for observation. Since things present themselves to us in such fashion that narrower and wider ranges, simpler and more complex ones, are readily distinguished, it would appear that metaphysical description and understanding is demarcated as that which has to do with the widest and fullest range of associated activity. And I remark that if the phrase "degrees of reality" can be given an empirically intelligible meaning, that meaning would seem to depend upon following out the line of thought thus suggested.[2] In short, there appears to be a fairly straight road to the conclusion that a just gauge of the adequacy of any philosophic account of things is found in the extent to which that account is based upon taking things in the widest and most complex scale of associations open to observation.

In making this statement I am not unaware that the opposite method has been pursued and is still recommended by philosophers in good repute; namely, a method based on predilection for ultimate and unattached simples, called by various writers essences, data, etc. The question of whether

---

[1] In case there is objection to the use of the conceptions of potentiality and actualization, it may be pointed out that the same facts may be stated, though as it seems to me more awkwardly, by saying that things in different modes of association occasion different effects, and that our knowledge of them is adequate in the degree in which it includes a broad range of effects due to a variety of associated operations.

[2] It is perhaps worth while in passing to note also that such concepts as "levels" and "emergence" seem to be most readily definable upon the basis of this consideration.

we should begin with the simple or the complex appears to me the most important problem in philosophic method at the present time, cutting under, for example, the traditional distinctions of real and ideal. Or, if it be said that while perforce we are compelled psychologically and practically to begin with the complex, *philosophy* begins only when we have come upon simples, the problem of method still remains. Are these simples isolated and self-sufficient, or are they the results of intellectual analysis, themselves intellectual rather than existential in quality, and therefore of value only in the degree in which they afford us means of arriving at a better understanding of the complex wholes with which we began? Time forbids consideration of this fundamental question. I content myself with observing that the hypothesis that ultimate and detached simples are the only reals for philosophy seems to be the sole logical alternative to the position that the wider and more complex the range of associated interaction with which we deal, the more fully is the nature of the object of philosophic thought revealed to us. Hence, the issue as to method reduces itself to the question whether isolated simples can be asserted without self-contradiction to be ultimate and self-sufficient on their own account. Those who do not accept them as the real, appear committed to the position herein stated.

While the fact of association and of range of associations as determining "degrees of reality" gives us our starting point, it gives *only* a starting point for discussing the value of "social" as a philosophic category. For by the social as a distinctive mode of association is denoted specifically human forms of grouping, and these, according to the findings of science, appear only late in time. Hence, the objection which readily occurs to mind. The view that "social" in its characteristically human sense is an important category is met with the retort that, on the contrary, it is but a highly special case of association and as such is restricted in significance, humanly interesting of course, but a matter of detail rather than of an important principle. My introductory remarks were intended as an anticipatory reply to such an objection. Association barely by itself is a wholly formal category. It acquires content only by considering the different forms of association which constitute the material of experience. Thus, while it is admitted that society, in the human sense, is a form of association that is restricted in its space-time manifestation, it cannot be placed in contrast with association in general. Its import can be determined not by comparing it with association in its generic formal sense, but only by comparing and contrasting it with other special types of association.

This fact gives what has been said regarding the importance of range and complexity of association as a philosophic measure its special import. If reference to association is to be anything more than a ceremonial and barren act of deference, if it is to be used in an enterprise of philosophic description and understanding, it indicates the necessity of study and analysis of the different modes of association that present themselves in experience. And the implication of our argument is that in such a comparison of definite types of association, the social, in its human sense, is the richest, fullest and most delicately subtle of any mode actually experienced. There is no need to go through the form of discovering, as if for the first time, the different typical modes which are to be compared and contrasted. They have been made familiar enough in the course of thought. Aside from social, whose thoroughgoing admission still awaits adequate acknowledgment, they are the physical, the vital or organic, and the mental. The gist of our problem consists in deciding which of these forms presents the broader and fuller range of associations. Association in general is but a matrix; its filling is the facts of association actually displayed in nature. Indeed, the category of association is but a highly abstract notation of what is formally common to the special modes.

Before coming, however, to this affair of comparison, which constitutes the main topic of this paper, it will be well to clear the ground of certain notions which led to misconstruction and depreciation of the meaning of "social" as a category. A moment ago I referred to the facts of association as they are actually displayed in human life. The reference implied that social facts are themselves natural facts. This implication goes against preconceptions engendered by the common opposition of the physical and the social sciences; by the tacit identification, in other words, of the natural sciences with the purely physical. As far as this idea lingers in the back of the head, social and natural are oppositional conceptions; the attempt to find a key by which to read the cipher of nature in the social is then immediately felt to be absurd; this feeling then operates to effect the contemptuous dismissal of the "social." Denial of opposition between the social and natural is, however, an important element of the *meaning* of "social" as a category; and if anyone is interested in finding out the intent of those who would employ "social" as a philosophic category, that one should begin by asking himself what are the implications of the current separation of natural and social sciences, and whether upon reflection he is willing to stand by them. A denial of the separation is not only possible to a sane mind, but is demanded by any methodological adoption of the principle of continuity, and also, as will be indicated later, by social phenomena themselves. Upon the hypothesis of continuity—if that is to be termed a hypothesis which cannot be denied without self-contradiction—the social, in spite of whatever may be said regarding the temporal and spatial limitation of its manifestations, furnishes philosophically the inclusive category.

A two-fold harm is wrought by the current separation of

social and natural science and by accepting the meaning which attaches to social after it has been thus divorced. The chief point at which philosophy may be of aid in the pursuits of the social sciences lies precisely here. In the degree in which what passes for social science is built upon the notion of a gap between natural and social phenomena, that science is truncated, arbitrary and insecure. An analytic survey of the present status of the social sciences would be needed to justify this remark. But there are only a few sociologists who have ventured as yet to assert that there is something distinctive or unique in social phenomena; so we are met with a paradoxical situation in which social phenomena are isolated from physical and organic considerations and yet are explained in physical, organic or psychological terms instead of in characteristically social terms. In psychology the persisting tradition of a purely individualistic and private subject-matter is to be attributed directly to neglect of the social conditions of mental phenomena, while indirectly this neglect goes back to a separation of social from natural; since only acknowledgment of the continuity of the social and the natural provides the intermediary terms which link psychological phenomena with others. Some forms of behaviorism, in reaction against the unnatural isolation of the physical and mental, merely throw the latter overboard entirely, and reduce them to the terms of the material dealt with in purely physical science. In political science may be noted an oscillation between the adoption of non-natural categories, such as a transcendent "will", and the resolution of political phenomena into physical terms of conflict and adjustment of forces. A recent economic writer has asserted that economic science has so neglected the place of technology in industry that a generation has gone forth which, although "educated" in economic science, is almost wholly ignorant of economic affairs.[1] Technology is

[1] Tugwell, *Industry's Coming of Age*, p. vii.

evidently a matter that connects directly with the development of physical science; the point, instead of being an incidental one, can be shown to be intimately connected with all the sound objections brought against the abstraction of the "economic man." The economic man cannot be set in his place in social phenomena, in his actual relations to legal, political, technological and other cultural institutions, until these are connected with natural phenomena.

These are but too casual and abbreviated hints of the meaning of the assertion that the performance of the service which philosophy might theoretically render to the social sciences waits upon the frank acknowledgment of the social as a category continuous with and inclusive of the categories of the physical, vital and mental.

This reference to the sciences is not to be regarded, however, as implying an adoption of that conception of philosophy which identifies it exclusively with either an analysis or a synthesis of the premises or results of the special sciences. On the contrary, the sciences themselves are outgrowths of some phase of social culture, from which they derive their instruments, physical and intellectual, and by which their problems and aims are set. The only philosophy which can "criticize" the premises of the special sciences, without running the danger of being itself a pseudo-science, is that which takes into account the anthropological (in its broadest sense) basis of the sciences, just as the only one that can synthesize their conclusions, without running a like danger, is the one which steps outside these conclusions to place them in the broader context of social life.

In now turning to the main point, the social as a ranking philosophic category, on the ground that it is indicative of the widest and richest range of association empirically accessible (and no apology is offered for basing philosophy upon the empirically manifest rather than upon the occult), it is necessary to point out a certain ambiguity of language which because of brevity of exposition, necessarily attaches to our statement. Social *phenomena* are not of themselves, of course, equivalent to social as a *category*. The latter is derived from the former by means of an intellectual analysis which determines what is their distinctive character. Now I am not here dealing with the important and eventually imperative problem of the category *of* the social, or the determination of the characteristics which constitute the distinguishing nature of the social, but rather with social phenomena *en gross* as comprehending, for philosophic analysis, physical, organic and mental phenomena in a mode of association in which the latter take on new properties and exercise new functions. In other words, I am here implying that social phenomena do as a matter of fact manifest *something* distinctive, and that that something affords the key to a naturalistic account of phenomena baffling philosophic interpretation when it is left out of account. To those who accept this view, the burden of proof as to the value of "social" as a metaphysical category lies upon those who habitually treat its worth as trivial. For what do *they* mean by social phenomena? If social phenomena are not an exemplification upon the widest and most intricate scale of the generic trait of associated behavior or interaction, what do they signify? I see but one kind of answer open to them, covering two alternatives: Either social phenomena are anomalous, an excrescence or intrusion, supervening in an accidental and meaningless way upon other phenomena, or else they have no distinctive import, being in reality *nothing but* physical, vital or psychological phenomena. Does not each of these views contradict the observable traits of social phenomena?

Upon a *prima facie* view, social phenomena take up and incorporate within themselves things associated in the narrower way which we term the physical. It gives a ludicrous result to think of social phenomena merely as lying on top of physical phenomena; such a notion is negated by the most casual observation of the facts. What would social phenomena be without the physical factor of land, including all the natural resources (and obstacles) and forms of energy for which the word "land" stands? What would social phenomena be without the tools and machines by which physical energies are utilized? Or what would they be without physical appliances and apparatus, from clothes and houses to railways, temples and printing-presses? No, it is not the social which is a superficial category. The view is superficial of those who fail to see that in the social the physical is taken up into a wider and more complex and delicate system of interactions so that it takes on new properties by release of potentialities previously confined because of absence of full interaction.

The same consideration applies to the inclusion within the social of the vital or organic. The members of society are living human beings with the characteristics of living creatures; but as they enter into distinctively human associations strictly organic properties are modified and even transformed. Certain physiological factors of sex, of procreation, immaturity and need of care, are assuredly implicated in the functions expressed in family life. But however great the rôle of animal lust, there is something more in any family association than bare physiological factors. The fact of transformation of the purely organic by inclusion within the scope of human association is so obvious—note the significant case of change of cries into speech—that it has indeed led to belief in the intrusive intervention of unnatural and supernatural factors in order to account for the differences between the animal and the human. The disjunction between the assertion that the human is the merely animal and the assertion that an extraneous force is obtruded is not, however, exhaustive. There remains an alternative which is most fully confirmed by empirical fact, namely that the difference is made when new

[85]

potentialities are actualized, when the range of interactions that delimits the organic is taken up into the wider and more subtly complex association which forms human society.

Since traits derived from the physical mode have been admitted into philosophy (materialism in other words is at least grudgingly admitted into philosophic companionship) ; and since organic philosophies, framed on the pattern of vital phenomena, upon conceptions of species, development and purpose, are freely admitted, it seems arbitrary, to say the least, to exclude the social from the rôle of a legitimate category.

That the mental has a recognized claim to serve as a category of description and interpretation of natural existence is evident in the very existence of idealistic philosophies. There are those who deny the ability of these theories to execute their claim, just as there are those who deny the capacity of the physical and vital to make good. But thought, as well as matter and life, is at least admitted to rank as a respectable figure in the gallery of categories. Now of the mental as of the physical and organic it may be said that it operates as an included factor within social phenomena, since the mental is empirically discernible only where association is manifested in the form of participation and communication. It would therefore appear legitimate to adopt as a hypothesis worthy of being tried out, the idea that the ulterior meaning of the mental as well as of the physical and vital is revealed in this form of associational interaction. The implication is not that they have no describable *existence* outside the social, but that in so far as they appear and operate outside of that large interaction which forms the social they do not reveal that full force and import with which it is the traditional business of philosophy to occupy itself.

After this statement of the intent of the enterprise of employing the social as a category, it remains to sketch in a summary fashion a few specimens of its implications which are relevant to the clarification of some outstanding philosophic issues. We may conveniently begin with the matter just referred to, the place of the mental in the existential scheme of things, using for purposes of our discussion as the equivalent of "mental" the fact of *meaning,* whether direct as in cognition of objects, or indirect as in esthetic, affectional and moral relations. The state of philosophic discussion exhibits a dilemma, or rather a trilemma. The mental is viewed (i) as a mysterious intrusion occurring in some unaccountable way in the order of nature; (ii) as illusory, or, in current language, as an epiphenomenon; and (iii) as ontological, whether as a section of being on the same level with the physical section, or as the Being of which so-called physical things are but disguised forms or "appearances." It may be argued that the persistence of the problem and of these widely opposed modes of solution is itself strongly indicative that some factor of the situation, the one which is the key to understanding, has been omitted. In any case, the persistence of these irreconcilable conceptions is a challenge to search for something which will eliminate the scandal of such sharp antagonisms in interpretation. Now when we turn to the social, we find *communication* to be an existential occurrence involved in all distinctively communal life, and we find that communication requires meaning and understanding as conditions of unity or agreement in conjoint behavior. We find, that is, meaning to be not an anomaly nor an accidentally supervening quality but a constitutive ingredient of existential events. We find meaning as a describable, verifiable empirical phenomenon whose genesis, modes and consequences can be concretely examined and traced. It presents itself not as an intrusion, nor as an accidental and impotent iridescence, nor as the reduplication of a structure already inhering in antecedent existence, but as an additive quality realized in the process of

[87]

wider and more complex interaction of physical and vital phenomena; and as having a distinctive and concretely verifiable office in sustaining and developing a distinctive kind of observable facts, those namely which are termed social. We do not then have to resort to purely metaphysical and dialectical considerations, adopted *ad hoc,* in order to "save" the reality and importance of the mental. The realm of meanings, of mind, is at home, securely located and anchored in an empirically observable order of existence. And this order stands in genetic continuity with physical and vital phenomena, being, indeed, these phenomena taken up into and incorporated within a wider scope of associated interactions. We do not have to read the mental back into the antecedent physical, much less resort to the desperate measure of making it so all-inclusive that the physical is treated as a disguised and illusory "appearance" of the mental. The social affords us an observable instance of a "realm of mind" objective to an individual, by entering into which, as a participating member, organic activities are transformed into acts having a mental quality.

These considerations are not supposed to demonstrate the truth of the position taken; but they are seriously proposed to indicate a hypothesis which is worthy of trial; as a hypothesis which starts from a *vera causa,* that is, from an empirically verifiable fact, instead of from concepts which have no such observed locus of their own but which are invented simply to account for facts otherwise inexplicable. In the second place, the actual structure of knowledge viewed in relation to the operations by which it is concretely established to be knowledge in the honorific sense, that is as tested and justified, as grounded, instead of as mere opinion and fantastic belief, can be understood only in social terms. By knowledge as grounded I mean belief in relation to evidence that substantiates it. Now the simplest distinction that can be drawn between objects of knowledge in this sense and mere matters of opinion and credulity, or even of thought however internally self-consistent and formally valid, is the distinction between the socially confirmed and the privately entertained. Opinion and theory as long as they are uncommunicated, or as long as, even if communicated and shared, they are unconfirmed in conjoint behavior are at best but candidates for membership within the system of knowledge. To labor this point is to weaken it. It is a truism that science is science because observations, experiments and calculations are so conducted as to be capable of report to others and repetition by others. Now this report and repetition are wholly misconceived when thought of simply as external additions to a thought complete in itself. They signify that thought itself is conceived and developed in such terms as to be capable of communication to others, of understanding by them, and of adoption and utilization in cooperative action. Report, communication, is not a bare emission of thoughts framed and completed in private soliloquy or solipsistic observation. The entire operation of individual experimentation and soliloquizing has been influenced at every point by reference to the social medium in which their results are to be set forth and responded to. Indeed what has been said is an understatement. It is not simply that the characteristic findings of thought cannot pass into knowledge save when framed with reference to social submission and adoption, but that language and thought in their relation to signs and symbols are inconceivable save as ways of achieving concerted action.

In passing, it may also be remarked that the reference to private thought as a *candidate* for knowledge through incorporation into conjoint associated action (which also involves, be it recalled, physical conditions and hence is subject to test by physical consequences), throws light upon and may give the key to another mystery of philosophic speculation—namely the nature of mind as subjective. For the latter when it is interpreted from the standpoint of the social as a category, does not appear as an anomaly, much less as a bogey, an intrusive and wholly undesirable source of error. Thinking and its results present themselves as indeed hypothetical, demanding trial in terms of social action, and hence as subject to error and defeat. But they also offer themselves as having a positive and constructive office. For they are not merely candidates for reception into the social *status quo,* the received and established order of associated behavior; they are rather claimants for a changed social order to be effected in the very action which they promote and by which they are to be tested. Sometimes the claim is narrow, affecting only the behavior of a selected group who are experts in the particular field; sometimes, as in the proposal of new policies, it is wide in the appeal which it virtually makes. But the former type, addressed primarily say to a group of scientific specialists, has a way of expanding; it cannot be kept cooped up; and in any case there is no difference in principle.

In giving illustrations, one is embarrassed by the range of philosophic problems, which suggest themselves as receiving illumination and clarification when the social is employed as a category of description and interpretation. We may, however, draw, almost at random, upon the moral field. Consider the recurrent discussion concerning the objectivity of moral distinctions and judgments, with its ceaseless vibration between reduction of them to private preferences, none the less private when they happen to be collectively entertained, and recourse to purely transcendent considerations in order to "secure" their objectivity. It would be dogmatic to assert in this casual allusion that the problem is solved when the social is used as a category, and the social is seen to incorporate the physical, organic and psychological; but no one can reasonably deny that the whole problem takes on a very different aspect when its elements are placed in this context.[1]

An allied topic concerns the "naturalness" of the moral life of man. Those who assert that it is natural are met by the counter-assertion that such a view reduces the moral life to a strictly animal plane. This sharp disjunction falls to the ground, however, when the distinctive forms of association characteristic of the life of man in social relations are recognized, for this recognition not only admits but asserts that these relations realize new and unique qualities not manifested in the lesser areas of natural association. A generalization of what is involved in this issue is found in a theory familiar to students of the history of thought. A succession of thinkers, from Herder and Kant to Hegel, have asserted that the significance of the history of humanity is found in the struggle of man to emerge from a state in which he was wholly immersed in "nature" to a state in which "spirit" is wholly triumphant, and where triumph involves a sublimated cancellation of the physical and animal. It is submitted that whatever is empirically verifiable in such a doctrine is better stated in terms of the constant remaking of the physical environment and the living organism which occurs when the latter come within the scope of the culture carried in human society. It is a fact rather than a speculation that physical and animal nature are transformed in the process of education, and of incorporation in the means and consequences of associated political, legal, religious, industrial, and scientific and artistic institutions. "Spirit" in the doctrine referred to is a transcendent and blind name for something which exhibits itself empirically as that phase of social phenomena called civilization.

[1] Compare the treatment of the objectivity of esthetic judgments in the article "On the Genesis of the Æsthetic Categories" by J. H. Tufts, *Decennial Publications of the University of Chicago*, Volume III.

The philosophic issues mentioned are cited only as illustrative specimens. They afford at most but a skeleton-like table of contents and a highly incomplete one at that. They are given as indications of a scheme of philosophic description and interpretation that has to be rounded out and filled in in order to realize and to test what is signified by "social" as a philosophic category. It is the historic claim of philosophy that it occupies itself with the ideal of wholes and the whole. It is submitted that either the whole is manifested in concretely empirical ways, and in ways consonant with infinite variety, or else wholeness is but a dialectical speculation. I do not say that the social as we know it *is* the whole, but I do emphatically suggest that it is the widest and richest manifestation of the whole accessible to our observation. As such it is at least the proper point of departure for any more imaginative construings of the whole one may wish to undertake. And in any case it furnishes the terms in which any consistent *empirical* philosophy must speak. Only by whole-hearted adoption of it as a ranking fact and idea can empirical philosophy come into its own, and escape the impotency and one-sidedness which has dogged the traditional sensationalistic empiricism. The commitment of Lockean empiricism to a doctrine that ignored the associative property of all things experienced is the source of that particularistic nominalism whose goal is solipsistic skepticism. In consequence, empiricism ceased to be empirical and became a dialectic construction of the implications of absolute particularism. By rebound, it induced recourse to principles of connection extraneously supplied, whether by "synthetic action of thought" or by eternal essences. In the end, these systems rise or fall with the truth of the empirical particularism against which they have reacted. Thus the social as a category is as important in the critical evaluation of recent systems of thought as it is in direct application to problems of matter, life and mind.

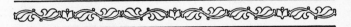

Qualitative Thought

THE world in which we immediately live, that in which we strive, succeed, and are defeated is pre-eminently a qualitative world. What we act for, suffer, and enjoy are things in their qualitative determinations. This world forms the field of characteristic modes of thinking, characteristic in that thought is definitely regulated by qualitative considerations. Were it not for the double and hence ambiguous sense of the term "common-sense," it might be said that common-sense thinking, that concerned with action and its consequences, whether undergone in enjoyment or suffering, is qualitative. But since "common-sense" is also used to designate accepted traditions and is appealed to in support of them, it is safe at the outset to refer simply to that thought which has to do with objects involved in the concerns and issues of living.

The problem of qualitative objects has influenced metaphysics and epistemology but has not received corresponding attention in logical theory. The propositions significant in physical science are oblivious of qualitative considerations as such; they deal with "primary qualities" in distinction from secondary and tertiary; in actual treatment, moreover, these primary qualities are not qualities but relations. Consider the difference between movement as qualitative alteration, and motion as $F=ma$; between stress as involving effort and tension, and as force per unit surface; between the red of the blood issuing from a wound, and red as signifying 400 trillion vibrations per time unit. Metaphysics has been concerned with the existential status of qualitative objects as contrasted with those of physical science, while epistemology, having frequently decided that qualities are subjective and psychical, has been concerned with their relation in knowing to the properties of "external" objects defined in non-qualitative terms.

But a logical problem remains. What is the relation or lack of relations between the two types of propositions, one which refers to objects of physical science and the other to qualitative objects? What, if any, are the distinguishing logical marks of each kind? If it were true that things as things, apart from interaction with an organism, are qualityless, the logical problem would remain. For the truth would concern the mode of production and existence of qualitative things. It is irrelevant to their logical status. Logic can hardly admit that it is concerned only with objects having one special mode of production and existence, and yet claim universality. And it would be fatal to the claims of logic to say that because qualities are psychical—supposing for the moment that they are—therefore logical theory has nothing to do with forms of thought characteristic of qualitative objects. It is even possible that some of the difficulties of metaphysical and epistemological theory about scientific and ordinary objects spring from neglect of a basic logical treatment.

A preliminary introduction to the topic may be found in the fact that Aristotelian logic, which still passes current nominally, is a logic based upon the idea that qualitative objects are existential in the fullest sense. To retain logical principles based on this conception along with the acceptance of theories of existence and knowledge based on an opposite conception is not, to say the least, conducive to clearness—a consideration that has a good deal to do with the existing dualism between traditional and the newer relational logics. A more obviously pertinent consideration is the fact that the interpretation of classic logic treats qualitative determinations as fixed properties of objects, and thus is committed to either an attributive or a classicatory doctrine of the import of propositions. Take the proposition: "The red Indian is stoical." This is interpreted either as signifying that the Indian in question is characterized by the property of stoicism in addition to that of redness, or that he belongs to the class of stoical objects. The ordinary direct sense of the proposition escapes recognition in either case. For this sense expresses the fact that the indigenous American was permeated throughout by a certain quality, instead of being an object possessing a certain quality along with others. He lived, acted, endured stoically.

If one thinks that the difference between the two meanings has no logical import, let him reflect that the whole current subject-predication theory of propositions is affected by the "property" notion, whether the theory speaks in the language of attribution or classification. A subject is "given"—ultimately apart from thinking—and then thought adds to what is given a further determination or else assigns it to a ready-made class of things. Neither theory can have any place for the integral development and reconstruction of subject-matter effected by the thought expressed in propositions. In effect it excludes thought from any share in the determination of the subject-matter of knowledge, confining it to setting forth the results (whether conceived as attributive or classificatory) of knowledge already attained in isolation from the method by which it is attained.

Perhaps, however, the consideration that will appeal to most people is the fact that the neglect of qualitative objects and considerations leaves thought in certain subjects without any logical status and control. In esthetic matters, in morals and politics, the effect of this neglect is either to deny (implicitly at least) that they have logical foundation or else, in order to bring them under received logical categories, to evacuate them of their distinctive meaning—a procedure which produces the myth of the "economic man" and the reduction of esthetics and morals, as far as they can receive any intellectual treatment at all, to quasi-mathematical subjects.

Consider for example a picture that is a work of art and not just a chromo or other mode of mechanical product. Its quality is not a property which it possesses in addition to its other properties. It is something which externally demarcates it from other paintings, and which internally pervades, colors, tones, and weights every detail and every relation of the work of art. The same thing is true of the "quality" of a person or of historic events. We follow, with apparently complete understanding, a tale in which a certain quality or character is ascribed to a certain man. But something said causes us to interject, "Oh, you are speaking of Thomas Jones, I supposed you meant John Jones." Every detail related, every distinction set forth remains just what it was before. Yet the significance, the color and weight, of every detail is altered. For the quality that runs through them all, that gives meaning to each and binds them together, is transformed.

Now my point is that unless such underlying and pervasive qualitative determinations are acknowledged in a distinct logical formulation, one or other of two results is bound to follow. Either thought is denied to the subject-matter in question, and the phenomena are attributed to "intuition" or "genius" or "impulse" or "personality" as ultimate and unanalyzable entities; or, worse yet, intellectual analysis is reduced to a mechanical enumeration of isolated items or "properties." As a matter of fact, such intellectual definiteness and coherence as the objects and criticisms of esthetic and moral subjects possess is due to their being controlled by the quality of subject-matter as a whole. Consideration of the meaning of regulation by an underlying and pervasive quality is the theme of this article.

What is intended may be indicated by drawing a distinction between something called a "situation" and something termed an "object." By the term situation in this connection is signified the fact that the subject-matter ultimately referred to in existential propositions is a complex existence that is held together, in spite of its internal complexity, by the fact that it is dominated and characterized throughout by a single quality. By "object" is meant some element in the complex whole that is defined in abstraction from the whole of which it is a distinction. The special point made is that the selective determination and relation of objects in thought is controlled by reference to a situation—to that which is constituted by a pervasive and internally integrating quality, so that failure to acknowledge the situation leaves, in the end, the logical force of objects and their relations inexplicable.

Now in current logical formulations, the beginning is always made with "objects." If we take the proposition "the stone is shaly," the logical import of the proposition is treated as if something called "stone" had complete intellectual import in and of itself and then some property, having equally a fixed content in isolation, "shaly" is attributed to it. No such self-sufficient and self-enclosed entity can possibly lead anywhere nor be led to; connection among such entities is mechanical and arbitrary, not intellectual. Any proposition about "stone" or "shaly" would have to be analytic in the Kantian sense, merely stating part of the content already known to be contained in the meaning of the terms. That a tautological proposition is a proposition only in name is well recognized. In fact, "stone," "shaly" (or whatever are subject and predicate) are determinations or distinctions instituted within the total subject-matter to which thought refers. When such propositions figure in logical textbooks, the actual subject-matter referred to is some branch of logical theory which is exemplified in the proposition.

This larger and inclusive subject-matter is what is meant by the term "situation." Two further points follow. The situation as such is not and cannot be stated or made explicit. It is taken for granted, "understood," or implicit in all propositional symbolization. It forms the universe of discourse of whatever is expressly stated or of what appears as a term in a proposition. The situation cannot present itself as an element in a proposition any more than a universe of discourse can appear as a member of discourse within that universe. To call it "implicit" does not signify that it is implied. It is present throughout as that of which whatever is explicitly stated or propounded is a distinction. A quart bowl cannot be held within itself or in any of its contents. It may, however, be contained in another bowl, and similarly what is the "situation" in one proposition may appear as a term in *another* proposition—that is, in connection with some *other* situation to which thought now refers.

Secondly, the situation controls the terms of thought; for they are *its* distinctions, and applicability to it is the ultimate test of their validity. It is this phase of the matter which is suggested by the earlier use of the idea of a pervasive and underlying quality. If the quart container affected the import of everything held within it, there would be a physical analogy; a consideration that may be awkwardly hinted at by the case of a person protesting to a salesman that he has not received a full quart; the deficiency affects everything that he has purchased. A work of art provides an apter illustration. In it, as we have already noted, the quality of the whole permeates, affects, and controls every detail. There are paintings, buildings, novels, arguments, in which an observer notes an inability of the author to sustain a unified attention throughout. The details fall to pieces; they are not distinctions of one subject-matter, because there is no qualitative unity underlying them. Confusion and incoherence are always marks of lack of control by a single pervasive quality. The latter alone enables a person to keep track of what he is doing, saying, hearing, reading, in whatever explicitly appears. The underlying unity of qualitativeness regulates pertinence or relevancy and force of every distinction and relation; it guides selection and rejection and the manner of utilization of all explicit terms. This quality enables us to keep thinking about one problem without our having constantly to stop to ask ourselves what it is after all that we are thinking about. We are aware of it not by itself but as the background, the thread, and the directive clue in what we do expressly think of. For the latter things are *its* distinctions and relations.[1]

If we designate this permeating qualitative unity in psychological language, we say it is felt rather than thought. Then, if we hypostatize it, we call it *a* feeling. But to term it a feeling is to reverse the actual state of affairs. The existence of unifying qualitativeness in the subject-matter defines the meaning of "feeling." The notion that "a feeling" designates a ready-made independent psychical entity is a product of a reflection which presupposes the direct presence of quality as such. "Feeling" and "felt" are names for a *relation* of quality. When, for example, anger exists, it is the pervading tone, color, and quality of persons, things, and circumstances, or of a situation. When angry we are not aware of anger but of these objects in their immediate and unique qualities. In another situation, anger may appear as a distinct term, and analysis may then call it a feeling or emotion. But we have now shifted the universe of discourse, and the validity of the terms of the later one depends upon the existence of the direct quality of the whole in a former one. That is, in saying that something was *felt,* not thought of, we are analyzing, in a new situation having its own immediate quality, the subject-matter

[1] The "fringe" of James seems to me to be a somewhat unfortunate way of expressing the rôle of the underlying qualitative character that constitutes a situation—unfortunate because the metaphor tends to treat it as an additional element instead of an all-pervasive influence in determining other contents.

of a prior situation; we are making anger an object of analytic examination, not being angry.

When it is said that I have a feeling, or impression, or "hunch," that things are thus and so, what is actually designated is primarily the presence of a dominating quality in a situation as a whole, not just the existence of a feeling as a psychical or psychological fact. To say I have a feeling or impression that so and so is the case is to note that the quality in question is not yet resolved into determinate terms and relations; it marks a conclusion without statement of the reasons for it, the grounds upon which it rests. It is the first stage in the development of explicit distinctions. All thought in every subject begins with just such an unanalyzed whole. When the subject-matter is reasonably familiar, relevant distinctions speedily offer themselves, and sheer qualitativeness may not remain long enough to be readily recalled. But it often persists and forms a haunting and engrossing problem. It is a commonplace that a problem *stated* is well on its way to solution, for statement of the nature of a problem signifies that the underlying quality is being transformed into determinate distinctions of terms and relations or has become an object of articulate thought. But something presents itself as problematic before there is recognition of *what* the problem is. The problem is had or experienced before it can be stated or set forth; but it is had as an immediate quality of the whole situation. The sense of something problematic, of something perplexing and to be resolved, marks the presence of something pervading all elements and considerations. Thought is the operation by which it is converted into pertinent and coherent terms.

The word "intuition" has many meanings. But in its popular, as distinct from refined philosophic usage, it is closely connected with the single qualitativeness underlying all the details of explicit reasoning. It may be relatively dumb and inarticulate and yet penetrating; unexpressed in definite ideas which form reasons and justifications and yet profoundly right. To my mind, Bergson's contention that intuition precedes conception and goes deeper is correct. Reflection and rational elaboration spring from and make explicit a prior intuition. But there is nothing mystical about this fact, and it does not signify that there are two modes of knowledge, one of which is appropriate to one kind of subject-matter, and the other mode to the other kind. Thinking and theorizing about physical matters set out from an intuition, and reflection about affairs of life and mind consists in an ideational and conceptual transformation of what begins as an intuition. Intuition, in short, signifies the realization of a pervasive quality such that it regulates the determination of relevant distinctions or of whatever, whether in the way of terms or relations, becomes the accepted object of thought.

While some ejaculations and interjections are merely organic responses, there are those which have an intellectual import, though only context and the total situation can decide to which class a particular ejaculation belongs. "Alas," "Yes," "No," "Oh" may each of them be the symbol of an integrated attitude toward the quality of a situation as a whole; that it is thoroughly pitiful, acceptable, to be rejected, or is a matter of complete surprise. In this case, they characterize the existent situation and as such have a cognitive import. The exclamation "Good!" may mark a deep apprehension of the quality of a piece of acting on the stage, of a deed performed, or of a picture in its wealth of content. The actual judgment may find better expression in these symbols than in a long-winded disquisition. To many persons there is something artificial and repellent in discoursing about any consummatory event or object. It speaks so completely for itself that words are poor substitutes—not that thought fails, but that thought so completely grasps the dominant quality that translation into explicit terms gives a partial and inadequate result.

Such ejaculatory judgments supply perhaps the simplest example of qualitative thought in its purity. While they are primitive, it does not follow that they are always superficial and immature. Sometimes, indeed, they express an infantile mode of intellectual response. But they may also sum up and integrate prolonged previous experience and training, and bring to a unified head the results of severe and consecutive reflection. Only the situation symbolized and not the formal and propositional symbol can decide which is the case. The full content of meaning is best apprehended in case of the judgment of the esthetic expert in the presence of a work of art. But they come at the beginning and at the close of every scientific investigation. These open with the "Oh" of wonder and terminate with the "Good" of a rounded-out and organized situation. Neither the "Oh" nor the "Good" expresses a mere state of personal feeling. Each characterizes a subject-matter. "How beautiful" symbolizes neither a state of feeling nor the supervening of an external essence upon a state of existence but marks the realized appreciation of a pervading quality that is now translated into a system of definite and coherent terms. Language fails not because thought fails, but because no verbal symbols can do justice to the fullness and richness of thought. If we are to continue talking about "data" in any other sense than as reflective distinctions, the original datum is always such a qualitative whole.

The logic of artistic construction is worth more than a passing notice, whether its product be a painting, a symphony, a statue, a building, a drama, or a novel. So far as it is not evidence of conceit on the part of a specialized class, refusal to admit thought and logic on the part of those who make these constructions is evidence of the breakdown of traditional logic. There are (as we previously noted) alleged works of art in which parts do not hang together and in which the quality of one part does not reinforce and expand the quality of every other part. But this fact is itself a manifestation of the defective character of the thought involved in their production. It illustrates by contrast the nature of such works as are genuine intellectual and logical wholes. In the latter, the underlying quality that defines the work, that circumscribes it externally and integrates it internally, controls the thinking of the artist; his logic is the logic of what I have called qualitative thinking.

Upon subsequent analysis, we term the properties of a work of art by such names as symmetry, harmony, rhythm, measure, and proportion. These may, in some cases at least, be formulated mathematically. But the apprehension of these formal relationships is not primary for either the artist or the appreciative spectator. The subject-matter formulated by these terms is primarily qualitative, and is apprehended qualitatively. Without an independent qualitative apprehension, the characteristics of a work of art can be translated into explicit harmonies, symmetries, etc., only in a way which substitutes mechanical formulæ for esthetic quality. The value of any such translation in esthetic criticism is measured, moreover, by the extent to which the propositional statements return to effect a heightening and deepening of a qualitative apprehension. Otherwise, esthetic appreciation is replaced by judgment of isolated technique.

The logic of artistic construction and esthetic appreciation is peculiarly significant because they exemplify in accentuated and purified form the control of selection of detail and of mode of relation, or integration, by a qualitative whole. The underlying quality demands certain distinctions, and the degree in which the demand is met confers upon the work of art that necessary or inevitable character which is its mark. Formal necessities, such as can be made explicit, depend upon the material necessity imposed by the pervasive and underlying quality. Artistic thought is not however unique in this respect but only shows an intensification of a characteristic of all thought. In a looser way, it is a characteristic of all non-technical, non-"scientific" thought. Scientific thought is, in its turn, a specialized form of art, with its own qualitative control. The more formal and mathematical science becomes, the more it is controlled by sensitiveness to a special kind of qualitative considerations. Failure to realize the qualitative and artistic nature of formal scientific construction is due to two causes. One is conventional, the habit of associating art and esthetic appreciation with a few popularly recognized forms. The other cause is the fact that a student is so concerned with the mastery of symbolic or propositional forms that he fails to recognize and to repeat the creative operations involved in their construction. Or, when they are mastered, he is more concerned with their further application than with realization of their intrinsic intellectual meaning.

The foregoing remarks are intended to suggest the significance to be attached to the term "qualitative thought." But as statements they are propositions and hence symbolic. Their meaning can be apprehended only by going beyond them, by using them as clues to call up qualitative situations. When an experience of the latter is had and they are relived, the realities corresponding to the propositions laid down may be had. Assuming that such a realization has been experienced, we proceed to consider some further questions upon which qualitative thought throws light.

First as to the nature of the predication. The difficulties connected with the problem of predication are of long standing. They were recognized in Greek thought, and the skepticism they induced was a factor in developing the Platonic theory of the same-and-the-other and the Aristotelian conception of potentiality-and-actuality. The skeptical difficulty may be summed up in the statement that predication is either tautological and so meaningless, or else falsifying or at least arbitrary. Take the proposition "that thing is sweet." If "sweet" already qualifies the meaning of "that thing," the predication is analytic in the Kantian sense, or forms a trivial proposition in the sense of Locke. But if "sweet" does not already qualify "that thing" what ground is there for tacking it on? The most that can be said is that some one who did not know before that it was sweet has now learned it. But such a statement refers only to an episode in the some one's intellectual biography. It has no logical force; it does not touch the question of predication that has objective reference and possible validity.

When, however, it is recognized that predication—any proposition having subject-predicate form—marks an attempt to make a qualitative whole which is directly and non-reflectively experienced into an object of thought for the sake of its own development, the case stands otherwise. What is "given" is not an object by itself nor a term having a meaning of its own. The "given," that is to say the existent, is precisely an undetermined and dominant complex quality. "Subject" and "predicate" are correlative determinations of this quality. The "copula" stands for the fact that one term is predicated of the other, and is thus a sign of the development of the qualitative whole by means of their distinction. It is, so to speak, the assertion of the fact that the distinctions designated in subject and predicate are correlative and work together in a common function of determination.

A certain quality is experienced. When it is inquired into or thought (judged), it differentiates into "that thing" on the one hand, and "sweet" on the other. Both "that thing" and "sweet" are analytic of the quality, but are additive, synthetic, ampliative, with respect to each other. The copula "is" marks just the effect of this distinction upon the correlative terms.

They mark something like a division of labor, and the copula marks the function or work done by the structures that exhibit the division of labor. To say that "that thing is sweet" means "that thing" will *sweeten* some other object, say coffee, or a batter of milk and eggs. The intent of sweetening something formed the ground for converting a dumb quality into an articulate object of thought.

The logical force of the copula is always that of an active verb. It is merely a linguistic peculiarity, not a logical fact, that we say "that is red" instead of "that reddens," either in the sense of growing, becoming, red, or in the sense of making something else red. Even linguistically our "is" is a weakened form of an active verb signifying "stays" or "stands." But the nature of any act (designated by the true verbal form) is best apprehended in its effect and issue; we say "is sweet" rather than "sweetens," "is red" rather than "reddens" because we define the active change by its anticipated or attained outcome. To say "the dog is ugly" is a way of setting forth what he is likely to *do,* namely to snarl and bite. "Man is mortal" indicates what man does or what actively is done to him, calling attention to a consequence. If we convert its verbal form into "men die," we realize the transitive and additive force of predication and escape the self-made difficulties of the attributive theory.

The underlying pervasive quality in the last instance, when it is put in words, involves care or concern for human destiny. But we must remember that this exists as a dumb quality until it is symbolized in an intellectual and propositional form. Out of this quality there emerges the idea of man and of mortality and of their existential connection with each other. No one of them has any meaning apart from the others, neither the distinctions, the terms, nor their relation, the predication. All the difficulties that attend the problem of predication spring from supposing that we can take the terms and their connection as having meaning by themselves. The sole alternative to this supposition is the recognition that the object of thought, designated propositionally, is a quality that is first directly and unreflectively experienced or had.

One source of the difficulty and the error in the classic theory lies in a radical misconception of the treacherous idea of the "given." The only thing that is unqualifiedly given is the total pervasive quality; and the objection to calling it "given" is that the word suggests something *to* which it is given, mind or thought or consciousness or whatever, as well possibly as something that gives. In truth "given" in this connection signifies only that the quality immediately exists, or is brutely there. In this capacity, it forms that to which all objects of thought refer, although, as we have noticed, it is never part of the manifest subject-matter of thought. In itself, it is the big, buzzing, blooming confusion of which James wrote. This expresses not only the state of a baby's experience but the first stage and background of all thinking on any subject. There is, however, no inarticulate quality which is merely buzzing and blooming. It buzzes to some effect; it blooms toward some fruitage. That is, the quality, although dumb, has as a part of its complex quality a movement or transition in some direction. It can, therefore, be intellectually symbolized and converted into an object of thought. This is done by statement of limits and of direction of transition between them. "That" and "sweet" define the limits of the moving quality, the copula "tastes" (the real force of "is") defines the direction of movement between these limits. Putting the nature of the two limits briefly and without any attempt to justify the statement here, the subject represents the pervasive quality as means or condition and the predicate represents it as outcome or end.

These considerations define not only the subject-predicate structure of categorical propositions but they explain why the

selective character of all such propositions with respect to the
fullness of existence is not falsifying in character. Idealistic
logicians, in calling attention to the partial or selective character of particular judgments, have used the fact to cast
logical aspersion upon them, and to infer their need of correction first by transformation into conditional propositions
and then finally into a judgment coextensive with the whole
universe, arguing that only the latter can be truly true. But
enough is always enough, and the underlying quality is itself
the test of the "enough" for any particular case. All that is
needed is to determine this quality by indicating the limits
between which it moves and the direction or tendency of its
movement. Sometimes the situation is simple and the most
meager indications serve, like the "safe" or "out" of a base-
ball umpire. At other times, a quality is complex and prolonged, and a multitude of distinctions and subordinate relations are required for its determinate statement. It would
have been logically vicious on one occasion to propound more
than "my kingdom for a horse," while under other circumstances it may need a volume to set forth the quality of the
situation so as to make it comprehensible. Any proposition
that serves the purpose for which it is made is logically adequate; the idea that it is inadequate until the whole universe
has been included is a consequence of giving judgment a
wrong office—an error that has its source in failure to see the
domination of every instance of thought by a qualitative
whole needing statement in order that it may function.

At this point a reference to what is termed association of
ideas is in place. For while the subject is usually treated as
psychological in nature, thinking as an existential process
takes place through association; existentially, thinking *is*
association as far as the latter is controlled. And the mechanics
of thinking can hardly be totally irrelevant to its *logical*
structure and function. I shall assume without much argu-

ment that "ideas" here signify objects, not psychical entities; objects, that is to say, as meanings to which reference may be made. When one, seeing smoke, thinks of fire he is associating objects, not just states in his own mind. And so when thinking of a hand, one thinks of grasping or of an organism. Thus, when association takes the form of thought, or is controlled and not loose day-dreaming, association is a name for a connection of objects or their elements in the total situation having a qualitative unity. This statement signifies something different than does a statement that associated objects are physical parts of a physical whole. It happens to hold in the case of "hand-organism" and with some qualifications in the case of "smoke-fire." But a philosophical student might be led by the thought of hand to the thought of Aristotle on the ground of a remark made by Aristotle.

In any case an original contiguity (or similarity) is not the cause of an association. We do not associate *by* contiguity, for recognition of a whole in which elements are juxtaposed in space or in temporal sequence is the *result* of suggestion. The absurdity of the preposition "by" when applied to similarity is still more obvious. It is the reason why some writers reduce similarity to identity in differences, a position that will be examined later. That by which association is effected, by which suggestion and evocation of a distinct object of thought is brought about, is some acquired modification of the organism, usually designated habit. The conditioning mechanism may not be known at present in detail, but it cannot be an original contiguity because that contiguity is apprehended only in consequence of association. It may well be an organic attitude formed in consequence of a responsive act to things once coexistent or sequential. But this act was unitary; reference to it only accentuates the fact that the quality attending it was spread over and inclusive of the two things in question.

That is, it was a response to a *situation* within which objects were related in space or time.

Given the conditions, the real problem is to say why objects once conjoined in a whole are now distinguished as two objects, one that which suggests, and the other that which is suggested. If I think of a chiffonier, the thought does not call up that of drawers as a distinct idea. For the drawers are a part of the object thought of. So when I originally saw, say a bird-in-a-nest, I saw a single total object. Why then does the sight or thought of a bird now call up that of a nest as a distinct idea? In general, the reason is that I have so often seen birds without seeing a nest and nests without birds. Moreover, it must be remembered that a person often sees a bird or nest, and instead of thinking of any other object, he reacts to it directly, as a man does when shooting at a bird or a boy climbing a tree to get the nest. While there is no association without habit, the natural tendency of habit is to produce an immediate reaction, not to evoke another distinct object of thought or idea. As the *dis*association of birds and nests in experience shows, this additional factor is some resistance to the attitude formed by the sight of nest-with-a-bird-in-it. Otherwise we should have the case over again of chiffonier and its drawers, or any object and its constitutive parts. Without the resistant or negative factor, there would be no tension to effect the change from a direct response, an immediate act, to an indirect one, a distinct object of thought.

Not only then is there no association *by* contiguity, but association is not *of* two objects separated yet contiguous in a prior experience. Its characteristic nature is that it presents as distinct but connected objects what originally were either two parts of one situational object, or (in the case that a man had previously always seen birds and nests separately from each other) that it presents in coexistence or sequence with one another objects previously separated in space and time.

This consideration is fatal to the notion that the associated objects account by themselves or in their own isolated nature for association. It indicates that coexistence or sequence as a physical existential fact is not the ground of association. What alternative remains save that the quality of a situation as a whole operates to produce a functional connection? Acceptance of this alternative implies that association is an *intellectual* connection, thus aligning association with thought, as we shall now see.

There is nothing intellectual or logical in contiguity, in mere juxtaposition in space and time. If association were, then, either *of* or *by* contiguity, association would not have any logical force, any connection with thought.[1] But in fact association of bare contiguities is a myth. There is an indefinite number of particulars contiguous to one another in space and time. When I think of a nest why does a bird come into my mind? As a matter of contiguity, there are multitudinous leaves and twigs which are more frequently and more obviously juxtaposed than is a bird. When I think of a hammer, why is the idea of nail so likely to follow? Such questions suggest, I hope, that even in seemingly casual cases of association, there is an underlying quality which operates to control the connection of objects thought of. It takes something else than contiguity to effect association; there must be relevancy of both ideas to a situation defined by unity of quality. There is coherence of some sort because of mutual pertinency of both ideas, (or of all ideas in train) to a basis beyond any of them and beyond mere juxtaposition of objects in space and time.

The usual notion that association is merely *de facto* receives a still more obvious shock in the case of similarity. When I associate bird with nest, there may have been at least

---

[1] The assumption that in the case of contiguity association is of a merely *de facto* or existential nature is the root of Lotze's (and others') theory that *a priori* logical forms are necessary in order to change juxtaposition of things into coherence of meaning.

some previous conjunction in experience of the two objects, even though that conjunction is not by itself a sufficient condition of the later association. But when troublesome thought suggests the sting of an insect, or when change of fortune suggests the ebb and flow of the sea, there is *no* physical conjunction in the past to which appeal can be made. To try to explain the matter by saying that two objects are associated *because* they are similar is either to offer the problem as a solution or to attribute causal efficacy to "similarity"—which is to utter meaningless words. So-called association "by" similarity is a striking example of the influence of an underlying pervasive quality in determining the connection essential in thought.

There is, as far as I am aware, but one serious attempt to explain such association on some other basis. This is found in the view that there is in what is called similarity an actual existential identity among differences and that this identity works and then reinstates differences by contiguity. I fail to see how the explanation applies in many cases—such as that of the troublesome thought and the sting of an insect, or Socrates and a gadfly. "Identity" seems to be the result rather than the antecedent of the association. But I shall confine the discussion to instances in which it is claimed to work. Bradley has stated the theory in question most clearly and I shall use his illustration.[1]

Walking on the shore of England, one sees a promontory and remarks how like it is to one in Wales. Bradley's explanation is that there is an actual identity of form in both and that this identical form suggests by contiguity in space certain elements which cannot be referred to the promontory now seen (size, color, etc., being incompatible) and thus constitutes in connection with identical form the content of the idea of the promontory in Wales. The seeming plausibility of this ex-

[1] Logic, Book II, Part 2, Ch. I, Sec. 30.

planation is shattered by the fact that form is not one isolated element among others, but is an arrangement or pattern of elements. Identity of pattern, arrangement of form is something that can be apprehended only *after* the other promontory has been suggested, by comparison of the two objects.

The only way that form or pattern can operate as an immediate link is by the mode of a directly experienced *quality,* something present and prior to and independent of all reflective analysis, something of the same nature which controls artistic construction. In psychological language, it is felt, and the feeling is made explicit or a term of thought in the idea of another promontory. What operates is not an external existential identity between two things, but a present immediate quality—an explanation which is the only one applicable to some cases already cited, and to being reminded of blotting paper by a certain voice. The priority of regulative quality of the situation as a whole is especially obvious in the case of esthetic judgments. A man sees a picture and says at first sight that it is by Goya or by some one influenced by him. He passes the judgment long before he has made any analysis or any explicit identification of elements. It is the quality of the picture as a whole that operates. With a trained observer such a judgment based on pervasive quality may lead later to definite analysis of elements and details; the result of the analysis may confirm or may lead to rejection of the original ascription. But the basic appreciation of quality as a whole is a more dependable basis of such point by point analysis and its conclusion than is an external analysis performed by a critic who knows history and mechanical points of brushwork but who is lacking in sensitiveness to pervasive quality.

Another instance of Bradley's refers to Mill's denial that the suggestion of another triangle by a given triangle can be reduced to contiguity. For, Mill says, "the form of a triangle is not one single feature among others." Bradley thinks such a view absurd; he cannot, he says, even tell what is meant. The use of the term "feature" may be unfortunate. For when we speak of a nose as a feature of a face, we have in mind one element or part among others. Now triangularity is not such an isolable element. It is a characteristic of the disposition, arrangement, or pattern of all elements, and it must be capable of immediate realization. Even a nose as a feature of a man's face is not completely isolable. For it is characterized by the whole face as well as characterizing that face. A better instance is found, however, when we speak of a man's *expression*. That assuredly is a total effect of all elements in their relation to one another, not a "single feature among others." And so is triangularity. Family resemblances are often detected, and yet one is totally unable to specify the points of resemblance. Unanalyzed quality of the whole accounts for the identification as a *result*, and it is a radically different thing from identification of a man by finger prints.

The outcome of this brief discussion, in revealing the significance of dominant qualitativeness in suggestion and connection of ideas, shows why thinking as an existential process is all one with controlled association.[1] For the latter is not explained by any merely external conjunction or any external identity in things. If it were, association would itself be merely another case of existential sequence, coexistence, or identity and would be lacking in intellectual and logical import. But selection and coherence determined by an immediate quality that constitutes and delimits a situation are characteristics of "association." These traits are different in kind from existential conjunction and physical sameness, and identical

[1] Were I to venture into speculative territory, I might apply this conception to the problem of "thinking" in animals, and what the *Gestalt* psychologists call "insight." That total quality operates with animals and sometimes secures, as with monkeys, results like those which we obtain by reflective analysis cannot, it seems to me, be doubted. But that this operation of quality in effecting results then goes out into symbolization and analysis is quite another matter.

with those of thought. The case of similarity or resemblance is almost uniquely significant. The problem of its nature is a crux of philosophies. The difficulty of dealing with it leads one on the one hand to thinking of it as purely psychical in nature, and, on the other hand, to the idealistic identification of the ontological and the logical *via* the principle of identity in difference. The recognition of pervasive quality enables us to avoid both extremes. By its means a voice is assimilated to blotting paper, and in more serious intellectual matters analogy becomes a guiding principle of scientific thought. On the basis of *assimilation* a further explicit recognition of similarity takes place. For assimilation is not itself the perception or judgment of similarity; the latter requires a further act made possible by symbols. It involves a proposition. The saying that there is a "tide in the affairs of men, etc.," does not of itself involve any direct comparison of human affairs with the ocean and an explicit judgment of likeness. A pervasive quality has resulted in an assimilation. If symbols are at hand, this assimilation may lead to a further act—the judgment of similarity. But *de facto* assimilation comes first and need not eventuate in the express conception of resemblance.[1]

"Assimilation" denotes the efficacious operation of pervasive quality; "similarity" denotes a *relation. Sheer* assimilation results in the presence of a single object of apprehension. To identify a seen thing *as* a promontory is a case of assimilation. By some physiological process, not exactly understood at present but to which the name "habit" is given, the net outcome of prior experiences gives a dominant quality, designated "promontory," to a perceived existence. Passage from this object to some other implies resistance to mere assimilation and results in making distinctions. The pervasive quality

[1] Thus, to recur to Bradley's example, one may pass directly from the promontory in England to one in Wales and become absorbed in the latter without any judgment of the likeness of the two.

is differentiated while at the same time these differentiations are connected. The result is an explicit statement or proposition.

I have touched, as I am well aware, only upon the fringes of a complex subject. But in view of the general neglect of the subject, I shall be satisfied if I have turned the attention of those interested in thought and its workings to an overlooked field. Omitting reference to ramifications, the gist of the matter is that the immediate existence of quality, and of dominant and pervasive quality, is the background, the point of departure, and the regulative principle of all thinking. Thought which denies the existential reality of qualitative things is therefore bound to end in self-contradiction and in denying itself. "Scientific" thinking, that expressed in physical science, never gets away from qualitative existence. Directly, it always has its own qualitative background; indirectly, it has that of the world in which the ordinary experience of the common man is lived. Failure to recognize this fact is the source of a large part of the artificial problems and fallacies that infect our theory of knowledge and our metaphysics, or theories of existence. With this general conclusion goes another that has been emphasized in the preceding discussion. Construction that is artistic is as much a case of genuine thought as that expressed in scientific and philosophical matters, and so is all genuine esthetic appreciation of art, since the latter must in some way, to be vital, retrace the course of the creative process. But the development of this point in its bearing upon esthetic judgment and theory is another story.

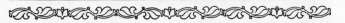

Affective Thought

TRADITIONAL theories in philosophy and psychology have accustomed us to sharp separations between physiological and organic processes on the one hand and the higher manifestations of culture in science and art on the other. The separations are summed up in the common division made between mind and body. These theories have also accustomed us to draw rigid separations between the logical, strictly intellectual, operations which terminate in science; the emotional and imaginative processes which dominate poetry, music and to a lesser degree the plastic art; and the practical doings which rule our daily life and which result in industry, business and political affairs. In other words, thought, sentiment or affectivity and volition have been marked off from one another. The result of these divisions has been the creation of a large number of problems which in their technical aspect are the special concern of philosophy, but which come home to every one in his actual life in the segregation of the activities he carries on, the departmentalizing of life, the pigeonholing of interests. Between science's sake, art for art's sake, business as usual or business for money-making, the relegation of religion to Sundays and holy-days, the turning over of politics to professional politicians, the professionalizing of sports, and so on, little room is left for living for the sake of living, a full, rich and free life.

Recent advances in some fundamental generalizations regarding biological functions in general and those of the nervous system in particular have made possible a definite conception of continuous development from the lower functions to the higher. Interestingly enough, this breaking-down of fixed barriers between physiological operations and the far

[117]

reaches of culture in science and art has also removed the underpinning from beneath the separation of science, art and practical activity from one another. There has long been vague talk about the unity of experience and mental life, to the effect that knowledge, feeling and volition are all manifestations of the same energies, etc.; but there has now been put in our hands the means by which this talk may be made definite and significant.

Naturally, the variety of physiological details involved has not yet been adequately organized nor has there been time to digest them and get their net results. In any case, the writer is not an expert in this field, and even if he were this would hardly be the place to expound them. But some of their net results are easy of comprehension and they have a definite bearing upon art and its connection with the normal processes of life.

We may begin with the field of reasoning, long supposed to be pre-empted by pure intellect, and to be completely severed, save by accident, from affectivity and desire and from the motor organs and habits by which we make our necessary practical adjustments to the world about us. But a recent writer, Rignano, working from a biological basis, has summed up his conclusions as follows: "The analysis of reasoning, the highest of our mental faculties, has led to the view that it is constituted entirely by the reciprocal play of the two fundamental and primordial activities of our psyche, the intellectual and the affective. The first consist in simple mnemonic evocations of perceptions or images of the past; the second appear as tendencies or aspirations of our mind towards a certain end to be attained, towards which reasoning itself is directed." [1]

An isolated quotation fails, of course, to bring out the full force of the points made. But what is summed up here under

[1] Rignano, *The Psychology of Reasoning*, p. 388.

the idea of "affectivity" is that an organism has certain basic needs which cannot be supplied without activity that modifies the surroundings; that when the organism is in any way disturbed in its "equilibration" with its environment, its needs show themselves as restless, craving, desiring activity which persists until the acts thus induced have brought about a new integration of the organism and its relation to the environment. Then it is shown that thinking falls within the scope of this principle; reasoning is a phase of the generic function of bringing about a new relationship between organisms and the conditions of life, and like other phases of the function is controlled by need, desire and progressive satisfactions.

Rignano calls the other phase "intellectual." But the context shows that the basic principle here is one of practical adjustments. Past experiences are retained so that they may be evoked and arranged when there is need to use them in attaining the new end set by the needs of our affective nature. But the retention is not intellectual. It is a matter of organic modifications, of change of disposition, attitude and habit. The "stuff" from which thinking draws its material in satisfying need by establishing a new relation to the surroundings is found in what, with some extension of the usual sense of the word, may be termed habits; namely, the changes wrought in our ways of acting and undergoing by prior experiences. Thus the material of thought all comes from the past; but its purpose and direction is future, the development of a new environment as the condition of sustaining a new and more fully integrated self.

It thus turns out, though the argument is too technical to be developed on this occasion, that the great gap which is traditionally made between the lower physiological functions and the higher cultural ones, is due first to isolating the organism from the environment, failing to see the necessity of its integration with environment; and secondly, to neglect of the function of needs in creating ends, or consequences to be attained. So when "ends" are recognized at all, it has been thought necessary to call in some higher and independent power to account for them. But the connection of ends with affectivities, with cravings and desires, is deep-seated in the organism, and is constantly extended and refined through experience. Desire, interest, accomplishes what in the traditional theory a pure intellect was evoked to accomplish. More and more expansive desires and more varied and flexible habits build up more elaborate trains of thought; finally, the harmonies, consistencies and comprehensive structures of logical systems result.

Reasoning and science are thus obviously brought nearer to art. The satisfaction of need requires that surroundings should be changed. In reasoning, this fact appears as the necessity for experimentation. In plastic art it is a commonplace. Art also explicitly recognizes what it has taken so long to discover in science; the control exercised by emotion in reshaping natural conditions, and the place of the imagination, under the influence of desire, in re-creating the world into a more orderly place. When so-called nonrational factors are found to play a large part in the production of relations of consistency and order in logical systems, it is not surprising that they should operate in artistic structures. Indeed, it may be questioned whether any scientific systems extant, save perhaps those of mathematics, equal artistic structure in integrity, subtlety and scope, while the latter are evidently more readily and widely understood, and are the sources of a more widespread and direct satisfaction. These facts are explicable only when it is realized that scientific and artistic systems embody the same fundamental principles of the relationship of life to its surroundings, and that both satisfy the same fundamental needs. Probably a time will come when it will be universally recognized that the differences between coherent logical schemes and artistic structures in poetry, music and the plastics are technical and specialized, rather than deep-seated.

In the past we have had to depend mostly upon phrases to explain the production of artistic structures. They have been referred to genius or inspiration or the creative imagination. Contemporary appeal to the Unconscious and the Racial Unconscious are the same thing under a new name. Writing the word with a capital letter and putting "the" before it, as if it were a distinct force, gives us no more light than we had before. Yet unconscious activities are realities, and the newer biology is making it clear that such organic activities are just of the kind to reshape natural objects in order to procure their adequate satisfaction, and that the reshaped object will be marked by the features known to belong to works of art.

It is a commonplace that recurrence in place and time, rhythm, symmetry, harmony, modulation, suspense and resolution, plot, climax and contrasting let-down, emphasis and intervals, action and retardation, unity, being "all of a piece," and inexhaustible variety, are means, in varying ways, to meet the requirements of different media, of all artistic productions. These are just the traits which naturally characterize objects when the environment is made over in consonance with basic organic requirements. On the other hand, the fact that the spectator and auditor "click" so intimately and intensely in the face of works of art is accounted for. By their means there are released old, deep-seated habits or engrained organic "memories"; yet these old habits are deployed in new ways, ways in which they are adapted to a more completely integrated world so that they themselves achieve a new integration. Hence the liberating, expansive power of art.

The same considerations explain the fact that works of art of a new style have to create their own audience. At first there is experienced largely the jar of dissonance with the superficial habits most readily called into play. But changes in the surroundings involve correlated changes in the organism, and so the eye and ear gradually become acclimatized. The organism is really made over, is reorganized in effecting an adequate perception of a work of art. Hence the proper effect of the latter is gradually realized, and then what was first condemned as *outré* falls into its serial place in the history of artistic achievement.

In *The Art in Painting,* Mr. Barnes has shown that plastic form is the *integration of all plastic means.* In the case of paintings, these are color, line, light and space. By means of their relations to one another, design is affected: design, namely in line patterns, in surface masses, in three-dimensional solids, and in spatial intervals—the "room" about objects whether up and down, side to side, front and back. And Mr. Barnes has shown that it is the kind and degree of integration of plastic means in achieving each of the elements of design taken by itself and also the integration of each with all the others, which constitutes the objective standard for value in painting. From the psychological standpoint, this integration in pictures means that a correlative integration is effected in the total set of organic responses; eye-activities arouse allied muscular activities which in turn not merely harmonize with and support eye-activities, but which in turn evoke further experiences of light and color, and so on. Moreover, as in every adequate union of sensory and motor actions, the background of visceral, circulatory, respiratory, functions is also consonantly called into action. In other words, integration in the object permits and secures a corresponding integration in organic activities. Hence, the peculiar well-being and rest in excitation, vitality in peace, which is characteristic of esthetic enjoyment.

Defective value can, of course, be judged by the same measure. Some one of the elements may be deficient; thereby adequate support is not given to the functioning of the other elements, and a corresponding lack of vitality in response occurs or even a feeling of frustration and bafflement. Or, what is more likely to happen in pictures that may conventionally attain celebrity for a time, some factor is overaccentuated— so that while vision is captured and impressed for the moment, the final reaction is partial and one-sided, a fatiguing demand being made upon some organic activities which are not duly nourished and reinforced by the others.

Thus it is not too much to say that the statement of an objective criterion of value in paintings set forth for the first time by Mr. Barnes will make possible in time an adequate psychological, even physiological, analysis of esthetic responses in spectators, so that the appreciation of paintings will no longer be a matter of private, absolute tastes and *ipse dixits*.

By the use of the same conception of integration of specified means, Mr. Barnes has also for the first time given us the clue to the historical development of modern painting in terms of paintings themselves. In the earlier period, integration is in considerable measure achieved by means extraneous to the painting itself, such as associated subject-matter in the religious or prior (academic) tradition, or by undue reliance upon familiar associations between light and shade and spatial positions. The history of art shows a tendency to secure variety and relationship in plastic form by means of the element most truly distinctive of painting, namely, color. Lines, for example, have ceased to be hard and fast clear-cut divisions (in which case they are more or less nonintegrative), and are determined by subtle meetings of color-masses which upon close examination are found to melt into one another. Similarly, light and shade were long employed on the basis of every-day practical associations to give the impression of solidity. But artists capable of greater differentiation and integration of their experiences in terms of color itself experimented in conveying tri-dimensional relationships by means of variations and juxtapositions in color. Then color was employed to build up structural solidity and its variations in single objects. Painters have also learned to render action and movement, not by depending upon associations with extraneous experiences—which always lead to an overaccentuation of some one feature, light or line, as in depicting exaggerated muscular poses—but by use of the relations of forms to one another, in connection with spatial intervals, this end being attained by use of color as means. The fact that this more subtle and complete integration usually involves deformation or distortion of familiar forms—that is, conflicts with associations formed outside the realm of painting—accounts for the fact that they are greeted at first with disdainful criticism. But in time a new line of organic associations is built up, formed on the basis of unalloyed esthetic experiences, and deformations—what are such from the practical every-day standpoint—cease to give trouble and to be annoying. They become elements in a genuine and direct æsthetic grasp.

From the standpoint of the analysis of pictures, there is nothing new in these remarks to any one familiar with Mr. Barnes' book. I have recurred to them only because the objective analysis of Mr. Barnes is in the first place so thoroughly in accord with the present trend of fundamental biological conceptions, and, secondly, because it makes possible an application of these biological conceptions to the whole field of artistic structures and esthetic criticism. It then becomes possible to break down the traditional separation between scientific and intellectual systems and those of art, and also to further the application of the principle of integration to the relationship of those elements of culture which are so segregated in our present life—to science, art in its variety of forms, industry and business, religion, sport and morals. And it is daily being more evident that unless some integration can be attained, the always increasing isolations and oppositions consequent upon the growth of specialization in all fields, will in the end disrupt our civilization. That art and its intelligent appreciation as manifested especially in painting is itself an integrating experience is the constant implication of the work of the Barnes Foundation as that is reflected in *The Art in Painting.* For to make of paintings an educational means is to assert that the genuine intelligent realization of pictures is not only an integration of the specialized factors found in the paintings as such, but is such a deep and abiding experience of the nature of fully harmonized experience as sets a standard or forms a habit for all other experiences. In other words, paintings when taken out of their specialized niche are the basis of an educational experience which counteracts the disrupting tendencies of the hard-and-fast specializations, compartmental divisions and rigid segregations which so confuse and nullify our present life.

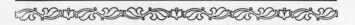

Logical Method and Law

HUMAN conduct, broadly viewed, falls into two sorts: Particular cases overlap, but the difference is discernible in any large scale consideration of conduct. Sometimes human beings act with a minimum of foresight, without examination of what they are doing and its probable consequences. They act not upon deliberation but from routine, instinct, the direct pressure of appetite, or a blind "hunch." It would be a mistake to suppose that such behavior is always inefficient or unsuccessful. When we do not like it, we condemn it as capricious, arbitrary, careless, negligent. But in other cases, we praise the marvelous rectitude of instinct or intuition; we are inclined to accept the offhand appraisal of an expert in preference to elaborately calculated conclusions of a man who is ill-informed. There is the old story of the layman who was appointed to a position in India where he would have to pass in his official capacity on various matters in controversy between natives. Upon consulting a legal friend, he was told to use his common-sense and announce his decisions firmly; in the majority of cases his natural decision as to what was fair and reasonable would suffice. But, his friend added: "Never try to give reasons, for they will usually be wrong."

In the other sort of case, action follows upon a decision, and the decision is the outcome of inquiry, comparison of alternatives, weighing of facts; deliberation or thinking has intervened. Considerations which have weight in reaching the conclusion as to what is to be done, or which are employed to justify it when it is questioned, are called "reasons." If they are stated in sufficiently general terms they are "principles." When the operation is formulated in a compact way, the decision is called a conclusion, and the considerations which led up to it are called the premises. Decisions of the first type may be reasonable: that is, they may be adapted to good results; those of the second type are reasoned or rational, increasingly so, in the degree of care and thoroughness with which inquiry has been conducted and the order in which connections have been established between the considerations dealt with.

Now I define logical theory as an account of the procedures followed in reaching decisions of the second type: in those cases in which subsequent experience shows that they were the best which could have been used under the conditions. This definition would be questioned by many authorities, and it is only fair to say that it does not represent the orthodox or the prevailing view. But it is stated at the outset so that the reader may be aware of the conception of logic which underlies the following discussion. If we take an objection which will be brought against this conception by adherents of the traditional notion, it will serve to clarify its meaning. It will be said that the definition restricts thinking to the processes antecedent to making a decision or a deliberate choice; and, thereby, in confining logical procedure to practical matters, fails to take even a glance at those cases in which true logical method is best exemplified: namely, scientific, especially mathematical, subjects.

A partial answer to this objection is that the especial topic of our present discussion is logical method in legal reasoning and judical decision, and that such cases at least are similar in general type to decisions made by engineers, merchants, physicians, bankers, etc., in the pursuit of their callings. In law we are certainly concerned with the necessity of settling upon a course of action to be pursued, giving judgment of one sort or another in favor of adoption of one mode of conduct and against another. But the scope of the position taken will appear more clearly if we do not content ourselves with this *ad hoc* reply.

If we consider the procedure of the mathematician or of any man of science, as it concretely occurs, instead of considering simply the relations of consistent implication which subsist between the propositions in which his finally approved conclusions are set forth, we find that he, as well as an intelligent farmer or business man or physician, is constantly engaged in making decisions; and that in order to make them wisely he summons before his mental gaze various considerations, and accepts and rejects them with a view to making his decision as rational as possible. The concrete subject with which he deals, the material he investigates, accepts, rejects, employs, in reaching and justifying his decision, is different from that of farmer, lawyer, or merchant, but the course of the operation, the form of the procedure, is similar. The scientific man has the advantage of working under much more narrowly and exactly controlled conditions, with the aid of symbols artfully devised to protect his procedure. For that reason it is natural and proper that we should, in our formal treatises, take operations of this type as standards and models, and should treat ordinary "practical" reasonings leading up to decisions as to what is to be done as only approximations. But every thinker, as an investigator, mathematician, or physicist as well as "practical man," thinks in order to determine *his* decisions and conduct—his conduct as a specialized agent working in a carefully delimited field.

It may be replied, of course, that this is an arbitrary notion of logic, and that in reality logic is an affair of the relations and orders of relations which subsist between propositions which constitute the accepted subject-matter of a science; that relations are independent of operations of inquiry and of reaching conclusions or decisions. I shall not stop to try to controvert this position, but shall use it to point the essential difference between it and the position taken in this article. According to the latter, logical systematization with a view to the utmost generality and consistency of propositions is indispensable but is not ultimate. It is an instrumentality, not an end. It is a means of improving, facilitating, clarifying the inquiry that leads up to concrete decisions; primarily that particular inquiry which has just been engaged in, but secondarily, and of greater ultimate importance, other inquiries directed at making other decisions in similar fields. And here at least I may fall back for confirmation upon the special theme of law. It is most important that rules of law should form as coherent generalized logical systems as possible. But these logical systematizations of law in any field, whether of crime, contracts or torts, with their reduction of a multitude of decisions to a few general principles that are logically consistent with one another while they may be an end in itself for a particular student, are clearly in last resort subservient to the economical and effective reaching of decisions in particular cases.

It follows that logic is ultimately an empirical and concrete discipline. Men first employ certain ways of investigating, and of collecting, recording and using data in reaching conclusions, in making decisions; they draw inferences and make their checks and tests in various ways. These different ways constitute the empirical raw material of logical theory. The latter thus comes into existence without any conscious thought of logic, just as forms of speech take place without conscious reference to rules of syntax or of rhetorical propriety. But it is gradually learned that some methods which are used work better than others. Some yield conclusions that do not stand the test of further situations; they produce conflicts and confusion; decisions dependent upon them have to be retracted or revised. Other methods are found to yield conclusions which are available in subsequent inquiries as well as confirmed by them. There first occurs a kind of natural selection of the methods which afford the better type of conclusion, better for subsequent usage, just as happens in the development of rules for conducting any art. Afterwards the methods are themselves studied critically. Successful ones are not only selected and collated, but the causes of their effective operation are discovered. Thus logical theory becomes scientific.

The bearing of the conception of logic which is here advanced upon legal thinking and decisions may be brought out by examining the apparent disparity which exists between actual legal development and the strict requirements of logical theory. Justice Holmes has generalized the situation by saying that "the whole outline of the law is the resultant of a conflict at every point between logic and good sense—the one striving to work fiction out to consistent results, the other restraining and at last overcoming that effort when the results become too manifestly unjust." [1] This statement he substantiates by a thorough examination of the development of certain legal notions. Upon its surface, such a statement implies a different view of the nature of logic than that stated. It implies that logic is not the method *of* good sense, that it has as it were a substance and life of its own which conflicts with the requirements of good decisions with respect to concrete subject-matters. The difference, however, is largely verbal. What Justice Holmes terms logic is formal consistency, consistency of concepts with one another irrespective of the consequences of their application to concrete matters-of-fact. We might state the fact by saying that concepts once developed have a kind of intrinsic inertia on their own account; once developed, the law of habit applies to them. It is practically economical to use a concept ready at hand rather than to take time and trouble and effort to change it or to devise a new one. The use of prior ready-made and familiar concepts also

[1] *Collected Legal Papers*, p. 50.

give rise to a sense of stability, of guarantee against sudden and arbitrary changes of the rules which determine the consequences which legally attend acts. It is the nature of any concept, as it is of any habit, to change more slowly than do the concrete circumstances with reference to which it is employed. Experience shows that the relative fixity of concepts affords men with a specious sense of protection, of assurance against the troublesome flux of events. Thus Justice Holmes says, "The language of judicial decision is mainly the language of logic. And the logical method and form flatter that longing for certainty and for repose which is in every human mind. But certainty generally is an illusion."[1] From the view of logical method here set forth, however, the undoubted facts which Justice Holmes has in mind do not concern logic but rather certain tendencies of the human creatures who use logic; tendencies which a sound logic will guard against. For they spring from the momentum of habit once forced, and express the effect of habit upon our feelings of ease and stability— feelings which have little to do with the actual facts of the case.

However this is only part of the story. The rest of the story is brought to light in some other passages of Justice Holmes. "The actual life of the law has not been logic: it has been experience. The felt necessities of the times, the prevalent moral and political theories, intuitions of public policy, avowed or unconscious, even the prejudices which judges share with their fellow-men, have had a good deal more to do than the syllogism in determining the rules by which men should be governed."[2] In other words, Justice Holmes is thinking of logic as equivalent with the syllogism, as he is quite entitled to do in accord with the orthodox tradition. From the standpoint of the syllogism as the logical model which was made current by scholasticism there *is* an antithesis

[1] *Ibid.*, p. 181. [2] *The Common Law*, p. 1.

between experience and logic, between logic and good sense. For the philosophy embodied in the formal theory of the syllogism asserted that thought or reason has fixed forms of its own, anterior to and independent of concrete subject-matters, and to which the latter have to be adapted whether or no. This defines the negative aspect of this discussion; and it shows by contrast the need of another kind of logic which shall reduce the influence of habit, and shall facilitate the use of good sense regarding matters of social consequences.

In other words, there are different logics in use. One of these, the one which has had greatest historic currency and exercised greatest influence on legal decisions, is that of the syllogism. To this logic the strictures of Justice Holmes apply in full force. For it purports to be a logic of rigid demonstration, not of search and discovery. It claims to be a logic of fixed forms, rather than of methods of reaching intelligent decisions in concrete situations, or of methods employed in adjusting disputed issues in behalf of the public and enduring interest. Those ignorant of formal logic, the logic of the abstract relations of ready-made conceptions to one another, have at least heard of the standard syllogism: All men are mortal; Socrates is a man; therefore, he is mortal. This is offered as the model of all proof or demonstration. It implies that what we need and must procure is first a fixed general *principle,* the so-called major premise, such as "all men are mortal;" then in the second place, a fact which belongs intrinsically and obviously to a class of things to which the general principle applies: Socrates is a man. Then the conclusion automatically follows: Socrates is mortal. According to this model every demonstrative or strictly logical conclusion "subsumes" a particular under an appropriate universal. It implies the prior and given existence of particulars and universals.

It thus implies that for every possible case which may

arise, there is a fixed antecedent rule already at hand; that the case in question is either simple and unambiguous, or is resolvable by direct inspection into a collection of simple and indubitable facts, such as, "Socrates is a man." It thus tends, when it is accepted, to produce and confirm what Professor Pound has called mechanical jurisprudence; it flatters that longing for certainty of which Justice Holmes speaks; it reinforces those inert factors in human nature which make men hug as long as possible any idea which has once gained lodgment in the mind.

In a certain sense it is foolish to criticize the model supplied by the syllogism. The statements made about men and Socrates are obviously true, and the connection between them is undoubted. The trouble is that while the syllogism sets forth the *results* of thinking, it has nothing to do with *operation* of thinking. Take the case of Socrates being tried before the Athenian citizens, and the thinking which had to be done to reach a decision. Certainly the issue was not whether Socrates was mortal; the point was whether this mortality would or should occur at a specified date and in a specified way. Now that is just what does not and cannot follow from a general principle or a major premise. Again to quote Justice Holmes, "General propositions do not decide concrete cases." No concrete proposition, that is to say one with material dated in time and placed in space, follows from any general statements or from any connection between them.

If we trust to an experimental logic, we find that general principles emerge as statements of generic ways in which it has been found helpful to treat concrete cases. The real force of the proposition that all men are mortal is found in the expectancy tables of insurance companies, which with their accompanying rates show how it is prudent and socially useful to deal with human mortality. The "universal" stated in the major premise is not outside of and antecedent to particular cases; neither is it a selection of something found in a variety of cases. It is an indication of a unified way of treating cases for certain purposes or consequences in spite of their diversity. Hence its meaning and worth are subject to inquiry and revision in view of what happens, what the consequences are, when it is used as a method of treatment.

As a matter of fact, men do not begin thinking with premises. They begin with some complicated and confused case, apparently admitting of alternative modes of treatment and solution. Premises only gradually emerge from analysis of the total situation. The problem is not to draw a conclusion from given premises; that can best be done by a piece of inanimate machinery by fingering a keyboard. The problem is to *find* statements of general principle and of particular fact, which are worthy to serve as premises. As matter of actual fact, we generally begin with some vague anticipation of a conclusion (or at least of alternative conclusions), and then we look around for principles and data which will substantiate it or which will enable us to choose intelligently between rival conclusions. No lawyer ever thought out the case of a client in terms of the syllogism. He begins with a conclusion which he intends to reach, favorable to his client, of course, and then analyzes the facts of the situation to find material out of which to construct a favorable statement of facts, to *form* a minor premise. At the same time he goes over recorded cases to find rules of law employed in cases which can be presented as similar, rules which will substantiate a certain way of looking at and interpreting the facts. And as his acquaintance with rules of law judged applicable widens, he probably alters perspective and emphasis in selection of the facts which are to form his evidential data. And as he learns more of the facts of the case he may modify his selection of rules of law upon which he bases his case.

I do not for a moment set up this procedure as a model of

scientific method; it is too precommitted to the establishment of a particular and partisan conclusion to serve as such a model. But it does illustrate, in spite of this deficiency, the particular point which is being made here: namely, that thinking actually sets out from a more or less confused situation, which is vague and ambiguous with respect to the conclusion it indicates; and that the formation of both major premise and minor proceed tentatively and correlatively in the course of analysis of this situation and of prior rules. As soon as acceptable premises are given—and of course the judge and jury have eventually to do with their becoming accepted—the conclusion is also given. In strict logic, the conclusion does not follow from premises; conclusions and premises are two ways of stating the same thing. Thinking may be defined either as a development of premises or development of a conclusion; as far as it is one operation it is the other.

Courts not only reach decisions; they expound them, and the exposition must state justifying reasons. The mental operations therein involved are somewhat different from those involved in arriving at a conclusion. The logic of exposition is different from that of search and inquiry. In the latter, the situation as it exists is more or less doubtful, indeterminate, and problematic with respect to what it signifies. It unfolds itself gradually and is susceptible of dramatic surprise; at all events it has, for the time being, two sides. Exposition implies that a definitive solution is reached, that the situation is now determinate with respect to its legal implication. Its purpose is to set forth grounds for the decision reached so that it will not appear as an arbitrary dictum, and so that it will indicate a rule for dealing with similar cases in the future. It is highly probable that the need of justifying to others conclusions reached and decisions made has been the chief cause of the origin and development of logical operations in the precise sense; of abstraction, generalization, regard for consistency of implications. It is quite conceivable that if no one had ever had to account to others for his decisions, logical operations would never have developed, but men would use exclusively methods of inarticulate intuition and impression, feeling; so that only after considerable experience in accounting for their decisions to others who demanded a reason, or exculpation, and were not satisfied till they got it, did men begin to give an account to themselves of the process of reaching a conclusion in a justified way. However this may be, it is certain that in judicial decisions the only alternative to arbitrary dicta, accepted by the parties to a controversy only because of the authority or prestige of the judge, is a rational statement which formulates grounds and exposes connecting or logical links.

It is at this point that the chief stimulus and temptation to mechanical logic and abstract use of formal concepts come in. Just because the personal element cannot be wholly excluded, while at the same time the decision must assume as nearly as possible an impersonal, objective, rational form, the temptation is to surrender the vital logic which has actually yielded the conclusion and to substitute for it forms of speech which are rigorous in appearance and which give an illusion of certitude.

Another moving force is the undoubted need for the maximum possible of stability and regularity of expectation in determining courses of conduct. Men need to know the legal consequences which society through the courts will attach to their specific transactions, the liabilities they are assuming, the fruits they may count upon in entering upon a given course of action.

This is a legitimate requirement from the standpoint of the interests of the community and of particular individuals. Enormous confusion has resulted, however, from confusion of *theoretical* certainty with practical certainty. There is a wide gap separating the reasonable proposition that judicial decisions should possess the maximum possible regularity, in order to enable persons in planning their conduct to foresee the legal import of their acts, and the absurd because impossible proposition that every decision should flow with formal logical necessity from antecedently known premises. To attain the former result there are required general principles of interpreting cases—rules of law—and procedures of pleading and trying cases which do not alter arbitrarily. But principles of interpretation do not signify rules so rigid that they can be stated once for all and then be literally and mechanically adhered to. For the situations to which they are to be applied do not literally repeat one another in all details, and questions of degree of this factor or that have the chief weight in determining which general rule will be employed to judge the situation in question. A large part of what has been asserted concerning the necessity of absolutely uniform and immutable antecedent rules of law is in effect an attempt to evade the really important issue of finding and employing rules of law, substantive and procedural, which will actually secure to the members of the community a reasonable measure of practical certainty of expectation in framing their courses of conduct. The mechanical ease of the court in disposing of cases and not the actual security of agents is the real cause, for example, of making rules of pleading hard and fast. The result introduces an unnecessary element of gamble into the behavior of those seeking settlement of disputes, while it affords to the judges only that factitious ease and simplicity which is supplied by any routine habit of action. It substitutes a mechanical procedure for the need of analytic thought.

There is of course every reason why rules of law should be as regular and as definite as possible. But the amount and kind of antecedent assurance which is actually attainable is a matter of fact, not of form. It is large wherever social conditions are pretty uniform, and when industry, commerce, transportation, etc., move in the channels of old customs. It is much less wherever invention is active and when new devices in business and communication bring about new forms of human relationship. Thus the use of power machinery radically modifies the old terms of association of master and servant and fellow-servants; rapid transportation brings into general use commercial bills of lading; mass production engenders organization of laborers and collective bargaining; industrial conditions favor concentration of capital. In part legislation endeavors to reshape old rules of law to make them applicable to new conditions. But statutes have never kept up with the variety and subtlety of social change. They cannot at the very best avoid some ambiguity, which is due not only to carelessness but also to the intrinsic impossibility of foreseeing all possible circumstances, since without such foresight definitions must be vague and classifications indeterminate. Hence to claim that old forms are ready at hand that cover every case and that may be applied by formal syllogizing is to pretend to a certainty and regularity which cannot exist in fact. The effect of the pretension is to increase practical uncertainty and social instability. Just because circumstances are really novel and not covered by old rules, it is a gamble which old rule will be declared regulative of a particular case, so that shrewd and enterprising men are encouraged to sail close to the wind and trust to ingenious lawyers to find some rule under which they can get off scot free.

The facts involved in this discussion are commonplace and they are not offered as presenting anything original or novel. What we are concerned with is their bearing upon the logic of judicial decisions. For the implications are more revolutionary than they might at first seem to be. They indicate either that logic must be abandoned or that it must be a logic *relative to consequences rather than to antecedents,* a logic of prediction of probabilities rather than one of deduction of certainties. For the purposes of a logic of inquiry into probable consequences, general principles can only be tools justified by the work they do. They are means of intellectual survey, analysis, and insight into the factors of the situation to be dealt with. Like other tools they must be modified when they are applied to new conditions and new results have to be achieved. Here is where the great practical evil of the doctrine of immutable and necessary antecedent rules comes in. It sanctifies the old; adherence to it in practice constantly widens the gap between current social conditions and the principles used by the courts. The effect is to breed irritation, disrespect for law, together with virtual alliance between the judiciary and entrenched interests that correspond most nearly to the conditions under which the rules of law were previously laid down.

Failure to recognize that general legal rules and principles are working hypotheses, needing to be constantly tested by the way in which they work out in application to concrete situations, explains the otherwise paradoxical fact that the slogans of the liberalism of one period often become the bulwarks of reaction in a subsequent era. There was a time in the eighteenth century when the great social need was emancipation of industry and trade from a multitude of restrictions which held over from the feudal estate of Europe. Adapted well enough to the localized and fixed conditions of that earlier age, they became hindrances and annoyances as the effects of new methods, use of coal and steam, emerged. The movement of emancipation expressed itself in principles of liberty in use of property, and freedom of contract, which were embodied in a mass of legal decisions. But the absolutistic logic of rigid syllogistic forms infected these ideas. It was soon forgotten that they were relative to analysis of existing situations in order to secure orderly methods in behalf of economic social welfare. Thus these principles became in turn so rigid as to be almost as socially obstructive as "immutable" feudal laws had been in their day.

That the remarks which have been made, commonplace as they are in themselves, have a profound practical import may also be seen in the present reaction against the individualistic formulæ of an older liberalism. The last thirty years has seen an intermittent tendency in the direction of legislation, and to a less extent of judicial decision, towards what is vaguely known as "social justice," toward formulæ of a collectivistic character. Now it is quite possible that the newer rules may be needed and useful at a certain juncture, and yet that they may also become harmful and socially obstructive if they are hardened into absolute and fixed antecedent premises. But if they are conceived as tools to be adapted to the conditions in which they are employed rather than as absolute and intrinsic "principles," attention will go to the facts of social life, and the rules will not be allowed to engross attention and become absolute truths to be maintained intact at all costs. Otherwise we shall in the end merely have substituted one set of formally absolute and immutable syllogistic premises for another set.

If we recur then to our introductory conception that logic is really a theory about empirical phenomena, subject to growth and improvement like any other empirical discipline, we recur to it with an added conviction: namely, that the issue is not a purely speculative one, but implies consequences vastly significant for practice. I should indeed not hesitate to assert that the sanctification of ready-made antecedent universal principles as methods of thinking is the chief obstacle to the kind of thinking which is the indispensable prerequisite of steady, secure and intelligent social reforms in general, and social advance by means of law in particular. If this be so, infiltration into law of a more experimental and flexible logic is a social as well as an intellectual need.

Corporate Personality

THE survey which is undertaken in this paper points to the conclusion that for the purposes of law the conception of "person" is a legal conception; put roughly, "person" signifies what law makes it signify. If this conclusion had not been disputed, if it were even now generally accepted, if even when it is accepted in substance it were not complicated by the use of non-legal concepts employed to justify certain reasonings and conclusions, this paper would have no particular excuse for being written. For in that case, being a legal concept, it would be one to be discussed by lawyers rather than by a layman. Accordingly, the justification for a layman venturing into the field is precisely the fact that discussions and theories which have influenced legal practice have, with respect to the concept of "person," introduced and depended upon a mass of non-legal considerations: considerations popular, historical, political, moral, philosophical, metaphysical and, in connection with the latter, theological.[1] So many of these

---

[1] Thus Geldart, an upholder of the doctrine of "real personality," says: "The question is at bottom not one on which law and legal conceptions have the only or the final voice: it is one which law shares with other sciences, political science, ethics, psychology, and metaphysics." Geldart, *Legal Personality* (1911) 27 L. QUART. REV. 90, at 94. On the next page he goes on to assert that "To say that all legal personality—whether of so-called natural or so-called juristic persons—is equally real because in fact the law gives it an existence, and equally artificial or fictitious because it is *only* the law which gives it an existence, is really to confound personality with capacity." But he makes no attempt to show the difference between them, nor to state what harm would result in law if the two were "confounded." That "artificial" is not synonymous with "fictitious" is shown by Machen, *Corporate Personality* (1910) 21 HARV. L. REV. 253, at 257: "That which is artificial is real, and not imaginary; an artificial lake is not an imaginary lake." Again he says: "A corporation cannot be at the same time 'created by the state' and fictitious. If a corporation is 'created' it is real, and therefore cannot be a purely fictitious body having no existence except in the legal imagination." Much the same points were made by Pollock. He says, that "artificial" means "in accordance with rules of art, lawyer-like, juridical," and that "fiction" should be derived from *fingere* in the sense of creating or making, not feigning. *Theory of Corporations in Common Law* (1911) 27 L. QUART. REV. 219, 220,

[141]

extraneous influences have received a formulation in philosophy and from thence have proceeded to affect legal doctrines that a student of philosophy does not have to travel far beyond his own field to discuss them.

As a starting point we may take the following statement from Maitland, who has done so much to bring the question of the nature of corporate legal personality to the attention of English readers: "The corporation is (forgive this compound adjective) a right-and-duty-bearing unit. Not all the legal propositions that are true of a man will be true of a corporation. For example, it can neither marry nor be given in marriage; but in a vast number of cases you can make a legal statement about x and y which will hold good whether these symbols stand for two men or for two corporations, or for a corporation and a man." [1] In saying that "person" might legally mean whatever the law makes it mean, I am trying to say that "person" might be used simply as a synonym for a right-and-duty-bearing unit. Any such unit would be a person; such a statement would be truistic, tautological. Hence it would convey no implications, except that the unit has those rights and duties which the courts find it to have. What "person" signifies in popular speech, or in psychology, or in philosophy or morals, would be as irrelevant, to employ an exaggerated simile, as it would be to argue that because a wine is called "dry," it has the properties of dry solids; or that, because it does not have those properties, wine cannot possibly be "dry." Obviously, "dry" as applied to a particular wine has the kind of meaning, and only the kind of meaning, which it has when applied to the class of beverages in general.

---

reprinted in *Essays in the Law* (1922) 153. Geldart's introduction of the word "only" in the phrase "because it is *only* the law" is like saying of a locomotive that "only" man gives it existence.

[1] 3 Maitland, *Collected Papers* (1911) 307. Throughout this paper "corporate" is used in its broad sense, of which a business corporation is but a species and which includes bodies not technically incorporated.

Why should not the same sort of thing hold of the use of "person" in law?

To take an illustration nearer to our theme, when the common law refused to recognize any paternity for an illegitimate son, and said he was *filius nullius,* it was not understood to deny the fact of physiological begetting; it was asserting that such a one did not possess the specific rights which belong to one who was *filius,* implying wedlock as a legal institution. That *filius* signifies a certain kind of heir, one implying a prior union of man and woman authorized by law, is an example of a term signifying what the system of rights and duties makes it signify. To take another illustration still nearer our topic, suppose that a number of married women, who, under common law suffered from disability to contract, had formed a corporation. It may be doubted whether even the most ardent disciple of the theory that the association is nothing but the sum of its individual members would infer that the corporation could not contract—although of course it might have been denied that the women could form a corporation. Admitting, however, the existence of the corporation, the right to contract would have been limited to the new relationship; because of it, the members of the corporation would possess a right *sui generis.* In a similar way, even if it were true, as it is not, that "natural person" is a wholly unambiguous term, to term a "natural" person a person in the legal sense is to confer upon him a new, additive and distinctive meaning; a meaning *sui generis,* as far as "natural person" is concerned.

If in justification of a particular decision in some particular and difficult controversy, a court supports itself by appealing to some prior properties of the antecedent non-legal "natural person," the appeal may help out the particular decision; but it either involves dependence upon non-legal theory, or else it extends the legal concept of "natural person," or it does both. This statement cuts in two ways. On the one hand, it indicates that much of the difficulty attending the recent discussion of the real personality of corporate bodies is due to going outside the strictly legal sphere so that legal issues have got complicated with other theories, and with former states of scientific knowledge; and on the other hand it suggests that law, at critical times and in dealing with critical issues, has found it difficult to grow in any other way than by taking over contemporary non-jural conceptions and doctrines. Just as the law has grown by taking unto itself *practices* of ante-cedent non-legal status, so it has grown by taking unto itself from psychology or philosophy or what not extraneous *dogmas* and *ideas*. But just as continued growth with respect to the former requires that law be again changed with great changes in further practices; just as, to be specific, the adoption of the law-merchant will not provide law adequate for the complex industrial relations of today, so it is even more markedly true that old non-legal doctrines which once served to advance rules of law may be obstructive today. We often go on discussing problems in terms of old ideas when the solution of the problem depends upon getting rid of the old ideas, and putting in their place concepts more in accord with the present state of ideas and knowledge. The root difficulty in present controversies about "natural" and associated bodies may be that while we oppose one to the other, or try to find some combining union of the two, what we really need to do is to overhaul the doctrine of personality which underlies both of them.

The purpose of the article is, in other words, to point out some of the non-legal factors which have found their way into the discussion of the personality of so-called natural and artificial persons, and to indicate the original conditions which gave these extraneous factors their efficacy. The postulate, which has unconsciously led to the merging of popular and philosophical notions of the person with the legal notion,

CORPORATE PERSONALITY

is the conception that before anything can be a jural person it
must intrinsically possess certain properties, the existence of
which is necessary to constitute anything a person. If the conception as to the nature of these inherent and essential attributes had remained constant perhaps no harm would have
resulted from shoving such a notion under the legal idea; the
legal doctrine would at least have remained as constant as
that of the nature of the seat of personality. But the history
of western culture shows a chameleon-like change in the latter
notion; this change has never, moreover, effected complete
replacement of an earlier by a later idea. Almost all concepts
have persisted side by side in a confused intermixture. Hence
their influence upon legal doctrine has necessarily been to
generate confusion and conflict.

We may illustrate by recourse to Maitland. The quotation
above made, taken apart from its context, would appear to
use "person" in a neutral sense, as signifying simply a right-
and-duty-bearing unit. But actually his discussion depends
upon an assumption that there are properties which any unit
must antecedently and inherently have in order to be a right-
and-duty-bearing unit. They are stated in his summary of
Gierke's position, although the statement is found in another
book. A "*universitas* (or corporate body) . . . is a living
organism and a real person, with body and members and a
will of its own. Itself can will, itself can act . . . it is a
group-person, and its will is a group-will." [1] I do not intend
to imply that Maitland or Gierke ever adopted into his corporate unit all the extreme analogies with an "organism,"
but a "will" he certainly thinks is presupposed for being a
legal person. In short, some generic or philosophic concept of
personality, that is, some concept expressing the intrinsic
character of personality *ueberhaupt,* is implied. And here is

[1] Gierke, *Political Theories of the Middle Age* (1902) xxvi (translated and
prefaced by Maitland).

[145]

room for questions of general theory and for the writing of many books to show that legal units do or do not have the properties required by the concept, and that "will" means this or that or the other thing.

Another example may make the implication more explicit. Michoud says: "For legal science, the notion of person is and should remain a purely juridical notion. The word signifies simply a *subject of rights-duties (sujet de droit),* a being capable of having the subjective rights properly belonging to him." [1] This sounds very much like saying "person" means what the law makes it mean in real distribution of rights and duties—although the word "subjective" prefixed to rights might make wary one who was acquainted with philosophical literature. But Michoud at once goes on to say: "To know if certain beings correspond to this definition, it is not necessary to ask if these beings constitute persons in the philosophical sense of the word. It is enough to ask if they are of such a *nature* that subjective rights may be attributed to them." Considerations extraneous to law are here nominally excluded, but they are actually taken in under the guise of the necessity of inquiring into the nature of the subjects, independently of and prior to the attribution of duty-rights. The word "subject" *might* have been used in legal theory simply as a descriptive term, denoting whatever is a right-and-duty-bearing unit. But in fact it has not been so used; it has been thought necessary— especially in German theory which has spread—first to define what makes anything properly a subject, as a *precondition* of having right-duties. And the German theory of "subjectivity" is itself a theme for volumes. This something-or-other must then be the same in whatever has rights and duties. The readiest starting point is a singular man; hence there is imposed the necessity of finding some nature or essence which belongs

---

[1] Michoud, *La Notion de Personalité Morale* (1889) 11 REVUE DU DROIT PUBLIC, 1, at 8.

both to men in the singular and to corporate bodies. If one denies that he can find such a common essence he holds that "person" as applied to corporate bodies denotes only a fiction. But if he denies the fictitious character of a corporate entity, then some personality identical in essence, or with respect to "subjectivity," must be discovered for all right-and-duty-bearing units, from the singular man on one side (including infants, born and unborn, insane, etc.) to the state on the other, together with all kinds of intervening corporate bodies such as "foundations," "associations" and corporations in the economic sense.[1] Clearly, this is not an easy task; it is so difficult of accomplishment that it accounts in the main for the voluminous Continental literature concerning juridical personality, or as French writers generally say, *"Les Personnes Morales."* But this is not the whole story. "Subject" and "Subjectivity" occupy in modern German philosophy (which directly and through writings on jurisprudence has had an enormous influence in Latin countries and considerable in England) the place taken in ancient metaphysics by "substance" and also by "subject" of a judgment in a logical sense. Thus the search for the common essence has been so affected by philosophical theories regarding "the subject" that it is extremely difficult to get the full force of the various solutions proffered for the problem without knowledge of German technical philosophy, that of Kant in particular.

It may be objected, however, that aside from all such philosophical theories regarding an "essence" or "nature" and regarding a "subject," it is only common-sense that whatever is a right-and-duty-bearing unit should have a character of its own in virtue of which it may possess rights—obligations;

[1] The first of these terms have their doctrinal significance in Continental rather than in Anglo-American law, the institution of trusteeship in the latter covering much of the ground. The theory of "associations" derived much of its point in the past from controversies regarding the legal status of religious congregations, to which is now added that of trade unions.

there *must* be a subject to which these legal relations belong or in which they inhere or to which, at all events, they are imputed. Otherwise why are not molecules, or trees or tables just as fit candidates for legal attributes as singular men and corporate bodies? The objection seems serious. But consider first an argument *ad hominem,* or rather *ad hoc.* There is no general agreement regarding the nature *in se* of the jural subject; courts and legislators do their work without such agreement, sometimes without any conception or theory at all regarding its nature; it can be shown that recourse to some theory has more than once operated to hinder rather than facilitate the adjudication of a special question of right or obligation. Moreover, English jurisprudence has accomplished by means of "trust" much that Continental law has accomplished by other means. One might then be justified in adopting a position of legal agnosticism, holding that even if there be such an ulterior subject *per se,* it is no concern of law, since courts can do their work without respect to its nature, much more without having to settle it.

It would, however, be retorted that such an attitude does not become jurisprudence, that some theory is *implied* in the procedure of courts, and that the business of the theory of law is to make explicit what is implied, particularly as false theories have done practical harm, while the lack of intelligent consensus of ideas has encouraged judicial empiricism, and thereby wrought confusion, conflict and uncertainty in specific decisions. This retort brings us to a deeper level. There are two radically different types of definitions; first, the type inherited from Greek logic, reflecting a definite metaphysical conception regarding the nature of things. This definition proceeds in terms of an essential and universal inhering nature. There is another mode of definition which proceeds in terms of *consequences.* In brief, for the latter a thing is—is defined as—what it does, "what-it-does" being stated in terms of

specific effects *extrinsically* wrought in other things. This
logical method was first stated by Charles S. Peirce as the
pragmatistic rule: "Consider what effects, which might conceivably have practical bearings, we conceive the object of
our conception to have. Then, our conception of these effects
is the whole of our conception of the object." [1] The mode of
definition, however, has no inherent dependence upon pragmatism as a philosophy. It has been stated and adopted on the
basis of analysis of mathematics and physics by writers who
would be horrified to be called pragmatists. Thus stated, it is
the principle known as "extensive abstraction," and assumes
this form: " . . . what really matters to science is not the
inner nature of objects but their mutual relations, and any
set of terms with the right mutual relations will answer all
scientific purposes as well as any other set with the same sort
of relations." [2]

From this point of view, the right-and-duty-bearing unit,
or subject, signifies whatever has consequences of a specified
kind. The reason that molecules or trees are not juridical "subjects" is then clear; they do not display the specified consequences. The definition of a legal subject is thus a legitimate,
and quite conceivably a practically important matter. But it
is a matter of analysis of facts, not of search for an inhering
essence. The facts in question are whatever specific consequences flow from being right-and-duty-bearing units. This
analysis is a matter to be conducted by one competent in law,
and not by the layman. But even a layman can point out the
field within which the search falls. The consequences must be
social in character, and they must be *such* social consequences

[1] *Chance, Love and Logic* (1923) 45, edited by Morris R. Cohen. The original
article was printed in the *Popular Science Monthly* for January, 1878.
[2] Broad, *Scientific Thought* (1923) 39. The idea and the name are taken, however, by him from A. N. Whitehead. This is a more general statement than Peirce's,
because it applies to mathematical concepts, such as "point," whose "consequences"
are not physical effects. In concrete matters, the "mutual relations" which count are,
however, of the nature of effects.

as are controlled and modified by being the bearing of rights and obligations, privileges and immunities. Molecules and trees certainly have social consequences; but these consequences are what they are irrespective of their having rights and duties. Molecules and trees would continue to behave exactly as they do whether or not rights and duties were ascribed to them; their consequences would be what they are anyway. But there are some things, bodies singular and corporate, which clearly act differently, and produce different consequences, depending upon whether or not they possess rights and duties, and according to what specific rights they possess and what obligations are placed upon them. If the logical principle be granted, it is a factual matter to decide what bodies have the specifiable consequences and what these consequences are; while it is a verbal matter whether we call them all "persons," or whether we call some of them persons and not others—or whether we abandon the use of the word entirely.[1]

The general statement as to the type of definition demanded may be made more specific by reference to Michoud. He finds what he is in search of primarily in "interests." Now while he had asserted the necessity of determining whether the beings who are "persons" are of such a nature that subjective rights may be attributed to them, his conclusion that

[1] English statutory law comes, in some respects, close to doing the latter by its very generalization of the term "person." In (1833) 3 & 4 Wm. IV, c. 74, it is said: "The Word 'Person' shall extend to a Body Politic, Corporate, or Collegiate, as well as an Individual." In the Interpretation Act of 1889, 52 & 53 Vict. c. 63, sec. 19, it is stated: "In this Act and in every Act passed after the commencement of this Act the expression 'person' shall, unless the contrary intention appears, include any body of persons corporate or unincorporate."

I owe the reference to Maitland, *op. cit. supra* note 2, at 401. He explains that the inclusion of "incorporate bodies" is probably due to the desire to include some organs of local government, such as boards of health, under their relevant legal rules. He adds: "It is not inconceivable that the above cited section of the Act of 1889 may do some work hereafter; but I have not heard of its having done any work as yet." This statement indicates what is meant by the assertion that a generalization of the term "person" may be equivalent to an abandonment of the term, the work being done by specific statutes and by judicial decisions bearing upon specific matters.

"interests" are primary shifts the logical ground. For "interests," whatever else they are or are not, fall within the region of consequences, not of "beings." Certain interests are protected by the rights and duties of charitable foundations; but these interests are those of recipients, who have no rights in the matter. Beings possessed of will, administrators, are necessary as the organs of the interest. His secondary mark or criterion may be said then to introduce an inherent factor, that of "will." But our former logical question recurs: Is "will" conceived or defined in terms of something intrinsic, or in terms of specifiable consequences? If the former, then we are at once involved in all the controversies regarding the nature of will found in psychology and philosophy:—there is no question upon which there is less consensus than upon the nature of will.[1] If the man of "common-sense" retorts, "Away with these metaphysical subtleties; everybody knows well enough the difference between a being with will and one without one," his retort may be true for most cases; but it involves more than "common-sense" is usually willing to acknowledge: namely, that "will" denotes certain empirically detectable and specifiable consequences, and not a force or entity, psychological or metaphysical. In other words, we determine the absence or presence of "intent," and the kind of "intent," by discrimination among concrete consequences, precisely as we determine "neglect," which by definition is not a peculiar kind of inhering agency. Neglect may, of course, be made into a positive and intrinsic force or agency by hypostatization, but this is parallel to the procedure of school-teachers who make a positive existential entity out of "inattention." If we recur to the logical method of conception by "extensive

[1] One illustration, trivial in itself, but significant in what it stands for, is the necessity the adherents of the "will" theory find themselves under, of distinguishing *volitions* from *volonté*. Volitions may proceed from the singular members of an association; *volonté* belongs to the association as such. Saleilles, *De la Personalité Juridique* (1910) 565.

abstraction," "will," like "interests," denotes a *function,* not an intrinsic force or structure.[1]

II

The foregoing section does not attempt to define what it is to be a "person" in the sense of a right-and-duty-bearing unit. Its purpose is to show the logical method by which such a definition should be arrived at; and, secondly, to show that the question has been enormously complicated by the employment of a wrong logical method, and by the introduction of irrelevant conceptions, imported into legal discussion (and often into legal practice) from uncritical popular beliefs; from psychology, and from a metaphysics ultimately derived from theology. It is not intended, however, to imply that these extraneous considerations have not been historically significant, nor that the causes of their emergence into law is not of importance for legal history. The reverse is the case. To the student, and not merely the historical student, of human cul-

---

[1] It would require an article longer than this one merely to list and describe various theories about will which, as held at one time or another, have influenced legal doctrines. One reference must suffice. Professor Pound has repeatedly shown how the conception of "will" was central in the Roman law idea of legal transactions and how it affected the nineteenth century theory of contracts and related subjects. The entire post-Kantian German concept of real personality is affected by Kant's theory of will. Practically, the movement fell in with another, quite different in character, which made "liberty" of will the central thing in order to find a universal basis of political liberty—as with Rousseau. Subsequently, the German and French ideas flowed together, and the conflux was affected by the notion of economic liberty, which readily rationalized itself by getting under the cover of the reigning theory of will. That the idea assisted in promoting movements which were socially useful there can be no doubt. To give one instance, Henderson has suggested its utility in liberalizing the treatment of foreign corporations, which upon the "concession" theory find the going very difficult. See Henderson, *Position of Foreign Corporations in American-Constitutional Law* (1918) 5.

My colleague, Professor H. W. Schneider, has called my attention to the important influence exercised upon theories of the "real" legal personality of corporate groups by the traditional association of the ideas of "agency," "responsibility" and "guilt" with will. I have omitted discussion of this point because its importance would demand an entire paper, at least, for adequate treatment. I would only suggest that the grouping of these ideas together is at present a matter of *historic* interest, but is unnecessary from the standpoint of contemporary thought.

ture, they afford a fascinating, if intricate, field of inquiry; and the history and present status of legal institutions are involved in this study of human culture. The sources, career and effects of the conceptions of "intent" and of "malicious" intent would alone lay bare an instructive cross-section of the whole history of religion, morals and psychology. Of more direct significance for our special theme is the fact that the underlying controversies, and their introduction into legal theory and actual legal relations, express struggles and movements of immense social import, economic and political. Such a formal or logical analysis as we have been engaged in is in fact but preliminary. What is back of these factors which are logically extraneous? What vital issues have led to their getting so thoroughly mixed up with questions of legal definition? To answer this question is to engage in a survey of the conflict of church and empire in the Middle Ages; the conflict of rising national states with the medieval Roman empire; the struggle between dynastic and popular representative forms of government; the conflict of feudal institutions, ecclesiastic and agrarian, with the economic needs produced by the industrial revolution and the development of national territorial states; the conflict of the "proletariat" with the employing and capitalist class; the struggle between nationalism and internationalism, or trans-national relations, to mention only a few outstanding movements.[1] These conflicts are primarily political

[1] Since the last-named topic will not concern us further, one illustration may be mentioned. A potent recent motive for the insistence upon the real "personality" of social groups, or corporate bodies, independent of the state, is opposition to the claim that the state is the sole or even supreme Person. The latter notion reflects the increase of importance of the national territorial state. Opposition from the side we are alluding to, is due to the fact that the doctrine of the ultimate personality of these states finds fitting expression in war. Moreover, war confers upon the states too unrestricted power over their citizens, and also unfavorably affects the complex economic interdependences wrought by modern methods of industry and commerce. In an article written before the war, Lindsay rightly cites Norman Angell as a factor "in the newest political gospel" which "makes open and declared war against the doctrine that the State is a personality." This attack is inspired "not by a belief in the isolation of individuals, but by a perception that the co-operation of

and economic in nature. But there is not one of them which has not left its profound impress upon the law, particularly upon the doctrines of the nature and seat of juridical personality. Discussions and concepts may have been in form intellectual, using a full arsenal of dialectical weapons; they have been in fact, where they have any importance, "rationalizations" of the positions and claims of some party to a struggle. It is this fact which gives such extraordinary interest to the history of doctrines of juridical personality. Add to this fact that the intellectual and scientific history of western Europe is reflected in the changing fortunes of the meanings of "person" and "personality," a history which has both affected and been affected by the social struggles, and the interest and complexity of the doctrines about juridical personality are sufficiently obvious.

For example, the "fiction" theory of the personality of corporate bodies, or *universitates,* was promulgated if not originated, by Pope Innocent IV (1243–1254. St. Thomas Aquinas died in 1274). It is hardly a coincidence that Pope Innocent was one of the strongest upholders of the supremacy of the spiritual over the temporal power, and that he was Pope immediately after the time of the greatest political power of the Papal Empire.[1] In outward form the doctrine that corporate bodies are *personæ fictæ* was directed at ecclesiastic bodies. The doctrine was stated as the reason why an ecclesiastic *collegium* or *universitas,* or *capitulum* could not be excommunicated, or be guilty of a delict. For *nomina sunt juris et non personarum;* they have neither a body nor a will.

---

individuals and their common dependence on one another extends beyond the bounds of the State." Lindsay, *The State in Recent Political Theory* (1914) 1 POLITICAL QUARTERLY, 128, at 130 and 132.

[1] Of a not far remote predecessor, it is said that "The fully rounded ecclesiastic theory, at the climax of actual ecclesiastic power, is to be found in the writings of Pope Innocent III (pontificate 1196–1216)." Dunning, *Political Theories, Ancient and Medieval* (1902) 162, 163.

A chapter was but a name and an incorporeal *res*. Other canonists declared that corporate bodies could not be punished or excommunicated because they had neither a soul nor a body, and carried their nominalism so far as to say that they had being only *in abstracto,* like "man" in respect to men. The doctrine did not imply, however, that excommunication was of no effect; on the contrary, it signified that, in order that a decree of punishment or excommunication should not lack effect, it was to be applied to all, *omnes singulos.* Even if Pope Innocent had not included *populus et gens et hujus modi* along with ecclesiastical groups (we cannot call them bodies on his theory), we may be sure that what applied to religious organizations applied *a fortiori* to civil. A chapter or a *populus* regarded as an entity would not suffer especially from excommunication; it was wholly different when the ban fell upon *"omnes singulos."* [1] The intellectual factor in the doctrine takes us to the fact that being a "person" was denied to these groups because of the dominant conception of person. The current idea is expressed in the definition of St. Thomas Aquinas, *vera persona est rei rationalis individua substantia.* In this definition every one of the three last words has a technical meaning that goes back to the metaphysical discussions of Aristotle; the problem of the nature of the "individual" being, indeed, for the Middle Age philosophers, even more of a problem than that of "substance," which had been decided once for all by Aristotle. [2] The consequences of including "rational individu-

---

[1] I have relied upon Gierke for the references (3 *Das deutsches Genossenschaftrecht,* 279–285.) Gierke says that Pope Innocent IV "was the father of the dogma of the purely fictitious and intellectual character of juridical persons which still rules." Even if this statement were not literally correct the reference would be of great importance because of the currency Maitland gave to the discussion and to Gierke, and because of the influence of Maitland upon Laski, one of the chief modern propounders of the doctrine that organized groups have personality independent of, and in many cases prior to, state action.

[2] We are far away from the Latin *persona* which when applied to a man in the concrete hardly meant more than a separate physical body. The change in meaning was undoubtedly of theological origin, the term *"persona"* having been applied by the fathers (first I believe by Tertullian) to the hyspostases of the Trinity.

PHILOSOPHY AND CIVILIZATION

ated substance" in the conception of "person" endured long
after the metaphysics and theology which gave it birth were
obscured if not forgotten; and they account for much of the
difficulty in even recent discussion in attributing "person" to
corporate as well as to single units.

The "concession" theory of juridical persons, while often
confused with the "fiction" theory, had a different origin, and
testifies to quite a different situation of conflict of interests. It
is essentially a product of the rise of the national state, with
its centralizing tendencies and its objection to *imperia in im-
perio* at a time when religious congregations and organizations of feudal origin (*communes* and guilds) were rivals of
the claim of the national state to complete sovereignty. The
shortest cut to making good this claim was to treat all minor
organizations as "conjurations" and conspiracies, except as
they derived all their powers from an express grant of a supreme power, the State. Certain classes were as much interested in magnifying the government and regulation by statute
law as Pope Innocent III was in magnifying the authority
and power of the Papacy. The choice of the word "concession" was probably influenced by Roman law.[1]

In lieu of an extended discussion of the practical motivation of the basic ideas of the concession theory, I shall give one
quotation. "In its various forms of ecclesiastical bodies and
foundations, guilds, municipalities, trading companies, or business organizations, the corporation has always presented the
same problem of how to check the tendency of group action

[1] Gaius, Digest, III, 4, 1. In all events, it is suggestive that the statements of
Gaius were made at a time (161 A.D.) when the Empire was in full centralizing
course. It should be noted, however, that Gaius is not referring explicitly to anything he calls persons. His point is that being a *universitas* or *collegium* is something dependent upon statutes, *sensatus consulta* and imperial constitutions. It is interesting, moreover, to note in connection with the efforts to bring Roman ideas into
the whole controversy that Maitland expressly says that "The admission must be
made that there is no text which directly calls the *universitas* a *persona,* and still
less any that calls it *persona ficta.*" Gierke (with preface by Maitland), *supra* note
3, at xviii.

[156]

to undermine the liberty of the individual or to rival the political power of the state. The somewhat vague theory of the later Middle Ages that communal organization not sanctioned by prescription or royal license was illegal was at least from the fifteenth century on supplemented by the technical doctrine, developed under canonist influences, that there is no capacity to act as a body corporate without positive authorization. To grant this authority has remained in England an attribute of the royal prerogative. . . . It is hardly possible to overestimate the theory that corporate existence depends on positive sanction as a factor in public and legislative policy. It is natural that the charter or incorporation law should be made the vehicle of restraints or regulations which might not be readily imposed upon natural persons acting on their own initiative, and the course of legislative history bears this out." [1]

It is clear that there is nothing essentially in common between the fiction and concession theories, although they both aimed toward the same general consequence, that of limitation of the power of corporate bodies. The fiction theory is ultimately a philosophical theory that the corporate body is but a name, a thing of the intellect; the concession theory may be indifferent as to the question of the reality of a corporate body; what it *must* insist upon is that its *legal power* is derived. In some respects, the concession theory is the more favorable to expanded power of corporations; a charter of broad powers might be granted and the courts might construe

[1] Freund, *Standards of American Legislation* (1917) 39. The quotation continues by indicating the restraints imposed on banking and insurance corporations, railways and express companies. Historically, the restrictive attitude towards at least business corporations finds its explanation and justification in the fact that they were few and exceptional, being usually huge trading companies, actually and often nominally, monopolies, whose "rights" were privileges and immunities. As so often happened, words, with associated ideas and temper of mind, persisted after corporations had become commonplace and, indeed, the usual means of carrying on business. Henderson, in the work already referred to, has shown the effect of possession of extraordinary privileges by early corporations in creating fear of them and the extent to which this fear influenced court decisions, as for example, that in the case of *The Bank of the United States v. Deveaux, op. cit. supra* note 10, at 19, 55, 56.

its terms liberally. Its promoteᴀ assimilation to the singular person; even when a corporation is called "artificial," it might even enlarge its rights, privileges and immunities. In an "individualistic" period—that is, an era chiefly concerned with rights of private property and contract—it is pretty sure to do so. Consider, for example, the court decisions that a business corporation is a "person" in the sense covered by the Fourteenth Amendment, and the effects of this decision. On the other hand, the fiction theory that a corporation having no soul cannot be guilty of delict gives a corporation considerable room in which to maneuver. Thus we cannot say, without qualification in respect of time and conditions, that either theory works out in the direction of limitation of corporate power.[1]

In spite of their historical and logical divergence, the two theories flowed together. Their conflux and its result is exhibited in many decisions of American judges. The practical key to the union, in which the feigned theory on the whole got the better of the concession theory, resides in the allusion just made to an "individualistic" age. When it is difficult to lay hands on the single persons who are said to be the only "real" persons, it is very convenient to do business on a fiction. With respect to its property, the fictitious entity has a clear title as an entity; with respect to its liabilities and burdens outside of property and contract, its position is not so clear; its fictitious character may be cited to relieve it of some obligations usually regarded as moral, and yet legally enforceable as regards single persons. Pope Innocent IV was under no such difficulty.

[1] Imaginary beings or fictions may not only gain privileges because of the absence of souls, but because of the unlimited elasticity of fictions. As Machen says, "If the corporate personality is imaginary, there is no limit to the characteristics and capacities which may be attributed to that personality. . . . If you can imagine a corporate entity is a person, you can also imagine that this person has a mind." Machen, *op. cit. supra* note 1, at 347, 348. The "fiction theory," if it had been separated wholly from the "concession theory," might have lent itself to liberalizing the theory of foreign corporations. Difficulties regarding "residence" and "migration" might easily have been got over; for imaginary creatures are notoriously nimble.

Excommunication could reach down to every part of the aggregate whole; it is not so easy to reach the fluctuating "real" persons who form that "merely collective aggregate," the shareholders in a joint-stock company, especially if they are "widows and orphans." To a considerable extent, the corporation has "had it both ways," when it was regarded as nothing but a name for an aggregate or collection of real persons. Adequately to develop this fact and the reasons for it would require an excursion into the change which took place in the eighteenth and nineteenth centuries in the concept of the "singular person," now become the full-fledged individual in his own right. The excursion cannot be undertaken. Suffice it to say that the single person, as the "real person," is no longer either a physical body or a rational substance. These two meanings persist, but they are covered up with vestments derived from the theory of natural rights inhering in individual persons as such. The contrast of "natural" and "artificial" persons got its point from the fact that "natural" connoted possession of inherent and inviolable rights. The dialectic of the courts, under the pressure of social facts, was equal to declaring that corporations, while artificial and fictitious, nevertheless had all the natural rights of an individual person, since after all they were legal persons.

Perhaps a reader may infer that the foregoing amounts to a plea for the "real" personality of corporate bodies. Recurrence to the introductory remarks should, however, dissipate this impression. As far as the historical survey implies a plea for anything, it is a plea for disengaging specific issues and disputes from entanglement with *any* concept of personality which is other than a restatement that such and such rights and duties, benefits and burdens, accrue and are to be maintained and distributed in such and such ways, and in such and such situations.

III

The fact of the case is that there is no clear-cut unity, logical or practical, throughout the different theories which have been advanced and which are still advanced in behalf of the "real" personality of either "natural" or associated persons. Each theory has been used to serve the same ends, and each has been used to serve opposing ends. The doctrine of the personality of the state has been advanced to place the state above legal responsibility on the ground that such a person has no superior person—save God—to whom to answer; and in behalf of a doctrine of the responsibility of the state and its officers to law, since to be a person is to have legal powers and duties. The personality of the state has been opposed to both the personality of "natural" singular persons and to the personality of groups. In the latter connection it has been employed both to make the state the supreme and culminating personality in a hierarchy, to make it but *primus inter paros,* and to reduce it to merely one among many, sometimes more important than others and sometimes less so. These are political rather than legal considerations, but they have affected law. In legal doctrines proper, all theories have been upheld for the same purpose, and each for opposed ends. Corporate groups less than the state have had real personality ascribed to them, both in order to make them more amenable to liability, as in the case of trade-unions, and to exalt their dignity and vital power against external control. Their personality has been denied for like reasons; they have been pulverized into mere aggregates of separate persons in order to protect other laborers from them, to make more difficult their unified action in trade disputes, as in collective bargaining, and to enable union property to escape liability, the associated individuals in their severalty having no property to levy upon. The group personality theory has been asserted both as a check upon what was regarded as anarchic and dissolving individualism, to set up something more abiding and worthful than a single human being, and to increase the power and dignity of the single being as over against the state. Even the doctrine that true personality resides only in the "natural" person has been worked in opposed directions. It was first used to give church or state a short and direct road of approach which would lessen the power of the singular being over against the collective being, while lately, through being affected by "natural" in the sense of natural rights, it has been employed to exalt private, at the expense of public, interests.

Unfortunately, the human mind tends toward fusion rather than discrimination, and the result is confusion. I quote at length from a recent writer: "A position intermediate between the biological and the psychological theories of the state is held by Gierke and Maitland, whose point of view is shared by such writers as Figgis, Laski and Duguit. The founder of this position was the German jurist, Johannes Althusius. . . . His theory of the state as a hierarchy of constituent groups was broadened out by his modern interpreter, Otto Gierke, in his *Genossenschaftslehre,* which was sponsored and clarified by the eminent English historian and jurist, F. W. Maitland. Briefly, the doctrine is that the state is not a collection of individuals but an aggregation of groups. These groups, in turn, are not merely a plural number of individuals, but an organization of individuals designed to achieve a definite purpose. As purposive groups they are psychic organisms, possessing not a fictitious but a real psychic personality. . . . The exponents of this doctrine of the reality and significance of the group range in their interpretation of the place and significance of the state all the way from the position of such writers as Ernest Barker, who supports an Aristotelian-Hegelian adulation of the state, to the extreme pluralists and the Syndicalists, who would eliminate the state altogether." [1]

[1] Barnes, *Sociology and Political Theory* (1924) 29–30.

The author is writing from the political point of view, not the legal; and the last sentence makes allowance for divergence of views as to the place of the state. But the passage gives the impression of a single school, coherent in its premises if not in its political conclusions. Analysis of the account, therefore, is not just for the sake of convicting Mr. Barnes of error, but for the sake of revealing the fate of any conception that, by ignoring context and purpose, tries to introduce unity into a conception where the facts show utmost divergence. There is a forced assemblage of persons. Laski, like Althusius, has a political interest; but the political interest of the former was to afford a basis for popular government, while that of Laski was to moralize the idea of the state, to attack the idea of irresponsible sovereignty, and, under the influence of the pluralistic philosophy of James, to utilize the importance of the group, assumed currently in the sociology of the period, so as to dwell upon the vitality and autonomy of group interests. Althusius, on the other hand, held that the latter, in contracting themselves into the state, lost their autonomous standing with respect to it.[1] The interest of Figgis in group-personality

[1] His (Laski's) article on *Personality of Associations* closes with a section introduced by these words: "If what we have here been urging is true, it reacts most forcibly upon our theory of the state. Thus far, for the most part, we have sought its unification. We have made it intolerant of associations within itself—associations that to Hobbes will appear comparable only to 'worms within the entrails of a natural man.' As a result we have made our state absorptive in a mystic, Hegelian fashion. It is all-sovereign and unchallengeable. . . . But sovereign your state no longer is if the groups within itself are thus self-governing. Nor can we doubt this polyarchism. Everywhere we find groups within the state which challenge its supremacy. They are, it may be, in relations with the state, a part of it; but one with it they are not. They refuse the reduction to unity. We find the state, in James' phrase, to be distributive and not collective." *Foundations of Sovereignty* (1921) 168–169, *originally printed in* (1916) 29 Harv. L. Rev. 404. The statements about the relation of groups and the state may be true, historically, sociologically and ethically. But they are an argument for the volitional personality of these associations only on the theory that the state is also a personal unified will. It was not the Hobbesian theory, or any similar theory, which produced the magnification of the state; the centralizing tendencies of the new national state produced the theory. Similarly, the rising social, economic and political importance of associations is producing, *in analogy with the concept of the older theory of the state,* a theory of *their* metaphysical personality. One can get the same practical results with a theory like

appears to be wholly conditioned upon his desire to preserve the autonomy of ecclesiastic organizations, especially that of the Church of England.[1]

Gierke's interest was primarily legal; he wrote at a time when no German writer of influence would have thought of depreciating the personality of the state; that was taken for granted. The practical issue was found in the quarrel between Romanists and Germanists; Savigny the great Romanist had come out for the *persona ficta* theory of corporate bodies. Gierke wrote as a Germanist to oppose him, and the quarrel found its practical bearing in the fact that the German Civil Code was being drawn. Maitland writes primarily as a historian of legal institutions, although his political interest is sufficient to make him remark that "the State's possession of a real will is insecure if no other groups may have wills of their own." [2] While he leans toward the real personality theory, it is safe to say that he is much more interested in a comparison of German and English theories and practices than he is in any theory; and any one interested in denying the theory can find much material in the rich store Maitland pro-

---

Duguit's, which denies not only the personality of both state and groups but also of the natural individual as a substratum of rights-duties. "Public law has become objective just as private law is no longer based on individual right or the autonomy of a private will, but upon the idea of a social function imposed on every person." Duguit, *Law in the Modern State* (1919, translated by Laski) 49. Again, "In private law the autonomy of the human will is in process of disappearance; the individual will is powerless by itself to create a legal situation." Duguit, *supra* at 243.

[1] It is interesting to note, as an instance of the particular and "pragmatic" origin of much of the English theorizing, the large part played by the case of the *Free Church of Scotland v. Overtown* [1904] A. C. 515, and of the trades-unions decisions in the *Taff Vale* case [1901] A. C. 426 and the *Osborne* case [1910] A. C. 87 or the former see Vinagradoff, *Juridical Persons* (1924) 24 Col. L. Rev. 594, at 597–599. Laski, *op. cit. supra* note 19, at 165–166 has a few comments on the latter two cases. There is a strange logic implied in the reasonings of the "real group personality" school that, since unwise decisions have been reached in a number of cases under cover of the "fictitious person" theory, the "real personality" view must be necessary to reach a correct decision. There is surely more than one alternative possibility omitted.

[2] Gierke (with preface by Maitland), *op. cit. supra* note 3, at xlii.

vides. [1] Duguit writes as a lawyer, and his political interest is in making the "state," all officers of government legally liable. He denies will and personality to both the state *and* all other groups. "Nor is it [fault] imputable to the collectivity since the latter outside the imagination of lawyers has no personal existence." [2] As for Ernest Barker, he is indeed strong for the personality of the state, but his purpose is identical with that of Duguit, who denies precisely what Barker asserts: "What is needed is, in the first place, the conception of the State or the Public as a legally responsible person; and, in the second place, the application to this person of the idea of agency in such sort that it shall admit responsibility for the acts of its servants done in its service." [3] Specifically he wants some kind of administrative and law courts, in which the state through its agents can be rendered liable, although not administrative law of the French type. Finally, the reference to "psychic organisms" is either gratuitous or highly misleading. It is not psychic personality which these writers—as far as they do hold to the personality of the state—are concerned with, but a moral personality, that is unity of organized action involving "will." The idea of psychic personality is read in from writers on social psychology and sociology.

I do not make this examination for the sake of indicating that Mr. Barnes sins above others. As already stated, the collection of commissions and omissions is the sort of thing which is bound to happen when one assumes that there is in existence

[1] Thus his whole discussion of trusts shows how much has been accomplished, avoiding some of the attending difficulties of German law, "without troubling the state to concede or deny the mysterious boon of personality." 3 *Collected Papers* 283. His remark that "it's often struck me that morally there is most personality where legally there is least" certainly cuts both ways. The fact that the family, which is the most intimate emotional and volitional unity, is not a jural personality, has given the adherents of the real personality theory much difficulty.

[2] Duguit, *Law in the Modern State* (1919) 205.

[3] Barker, *The 'Rule of Law'* (May, 1914) THE POLITICAL QUARTERLY, 117, at 123. For a full discussion of this matter see Borchard, *Government Liability in Tort* (1924) 34 YALE LAW JOURNAL, 1, 129, 229.

some single and coherent theory of personality and will, singular or associated. Nothing accurate or intelligible can be said except by specifying the interest and purpose of a writer, and his historical context of problems and issues. Thus we end where we began: with the statement that the entire discussion of personality, whether of single or corporate personality, is needlessly encumbered with a mass of traditional doctrines and remnants of old issues. Almost every English writer, beginning with Maitland, who has written in behalf of the doctrine of the "real personality" of corporate bodies, has felt obliged to quote the following from Dicey: "When a body of twenty or two thousand or two hundred thousand men bind themselves together to act in a particular way for some common purpose, they create a body which by no fiction of law but by the very nature of things, differs from the individuals of whom it is composed." Assuredly; but why should such a fact be thought to have any bearing at all upon the problem of personality? Only because the doctrine of "fictitious" personality had been employed, under the influence of the "individualistic" philosophy already referred to, to deny that there is any social reality at all back of or in corporate action. Hence the assertion of the simple fact that there is some social reality involved got bound up with the notion of a real, as distinct from fictitious, personality. The example, it seems to me, is sufficiently striking to enforce the value of eliminating the *idea* of personality until the concrete facts and relations involved have been faced and stated on their own account: retaining the *word* will then do no great harm.

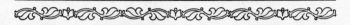

Nature and Reason in Law

IN Pollock's "Expansion of the Common Law," there is found the following interesting passage from St. German, written early in the sixteenth century: "It is not used among them that be learned in the laws of England, to reason what thing is commanded or prohibited by the Law of Nature and what not, but all the reasoning in that behalf is under this manner. As when anything is grounded upon the Law of Nature, they say that Reason will that such a thing be done; and if it be prohibited by the Law of Nature they say it is against Reason, or that Reason will not suffer that to be done."[1] It is a commonplace to the student of the history of law that this identification of natural and rational, and the equating of both with the morally right, has been at various times a source of great improvements in law. Professor Pound has recently designated the stage in the development of law that follows upon and corrects many of the abuses of the stage of strict law as that of equity or natural law. He says: "The capital ideas of the stage of equity or natural law are the identification of law with morals; the conception of duty and the attempt to make moral duties into legal duties, and reliance upon reason rather than upon arbitrary rule to keep down caprice and eliminate the personal element in the administration of justice."[2] Aside from the introduction of equity, the abolition of technicalities which obstruct rather than further justice, the adoption by the courts of usages that were more reasonable than those perpetuated in older law, the idea of the subordination of government to social ends, and the furtherance of humane international relations

[1] Pollock, *The Expansion of the Common Law*, p. 109.
[2] 27 *Harvard Law Review*, p. 213.

are a few of the many services rendered by the identification
of the natural with the reasonable. Looking back and taking
the intellectual temper and equipment of the times into
account, it is hard to see what other intellectual instrumentality could have done the work effected by the concept of
natural reason in the seventeenth and eighteenth centuries.
In the view of such facts the title given by Pollock to the Law
of Nature, "a living embodiment of the collective reason of
civilized mankind," [1] is not so much out of the way as it seems
to the philosopher who has been trained to look with suspi-
cion upon any reference to Nature as a norm; and who is
conscious of the seemingly individualistic, if not anti-social,
connotation of the term in political philosophy. But even in
Locke, careful analysis shows that the limitation of governmental action to the protection of pre-existent natural rights
is much more an assertion of the subordination of governmental action to ends that are reasonable, or moral, than
appears from a hasty reading. Restricting the action of
government by moral considerations, that is to say considerations of reason, is what Locke is chiefly concerned with.

But, unfortunately, nature and reason are ambiguous
terms; hence their use as equivalents of what is morally desirable is subject to diverse interpretations. Nature also means
the existent, the given, the antecedent state of things; or the
present state of things so far as that is connected with the
antecedent condition by casual laws. Appeal to nature may,
therefore, signify the reverse of an appeal to what is desirable
in the way of consequences; it may denote an attempt to settle
what is desirable among consequences by reference to an antecedent and hence fixed and immutable rule.

Accordingly, while at one time or with some people, or
with some persons part of the time, natural justice means that
which commends itself to the best judgment of the most expe-

[1] *Op. cit.*, p. 128.

rienced or to the collective common-sense of the race, as over against the conventional and technical justice of inherited legal rules; at other times it means acceptance of the given state of distribution of advantages and disadvantages. Such a view of natural justice finds, for example, a typical representative in Herbert Spencer. It is, so to speak, purely accidental that such philosophies have been what we lately call individualistic as against collective or socialistic. The essential thing in them is the subordination of the human, whether several or conjoint, to the given, to the physical. The central feature of the *laissez faire* doctrine is that human reason is confined to discovering what antecedently exists, the pre-existent system of advantages and disadvantages, resources and obstacles, with the intent of conforming action strictly to the given scheme. It is the abnegation of human intelligence save as a bare reporter of things as they are and as a power conforming to them. It is a kind of epistemological realism in politics. That such a doctrine should work out, no matter how personally benevolent its holders, in the direction of *Beati possidentes,* is inevitable.

This mode of interpretation affected the idea of Reason as well as of Nature, not merely because of the historic equating of Reason and Nature in judicial philosophy, but for special reasons. To the century that felt the influence of Newtonian science, Nature was more Reason than human reason itself. Human reason was reason only as a faculty of retracing the wisdom, harmony, the uniform and comprehensive laws, embodied in Nature—that is, in the physically given world. The Lockean and Deistic identification of Reason with God, the benevolent ordainer and arranger of things, flavored even the most free-thinking speculation of the times. Those who prided themselves that they had no fear of God attributed to Nature the same optimistic benevolence that had characterized the God of natural religion. In order to be really reasonable and moral in action, that is, to act in behalf of good consequences, one had but to get his own interfering intelligence out of the way, and permit Nature, true Reason, to execute her own harmonious and benevolent designs. With respect to Reason as to Nature, the emphasis upon individualism was extraneous and secondary; the intrinsic and primary thing was the denial of a characteristic, a unique function, to human intelligence. Nature, not human thought, determined the formation of true purposes.

If I trace an analogous movement in the decisions of the courts relative to due diligence and undue negligence, it is not for the sake of demonstrating a direct influence of this type of philosophy upon the minds of judges; that would be somewhat absurd. But there *is* demonstrable, in my opinion, a parity of logic; and in addition there was probably some indirect influence in so far as this mode of thought was in the air. Reason is appealed to as a standard of action. A man's liability depends upon whether he uses the proper degree of reasonable care and prudence. But what measures this? Obviously ordinary prudence is a vague and relative matter— relative in the sense of varying with the circumstances of the situations, as the courts have pointed out. But this very vagueness and variability make the more necessary some principle for detecting the meaning of reasonable in special cases. It is obvious at a glance that the reference to what reasonable and prudent men do or would do in similar cases, has exactly the ambiguity we have been dealing with. It may mean reasonable in the sense of involving the kind of foresight that *would*, in similar situations, conduce to desirable consequences; or it may mean the amount and kind of foresight that, as a matter of fact, are customary among men in like pursuits, even though it be demonstrable that, upon the whole, the customs involve deplorable consequences.

That this ambiguity is not merely a theoretical possibility

is evidenced by the course of court decisions in the matter of the due diligence of employers in the last half century. While, in some cases, the courts have taken the position which identifies reason with foresight of specific consequences, the general tendency for a long time was to identify reasonable prudence with the ruling customs of the trade, no matter how unreasonable those customs themselves were when looked at from the standpoint of the sort of consequences they tend to produce. For a long time the Supreme Court was almost alone in saying: "Ordinary care on the part of a railway company implies, as between it and its employees, not simply that degree of diligence which is *customary* among those intrusted with the management of railroad property, but such as having respect to the exigencies of the particular service, *ought* reasonably to be observed . . . such watchfulness, caution, and foresight as, under all the circumstances of the particular service, a corporation controlled by careful, prudent men *ought* to exercise." . . . The Court "cannot give their assent to the doctrine that ordinary care in such cases means only the degree of diligence which is customary, or is sanctioned by the general practice and usage which obtains." [1] Such a quotation, on the contrary side, as the following, from a federal court, shows well the different interpretations of reasonable care put upon the obligations of the corporation to the general public it served and to those for whose services it paid: "As respects travel on steam railways many of the courts of this country hold the carrier bound to keep pace with new inventions in the direction of safety. But this rule is an exceptional one, established upon grounds of public policy, and for the safety of human life. It has never been applied to the relation of master and servant." [2]

When we consider the implications of the contract from

---

[1] *Wabash Ry. Co.* v. *McDaniels,* 107 U. S. 454.; italics are mine.
[2] 40 Fed. 784.

the side of the employee, as these have been developed through
court decisions with respect to the assumption of risks, we find
yet another aspect of the same matter. No Kantian philosopher ever went further in ascribing a ready-made antecedent
faculty of reason to man than the courts have done in endow-
ing the laborers of this country with unbounded foresight of
the consequences implied in taking a job; and no transcenden-
talist ever went further in assuming that this antecedently
possessed reason was in a position to make itself effective in
action. As far as the workmen were concerned the courts were
committed to the idealistic assumption: *Mens agitat molem.*
In its application, this meant, that risks which the laborer ran
as matter of fact in the performance of his habitual duties
were assumed to have been deliberately or intentionally undertaken by him. The whole doctrine of the assumption of risk
was, in pragmatic effect, a rendering of brute physical situations in terms of purpose or reason.

In short, in substance although not in form, the reasonable or "natural" was identified with the antecedently given,
with the state of affairs that customarily obtained, not with
the exercise of intelligence to correct defects and to bring
about better consequences. From the side of the employer, it
meant *Beati possidentes,* To him that hath shall be given;
from the side of the employee, *Væ victis,* From him that hath
not shall be taken away even that which he seemeth to have.

It would not be difficult to trace the same logic in the
denial of the principle of liability without fault. Under certain conditions, the doctrine is doubtless reasonable, in the
sense in which reasonable means due foresight of consequences. Under other conditions, where industrial pursuits
bring about different consequences, the doctrine that in pure
accident of misadventure it is reasonable for the loss to lie
where it falls, is, when laid down as a dogma, the deliberate
identification of the reasonable with the physically existent,

and willful refusal to use intelligence in such a way as to ameliorate the impact of disadvantages.

Fortunately, many of the specific things dealt with in this paper are now by way of becoming historic reminiscences. But for this very reason they may the better illustrate the main thesis of this paper. The principle of natural law and justice in the sense that technical and official legal rules need to be adapted to secure desirable results in practice, may well be accepted. But we also find that one of the chief offices of "nature" in political and judicial practice has been to consecrate the existent state of affairs, whatever its distribution of advantages and disadvantages, of benefits and losses; and to idealize, rationalize, moralize, the physically given—for customs from a philosophical point of view are part of the physical state of affairs. By reading between the lines, moreover, we find that the chief working difference between moral philosophies in their application to law is that some of them seek for an antecedent principle by which to decide; while others recommend the consideration of the specific consequences that flow from treating a specific situation this way or that, using the antecedent material and rules as guides of intellectual analysis but not as norms of decision.

Interpretation of the Savage Mind

THE psychical attitudes and traits of the savage are more than stages through which mind has passed, leaving them behind. They are outgrowths which have entered decisively into further evolution, and as such form an integral part of the framework of present mental organization. Such positive significance is commonly attributed, in theory at least, to animal mind; but the mental structure of the savage, which presumably has an even greater relevancy for genetic psychology, is strangely neglected.

The cause of this neglect I believe lies in the scant results so far secured, because of the abuse of the comparative method —which abuse in turn is due to the lack of a proper method of interpretation. Comparison as currently employed is defective—even perverse—in at least three respects. In the first place, it is used indiscriminately and arbitrarily. Facts are torn loose from their context in social and natural environment and heaped miscellaneously together, because they have impressed the observer as alike in some respect. Upon a single page of Spencer,[1] which I chanced to open in looking for an illustration of this point, appear Kamschadales, Kirghiz, Bedouins, East Africans, Bechuanas, Damaras, Hottentots, Malays, Papuans, Fijians, Andamanese—all cited in reference to establishing a certain common property of primitive minds. What would we think of a biologist who appealed successively to some external characteristic of say snake, butterfly, elephant, oyster and robin in support of a statement? And yet the peoples mentioned present widely remote cultural resources, varied environments and distinctive institutions. What is the scientific value of a proposition thus arrived at?

[1] *Sociology*, I, p. 57.

In the second place, this haphazard, uncontrollable selection yields only static facts—facts which lack the dynamic quality necessary to a genetic consideration. The following is a summary of Mr. Spencer's characterizations of primitive men, emotional and intellectual:

He is explosive and chaotic in feeling, improvident, childishly mirthful, intolerant of restraint, with but small flow of altruistic feeling,[1] attentive to meaningless detail and incapable of selecting the facts from which conclusions may be drawn, with feeble grasp of thought, incapable of rational surprise, incurious, lacking in ingenuity and constructive imagination.[2] Even the one quality which is stated positively, namely, keenness of perception, is interpreted in a purely negative way, as a trait antagonistic to reflective development. "In proportion as the mental energies go out in restless perception, they cannot go out in deliberate thought."[3] And this from a sensationalist in psychology!

Such descriptions as these also bear out my first point. Mr. Spencer himself admits frequent and marked discrepancies (e.g., pp. 56, 59, 62, 65, etc.), and it would not be difficult to bring together a considerable mass of proof-texts to support the exact opposite of each of his assertions. But my point here is that present civilized mind is virtually taken as a standard, and savage mind is measured off on this fixed scale.

It is no wonder that the outcome is negative; that primitive mind is described in terms of "lack," "absence": its traits are incapacities. Qualities defined in such fashion are surely useless in suggesting, to say nothing of determining, progress, and are correspondingly infertile for genetic psychology, which is interested in becoming, growth, development.

The third remark is that the results thus reached, even passing them as correct, yield only loose aggregates of unre-

[1] *Sociology,* I, pp. 59, 60, 63, 69, 71.   [2] *Ibid.,* pp. 79, 82, 85–87.   [3] *Ibid.,* p. 77.

lated traits—not a coherent scheme of mind. We do not escape from an inorganic conglomerate conception of mind by just abusing the "faculty" psychology. Our standpoint must be more positive. We must recognize that mind has a pattern, a scheme of arrangement in its constituent elements, and that it is the business of a serious comparative psychology to exhibit these patterns, forms or types in detail. By such terms, I do not mean anything metaphysical; I mean to indicate the necessity of a conception such as is a commonplace with the zoölogist. Terms like articulate or vertebrate, carnivora or herbivora, are "pattern" terms of the sort intended. They imply that an animal is something more than a random composite of isolated parts, made by taking an eye here, an ear there, a set of teeth somewhere else. They signify that the constituent elements are arranged in a certain way; that in being co-adapted to the dominant functions of the organism they are of necessity co-related to one another. Genetic psychology of mind will advance only as it discovers and specifies generic forms or patterns of this sort in psychic morphology.

It is a method for the determination of such types that I wish to suggest in this paper. The biological point of view commits us to the conviction that mind, whatever else it may be, is at least an organ of service for the control of environment in relation to the ends of the life process.

If we search in any social group for the special functions to which mind is thus relative, occupations at once suggest themselves.[1] Occupations determine the fundamental modes of activity, and hence control the formation and use of habits. These habits, in turn, are something more than practical and overt. "Apperceptive masses" and associational tracts of necessity conform to the dominant activities. The occupations deter-

[1] We might almost say, in the converse direction, that biological genera are "occupational" classifications. They connote different ways of getting a living with the different instrumentalities (organs) appropriate to them, and the different associative relations set up by them.

mine the chief modes of satisfaction, the standards of success and failure. Hence they furnish the working classifications and definitions of value; they control the desire processes. Moreover, they decide the sets of objects and relations that are important, and thereby provide the content or material of attention, and the qualities that are interestingly significant. The directions given to mental life thereby extend to emotional and intellectual characteristics. So fundamental and pervasive is the group of occupational activities that it affords the scheme or pattern of the structural organization of mental traits. Occupations integrate special elements into a functioning whole.

Because the hunting life differs from, say, the agricultural, in the sort of satisfactions and ends it furnishes, in the objects to which it requires attention, in the problems it sets for reflection and deliberation, as well as in the psycho-physic co-ordinations it stimulates and selects, we may well speak, and without metaphor, of a hunting psychosis as a mental pattern. And so of the pastoral, the military, the trading, the manually productive (or manufacturing) occupations and so on. As a specific illustration of the standpoint and method, I shall take the hunting vocation, and that as carried on by the Australian aborigines. I shall try first to describe its chief distinguishing marks; and then to show how the mental pattern developed is carried over into various activities, customs and products, which on their face have nothing to do with the hunting life. If a controlling influence of this sort can be made out—if it can be shown that art, war, marriage, etc., tend to be psychologically assimilated to the pattern developed in the hunting vocation, we shall thereby get an important method for the interpretation of social institutions and cultural resources—a psychological method for sociology.

The Australian lives in an environment upon the whole benign, without intense or violent unfavorable exhibition of natural forces (save in alternations of drought and flood in some portions), not made dangerous by beasts of prey, and with a sufficient supply of food to maintain small groups in a good state of nutrition though not abundant enough to do this without continual change of abode. The tribes have no cultivated plants, no domesticated animals (save the dingo dog), hence no beasts of burden, and no knowledge or use of metals.[1]

Now as to the psychic pattern formed under such circumstances. How are the sensory-motor co-ordinations common to all men organized, how stimulated and inhibited into relatively permanent psychic habits, through the activities appropriate to such a situation?

By the nature of the case, food and sex stimuli are the most exigent of all excitants to psycho-physic activity, and the interests connected with them are the most intense and persistent. But with civilized man, all sorts of intermediate terms come in between the stimulus and the overt act, and between the overt act and the final satisfaction. Man no longer defines his end to be the satisfaction of hunger as such. It is so complicated and loaded with all kinds of technical activities, associations, deliberations and social divisions of labor, that conscious attention and interest are in the process and its content. Even in the crudest agriculture, means are developed to the point where they demand attention on their own account, and control the formation and use of habits to such an extent that they are the central interests, while the food process and enjoyment as such is incidental and occasional.

[1] All these points are important, for the general hunting psychosis exhibits marked differentiations when developed in relation to ferocious beasts; in relation to a very sparse or very abundant food supply; in relation to violently hostile natural forces; and when hunting is pursued in connection with various degrees of agriculture or domesticated herds or flocks. For economy of space, I have omitted reference to the few portions of Australia where the food supply (generally fish in such circumstances) is sufficiently abundant to permit quasi-permanent abodes, though the psychological variations thus induced are interesting.

The gathering and saving of seed, preparing the ground, sowing, tending, weeding, care of cattle, making of improvements, continued observation of times and seasons, engage thought and direct action. In a word, in all post-hunting situations the end is mentally apprehended and appreciated not as food satisfaction, but as a continuously ordered series of activities and of objective contents pertaining to them. And hence the direct and personal display of energy, personal putting forth of effort, personal acquisition and use of skill are not conceived or felt as immediate parts of the food process. But the exact contrary is the case in hunting. There are no intermediate appliances, no adjustment of means to remote ends, no postponements of satisfaction, no transfer of interest and attention over to a complex system of acts and objects. Want, effort, skill and satisfaction stand in the closest relations to one another. The ultimate aim and the urgent concern of the moment are identical; memory of the past and hope for the future meet and are lost in the stress of the present problem; tools, implements, weapons are not mechanical and objective means, but are part of the present activity, organic parts of personal skill and effort. The land is not a means to a result but an intimate and fused portion of life —a matter not of objective inspection and analysis, but of affectionate and sympathetic regard. The making of weapons is felt as a part of the exciting use of them. Plants and animals are not "things," but are factors in the display of energy and form the contents of most intense satisfactions. The "animism" of primitive mind is a necessary expression of the immediacy of relation existing between want, overt activity, that which affords satisfaction and the attained satisfaction itself. Only when things are treated simply as *means,* are marked off and held off against remote ends, do they become "objects."

Immediacy of interest, attention and deed is the essential trait of the nomad hunter. He has no cultivated plants, no system of appliances and tending and regulating plants and animals; he does not even anticipate the future by drying meat. When food is abundant, he gorges himself, but does not save. His habitation is a temporary improvised hut. In the interior, he does not even save skins for clothes in the cold of winter, but cooks them with the rest of the carcass. Generally even by the water he has no permanent boats, but makes one of bark when and as he needs it. He has no tools or equipment except those actually in use at the moment of getting or using food—weapons of the chase and war. Even set traps and nets which work for the savage are practically unknown. He catches beast, bird and fish with his own hands when he does not use club or spear; and if he uses nets he is himself personally concerned in their use.

Now such facts as these are usually given a purely negative interpretation. They are used as proofs of the incapacities of the savage. But in fact they are parts of a very positive psychosis, which, taken in itself and not merely measured against something else, requires and exhibits highly specialized skill and affords intense satisfactions—psychical and social satisfactions, not merely sensuous indulgences. The savage's repugnance to what we term a higher plane of life is not due to stupidity or dullness or apathy—or to any other merely negative qualities—such traits are a later development and fit the individual only too readily for exploitation as a tool by "superior races." His aversion is due to the fact that in the new occupations he does not have so clear nor so intense a sphere for the display of intellectual and practical skill, or such opportunity for a dramatic play of emotion. Consciousness, even if superficial, is maintained at a higher intensity.[1]

[1] For good statements by competent authorities of the Australian's aversion to agriculture, etc., see Hodkinsson, *Australia, from Port Macquarie to Moreton Bay*, p. 243; and Grey, *Two Expeditions*, etc., II, p. 279.

The hunting life is of necessity one of great emotional interest, and of adequate demand for acquiring and using highly specialized skills of sense, movement, ingenuity, strategy and combat. It is hardly necessary to argue the first point. Game and sport are still words which mean the most intense immediate play of the emotions, running their entire gamut. And these terms still are applied most liberally and most appropriately to hunting. The transferred application of the hunting language to pursuit of truth, plot interest, business adventur ⁀nd speculation, to all intense and active forms of amusement, to gambling and the "sporting life," evidences how deeply imbedded in later consciousness is the hunting pattern or schema.[1]

The interest of the game, the alternate suspense and movement, the strained and alert attention to stimuli always changing, always demanding graceful, prompt, strategic and forceful response; the play of emotions along the scale of want, effort, success or failure—this is the very type, psychically speaking, of the drama. The breathless interest with which we hang upon the movement of play or novel are reflexes of the mental attitudes evolved in the hunting vocation.

The savage loses nothing in enjoyment of the drama because it means life or death to him. [2] The emotional interest in the game itself is moreover immensely reinforced and deepened by its social accompaniments. Skill and success mean applause and admiration; it means the possibility of lavish generosity—the quality that wins all. Rivalry and emulation and vanity all quicken and feed it. It means sexual admiration and conquests—more wives or more elopements. It means, if

[1] See Thomas' *The Gaming Instinct, American Journal of Sociology,* Vol. VI, p. 750. I am indebted to Dr. Thomas (through personal conversation as well as from his articles) for not only specific suggestions, but for the point of view here presented to such an extent that this article is virtually a joint contribution.
[2] Though some writers even say that the savage's interest in the game of hunting is so great that he hunts for the excitement rather than for food. See Lumholtz, *Among Cannibals,* p. 161 and p. 191.

persistent, the ultimate selection of the individual for all tribal positions of dignity and authority.

But perhaps the most conclusive evidence of the emotional satisfactions that are involved is the fact that the men reserve the hunting occupation to themselves, and give to the women everything that has to do with the vegetable side of existence (where the passive subject-matter does not arouse the dramatic play), and all activity of every sort that involves the more remote adaptation of means to ends—and hence, drudgery. [1]

The same sort of evidence is found in the fact that, with change to agricultural life, other than hunting types of action are (if women do not suffice) handed over to slaves, and the energy and skill acquired go into the game of war. This also explains the apparent contradiction in the psychic retrogression of the mass with some advances in civilization. The gain is found in the freed activities of the few, and in the cumulation of the objective instrumentalities of social life, and in the final development, under the discipline of subjection, of new modes of interest having to do with remoter ends—considerations, however, which are psychologically realized by the mass only at much later periods.

As to the high degree of skill, practical and intellectual, stimulated and created by the hunting occupation, the case is equally clear—provided, that is, we bear in mind the types of skill appropriate to the immediate adjustments required, and do not look for qualities irrelevant because useless in such a situation.

No one has ever called a purely hunting race dull, apathetic or stupid. Much has been written regarding the aversion of savages to higher resources of civilization—their refusal to adopt iron tools or weapons, for example, and their sodden

[1] This collateral development of a different mental pattern in women is a matter of the greatest significance, in itself, in its relation to subsequent developments and in relation to present mental interests.

absorption in routine habits. None of this applies to the Australian or any other *pure* hunting type. Their attention is mobile and fluid as is their life; they are eager to the point of greed for anything which will fit into their dramatic situations so as to intensify skill and increase emotion. Here again the apparent discrepancies strengthen the case. It is when the native is forced into an alien use of the new resources, instead of adapting them to his own ends, that his workmanship, skill and artistic taste uniformly degenerate.

Competent testimony is unanimous as to the quickness and accuracy of apprehension evinced by the natives in coming in contact even for the first time with complicated constructive devices of civilized man, provided only these appliances have a direct or immediate action-index. One of the commonest remarks of travelers, hardly prepossessed in favor of the savage, is their superiority in keenness, alertness and a sort of intelligent good humor to the average English rustic. The accuracy, quickness and minuteness of perception of eye, ear and smell are no barren accumulation of meaningless sense detail as Spencer would have it; they are the cultivation to the highest point of skill and emotional availability of the instrumentalities and modes of a dramatic life. The same applies to the native's interest in hard and sustained labor, to his patience and perseverance as well as to his gracefulness and dexterity of movement—the latter extending to fingers and toes to an extent which makes even skilled Europeans awkward and clumsy. The usual denial of power of continued hard work, of patience and of endurance to the savage is based once more upon trying him by a foreign standard—interest in ends which involve a long series of means detached from all problems of purely personal adjustment. Patience and persistence and long-maintained effort, the savage does show when they come within the scope of that immediate contest situation with reference to which his mental pattern is formed.

I hardly need say, I suppose, that in saying these things I have no desire to idealize savage intelligence and volition. The savage paid for highly specialized skill in all matters of personal adjustment, by incapacity in all that is impersonal, that is to say, remote, generalized, objectified, abstracted. But my point is that we understand their incapacities only when we see them as the obverse side of positively organized developments; and, still more, that it is only by viewing them primarily in their positive aspect that we grasp the genetic significance of savage mind for the long and tortuous process of mental development, and secure from its consideration assistance in comprehending the structure of present mind.

I come now to a brief consideration of the second main point—the extent to which this psychic pattern is carried over into all the relations of life, and becomes emotionally an assimilating medium. First, take art. The art of the Australian is not constructive, not architectonic, not graphic, but dramatic and mimetic.[1] Every writer who has direct knowledge of the Australian corroborees, whether occasional and secular, or state and ceremonial, testifies to the remarkable interest shown in dramatic representation. The reproduction by dances, of the movements and behavior of the animals of the chase is startling. Great humor is also shown in adapting and reproducing recent events and personal traits. These performances are attended with high emotional attacks; and all the accompaniments of decoration, song, music, spectators' shouts, etc., are designed to revive the feelings appropriate to the immediate conflict-situations which mean so much to the savage. Novelty is at a distinct premium; old songs are discarded; one of the chief interests at an intertribal friendly

[1] There are of course pictures, but comparatively speaking, few and crude. Even the carvings, if originally pictorial, have mostly lost that quality, and become conventional.

meeting is learning new dance-songs; and acquisition of a new one is often sufficient motive for invitation to a general meeting.

The ceremonial corroborees are of course more than forms of art.[1] We have in them the sole exception to the principle that the activities of the hunter are immediate. Here they are weighted with a highly complicated structure of elaborated traditional rites—elaborated and complicated almost beyond belief.[2] But it is an exception which proves the rule. This apparatus of traditionary agencies has no reference to either practical or intellectual control, it gets nowhere objectively. Its effect is just to reinstate the emotional excitations of the food conflict-situations; and particularly to frame in the young the psychic disposition which will make them thoroughly interested in the necessary performances.[3]

There is a natural transition to religion. Totemism and the abundance of plant and animal myths (especially the latter) and the paucity of cosmic and cosmogonic myth testify to the centering of attention upon the content of the combat, or hunting situation. It would be absurd to attempt in a parenthesis an explanation of totemism, but certainly any explanation is radically defective which does not make much of the implication of tribe and animal in the same emotional situation. Hunter and hunted are the factors of a single tension; the mental situation cannot be defined except in terms of both. If animals get away, it is surely because they try; and if they are caught it is surely because after all they are not totally averse—they are friendly. And they seal their friendliness by sharing in one of the most intense satisfactions of life

[1] It is, of course, a historic fact that the actual origin of dramatic art (through the Greeks) is in mimetic dances of a festival and ceremonial sort.
[2] The best account is of course Spencer and Gillen. Certain ceremonies take weeks.
[3] Not, of course, that all these ceremonies are initiatory in character; on the contrary, many are "magical," intended to promote the productivity of their chief food-supplies. But even these were conducted in dramatic fashion, and in such way as to reproduce the emotional disposition involved in the actual occupational life.

—savory food to the hungry. They are, as a matter of fact, co-partners in the life of the group. Why then should they not be represented as of close kin? In any case, attention and interest center in animals more persistently than in anything else; and they afford the content of whatever concentrated intellectual activity goes on. The food taboos, with their supernatural sanctions, certainly create tensions, or reinstate conflict-situations, in the mind; and thus serve to keep alive in consciousness values which otherwise would be more nearly relegated to the mechanically habitual, or become sensuous, not idealized or emotionalized.

I turn now to matters of death and sickness, their cause, and cure, or, if cure is hopeless, their remedy by expiation. Here the assimilation to the psychosis of the hunting activity is obvious. Sickness and death from sickness are uniformly treated as the results of attacks of other persons, who with secret and strange weapons are hunting their victim to his death. And the remedy is to hunt the hunter, to get the aid of that wonderful pursuer and tracker, the medicine man, who by superior ability runs down the guilty party, or with great skill hunts out the deadly missile or poison lodged in the frame of his victim.

If death ensues, then we have the devices for tracking and locating the guilty party. And then comes actual conflict, actual man-hunting. Death can be avenged only by the ordeal of battle—and here we have the explanation of the wars and war-like performances of which so much has been made. It is, however, now generally admitted that the chief object of these war-like meetings is to reinstate the emotion of conflict rather than to kill. They are, so to speak, psychological duels on a large scale—as one observer says, they are "fights with a maximum of noise, boast, outward show of courage and a minimum of casualties." [1] But the maneuvering, throwing and

[1] Horn, *Expedition*, Vol. IV, p. 36.

dodging that take place are a positive dramatic exercise in the utilities of their occupational pursuits.

Finally, as to marriage, and the relations between the sexes. What was said concerning the impossibility of an adequate account of totemism applies with greater force to the problem of the system of group relationships which determine marital possibilities. It is clear, however, that the system of injunctions and restrictions serves to develop a scheme of inhibitions and intensified stimuli which makes sex-satisfaction a matter of pursuit, conflict, victory and trophy over again. There is neither complete absence of inhibition, which, involving little personal adjustment, does not bring the sexual sensations into the sphere of emotion as such; nor is there a system of voluntary agreement and affection, which is possible only with a highly developed method of intellectual control and large outlooks upon a long future. There is just the ratio between freedom and restraint that develops the dramatic instinct, and gives courtship and the possession of women all the emotional joys of the hunt—personal display, rivalry, enough exercise of force to stimulate the organism; and the emotion of prowess joined to the physical sensations of indulgence. Here, as elsewhere in the hunting psychosis, novelty is at a premium, for the mind is dependent upon a present or immediate stimulus to get activity going. It requires no deep scientific analysis to inform us that sex-relations are still largely in the dramatized stage; and the play of emotion which accompanies the enacting of the successive stages of the drama gives way to genuine affection and intelligent foresight only slowly through great modifications of the whole educative and economic environment. Recent writers, I think, in their interest on the institutional side of marriage (for we are going through a period of reading back Aryan legal relationships just as we formerly read back Aryan theogonies and mythologies) have overlooked the tremendous importance of the immediate play of psychic factors congruous to hunting as such.[1]

In conclusion, let me point out that the adjustment of habits to ends, through the medium of a problematic, doubtful, precarious situation, is the structural form upon which present intelligence and emotion are built. It remains the ground-pattern. The further problem of genetic psychology is then to show how the purely immediate personal adjustment of habit to direct satisfaction, in the savage, became transformed through the introduction of impersonal, generalized objective instrumentalities and ends; how it ceased to be immediate and became loaded and surcharged with a content which forced personal want, initiative, effort and satisfaction further and further apart, putting all kinds of social divisions of labor, intermediate agencies and objective contents between them. This is the problem of the formation of mental patterns appropriate to agricultural, military, professional and technological and trade pursuits, and the reconstruction and overlaying of the original hunting schema.

But by these various agencies we have not so much destroyed or left behind the hunting structural arrangement of mind, as we have set free its constitutive psycho-physic factors so as to make them available and interesting in all kinds of objective and idealized pursuits—the hunt for truth, beauty, virtue, wealth, social well-being, and even of heaven and of God.

[1] For a statement doing justice to the psycho-physic factors involved, see Thomas, Der Ursprung der Exogamie, *Zeitschrift für Socialwissenschaft,* Bd. V, 1.

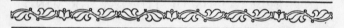

A Naturalistic Theory of Sense Perception

IN its primary and unsophisticated use, sense-perception signifies observation and recognition of objects by means of bodily organs, eyes, ears, hands, nose, *etc.* As a term, it is like pen-writing, brush-painting, hammer-pounding, steel-engraving. It tells nothing about the nature of perceiving, but conveys information about the means by which the act of perceiving occurs, just as the other phrases specify tools through which acts take place. However, in each case the act and its characteristic consequences are modified by the traits of the organs and means which are involved. Thus questions arise: In what way do the employed instrumentalities affect the act and thereby its results? In carrying on such inquiries, investigators are led to discoveries far outside the scope of the first question. In connection with acts performed by the use of tools, not only are their specific effects learned, but principles of friction, mechanical equivalents of heat, the correlation of energies are ascertained. Similarly, in connection with the use of the eyes, ears, *etc.,* in the act of perceiving, not only are the particular functions of different organic structures learned, but such things as the effects of color blindness, astigmatism, muscular adjustments, refraction by the lens. In short, we learn how nerve-elements interact with external physical changes in bringing about the occurrence of certain perceived qualities. But all this concerns the things perceived. It does not affect the act of perceiving. Hence such problems as present themselves are of the same order as those hit upon in any naturalistic inquiry. They do not concern the nature of perception, awareness, or knowledge. There is nothing peculiar, nothing unique, about them.

The adjectives "sense" and "sensory" are prefixed to qualities as well as to the act of perceiving. Colors, sounds, odors, rough, smooth, *etc.,* are named "sense qualities." Here the term "sense" is prefixed by a figure of speech. The qualities themselves are not sensory; "sensory" designates an important condition of their occurrence, not a constituent in their nature. By precisely a similar usage of speech, a house, factory, barn is called a building, meaning that which is the outcome of the operation of building; no one is misled by the word into transferring the properties of the act of building into the house or factory. So a picture is named a painting or an oil-color or a water-color. In each case the name is given because of the consequences of the means employed upon the object produced, yet its traits, uses, and career when produced are independent of the act of generation. We might also call "sense" qualities vibration qualities, or cerebral qualities, or by the name of any other factor which conditions their occurrence. In short, perception does not affect or infect the nature of the qualities perceived, although sense-*organs* and their structural connections, which are the means of perceiving, do affect the properties of the thing produced. But there is nothing unique or peculiar about this fact. The same thing happens in any natural sequence when traits of a consequence are correlated with traits of interacting antecedents.

The significance of the point of view thus briefly indicated lies in its contrast with the epistemological theory of sense perception; in contrast with that theory, the one set forth may be termed naturalistic. By the epistemological theory, sense perception means a unique kind of perception, and sense quality means a kind of quality so distinctive that it may be called psychical or mental. Upon the naturalistic theory, all perception is one and the same, and prefixed adjectives, like sensory, refer to its means or organs; the difference between an object perceived by means of the senses and an object recalled by means of some other organic structure is comparable to the difference between any two concrete things, say between a cat and dog, land and water. The difference is in one factual subject-matter, "sense-presentation" having for its subject-matter a thing in some *present* space-relation, memory-presentation that thing in a specified past temporal relation. But upon the other theory, perception is made unique and heterogeneous because of its "sense" nature, and hence the objects of the two modes of presentation are so different in kind that a problem is constituted. And the same thing occurs in the case of contrast of things presented as "conceptual" (or reflectively determined) objects in distinction from "sense" objects. In one theory the difference between colors and, say, electromagnetic disturbances is a difference in specified facts in one and the same world of objects, comparable again to the difference between land and water as objects of perception; on the other theory, there is a gulf in kind between them, and we have to decide which is "the reality," or else find some method of "reconciling" the reality of the one kind of object with that of the other kind of object.

There is, therefore, a question of fact behind the epistemological question. Until this question of fact has been decided the epistemological problem may possibly be a wholly artificial question due to assuming as a fact something which is not a fact. Is the prefixing of "sense" or "sensory" to "perception" metaphorical, transferring by an intrinsically harmless and common figure of speech traits of the tools and effects of an act to the act itself? Is it properly analogous to water-color painting and oil-painting, to etching and engraving, as names for pictures? [1] Or does it properly denote a distinctive and

---

[1] The implication of the question is not that reference to mode of production is an illegitimate way of distinguishing different specific qualities from one another.

unique kind of presentation, "sensory" affecting and qualifying throughout the intrinsic nature of the being aware, and thereby determining that of which we are aware to be a distinctive and unique kind of thing?

This question is primarily, as indicated, a question of fact. The factual reasons assigned for accepting the second alternative have to do with various "abnormalities" in connection with perception by means of sense-organs. There is an almost endless list of such occurrences, so that only a few samples need be given. They are such affairs as double images when the object remains one; the changes which take place in an image while the object remains unaltered—as seeing a thing dance when the eye-ball is pushed; a stick seemingly bent in water; the change in the visual form of things seen in different perspectives and angles; the change in apparent pitch of sound with velocity of approach or removal; converging railway tracks, *etc.*, to say nothing of outright illusions. In the words of a contemporary epistemological writer: "The point is, that all these cases can easily be described in terms of actual and potential *sensations,* while a description in terms of *objects* leads to grave difficulties." [2] The contrast drawn by the italicized words, "sensations" and "objects," is equivalent to the difference between statements in terms of specified subject-matters on one hand, and a unique peculiarity of perception on the other, "sensations" meaning, as here used, a peculiar kind of existence called psychical.

Discussion of facts is, however, bound up with difficulties

The nature of the difference between an engraving and an etching, a wood-engraving and a steel-engraving, may be more exactly and surely determined if we know the different ways in which they are produced. But this is an *added* knowledge about pictures; it does not create a problem as to the nature of pictorial representation *ueberhaupt.* Similarly the effect of sensory and other organic conditions upon the particular things which we perceive does not create a problem as to the nature of perception as such.

[2] Durant Drake, in an article entitled *What Kind of Realism,* in this Journal, Vol. IX, p. 150, italics mine.

arising from implications of terminology and from diverse theories inherited from previous philosophizing. This paper is given to an effort to clear away some of the underbrush which obscures vision.

In the first place, traditional ideas have had an effect because of language which persisted after the beliefs that had given it significance and pertinence had disappeared. "Sense qualities" is, historically, a survival of *sensible* qualities: but while "sense" prefixed to qualities has no import save that of casual reference, "sensible" was, given the metaphysical creed which once obtained, a genuine characterization of some qualities in distinction from others, namely, "intelligible" qualities. Nature was divided, cosmically, into kinds of objects, or at least of objects with two kinds of properties. One set was permanent; the other was of nature in movement or change; one was of things as actualized, the other of things *qua* potential. Since the properties of natural change were actualized in animals, including man, through sense-organs, these qualities were fittingly called sensible. The "ible" clearly implies potentiality, requiring sense for their actualization into sense-forms or sensory essences. Intelli*gible* forms, on the other hand, were actualized through the intellect. Thus the term "sensible qualities" had a characteristic and, given the premises, legitimate meaning. When modern physical science asserted the homogeneity of all things in the physical world and abandoned the category of potentiality and actuality for that of physical contact and motion ("efficient causality"), the term "sensible qualities" still continued in use. It was "rationalized" by interpreting it to mean qualities due to perception in distinction from qualities belonging to things themselves.[1]

[1] Locke, for example, does not use the expression "sense" or "sensory" qualities, but retains the older terminology, "sensible qualities," although repudiating the science and metaphysics which gave it significance. But it should also be noted that Locke uses "sensation" not to denote an existence, but an *operation* of mind. It is

Secondly, epistemological arguments that make qualities in the generation of which sense-organs play a part to be of a different order from things, are pervasively infected with an ambiguity. This consists in treating empirical things (trees, stones, stars, candle-flames, *etc.,* all the things designated by ordinary common nouns) now as the causes of qualities, and now as correlated groups of the qualities. Thus we are told that a *tree* affects the *optic nerve*—(or the light reflected from a tree), giving rise to "sensations" of light and color; that a *stick,* partly in the *air* and partly in the *water,* through inter-action with *sense-organs* and *brain,* occasions "sensations" which in turn give rise to a perception of a bent stick. Now it is clear that all the italicized words, whether naming things within or without the organism, designate empirical objects, not the objects of distinctively physical science. They are all, so to speak, in the same boat with colors and figures. The same is true, of course, when the finger pressing upon the eye-balls is said to cause the perception of double images, *etc., etc.* Now a moment's reflection shows that tree, stick, water, air, finger, and all such objects as figure in these arguments can not be opposed as real or as physical objects to sensations as mental. For these things, by the logic of the epistemologists, are them-selves groups or combinations of "sensations," or of their equivalent mental "images." They are, in Locke's language, themselves complex modes, and can be distinguished from the sensation or sense quality only as the compound from the simple. They are of the same order, not of a different order. And if we do not use the language of epistemology, but of common sense, we are dealing with things and *their* qualities.

The thing which is to be distinguished from a quality as

---

the act of mind which takes place when the mind perceives an idea upon occasion of changes in sense organs, themselves due to changes of objects which affect the sense organs. We get the idea of sensation, therefore, not from sensation, but, as in the case of all ideas of operations of the mind, from "reflection." See Book II of the *Essay,* Chaps. 9 and 19.

its cause is not tree, finger, water, etc., but certain molecular disturbances. The latter are contrasted with the empirical thing, the finger, as well as with the immediate color quality. The bearing of this fact upon our present topic may be seen by taking the well-worn illustration of a penny seen now as a round flat disc, now as an ellipse with various degrees of distortion, and now, seen edgewise, as a curved line—or from a distance as a straight line. Unless there is a passage from one genus, from one universe of discourse, to another the facts must be stated in one or other of the two following ways: (1) Certain molecular disturbances in interaction with another set of molecular arrangements—empirically identified as the human organism—*cause* various phenomena of shape to appear. The round, flat form is no more the "real" (physical) object than are the ellipses and lines; the latter are not appearances of it, but they and it alike are "appearances" due to physical, or physical and physico-chemical changes. "Appearance" here has no other meaning than *effects,* effects used, as effects are everywhere used in scientific inquiry, to make inferences regarding their cause. In this case, the problems involved are similar to those found in any scientific inquiry where certain facts serve as evidence from which to infer something else, externally of quite a different sort. Thus a form in a rock is used to tell of the presence and traits of an animal which lived in some by gone age. It is thus an "appearance" of that animal: that is, it is an effect which gets its full meaning only when placed in connection with something else of which it serves as sign or evidence.

(2) The other mode of statement is concerned simply with empirical relations between what is empirically perceived. The relations with which it deals are those of whole and part, or of a thing and its "belongings," not those of inference from what is perceived to some hypothetical or inferred cause. Thus an object when placed in a certain posi-

tion with reference to the body presents a flat, round form, while when otherwise placed, it presents an elliptical form, or that of a curved edge. Or, suppose we begin with a form like that of a narrow curved band; we find that it can be placed in a serial order of other forms, some elliptical and some round and that a single formula can be found for the entire serial order, just as some numbers which first present themselves at random, or as a jumble, are finally arranged in a series having a principle of connection. There is no question of cause and effect, of "reality" and "appearance," even in the logical, non-epistemological sense found in our previous case. There is simply and only a question of the correlation, according to a constant formula, of various qualities, the total correlated series constituting the object, say a penny. "It," the penny, has or is a series of phases, and physical conditions are such that the phases can not occur simultaneously but only serially—just as there is a series of phases by a determinable formula of gas, liquid, and solid. We may ask which most frequently occurs, and we may take, if we please, the frequency mode, for *practical* purposes, as the standard. But there is no sense in regarding one of them exclusively as the real and the others as its appearances. Every conceivable form or phase may, by the formula of the series, be taken as real in turn and the others as its appearances. But the fact denoted by this language is simply the existence of a series of a determined type.

There are thus two universes of discourse. In one we deal with the physical, existential relation of causal connection, as between colors, sounds, *etc.,* and their conditions, such as vibrations of a physical medium. In the other, we deal with the integrations of various perceptual objects into a whole. The problem is not one of causation, but neither is it one of the connection of a perceived object with an inferred object. It is like the problem of, say, getting the meaning of a sentence by integrating the meaning of words, or, *vice-versa,* of defining the meaning of a word otherwise unknown by considering its contextual connections. A problem different from the problems of physical science and from those of ordinary empirical interpretation arises only if we mix and confuse terms taken from the two different universes of discourse.

Let "real object" be taken at one juncture in the discussion to signify the cause of certain qualitative and immediate effects, and at another juncture as the correlation of these effects into a single whole, and the confusion will generate the epistemological problem of perception as that is ordinarily stated. The confusion is increased by the ambiguities of the word "appear." Sometimes it signifies "be the effect of," as color is the effect of physical rays, or a fossil stone is the "appearance" of a once living animal; sometimes it signifies "be evident, apparent, immediately open to perception," like something before me in contrast with something in the next room, or the edge of a coin in contrast with the entire coin, or a particular rôle of an actor in contrast with the whole set of rôles which define the actor. Then the confused mixture of the two senses generates the idea of "appearance" as distinct from the "real," and hence the problem of the relation of the perceived object as, metaphysically, an appearance in contrast with the unperceived but real object.

In the third place, there is the persistent notion, taken over from Locke by psychological doctrine, that the first qualities perceived are simple and independent: that "red" is sensed before blood or a dress is perceived; blue before the sky, sweet before sugar, orange color and a peculiar odor before *an* orange, *etc.* This is pure superstition. Yet if it is surrendered, the whole current distinction between sensation and perception as modes of "consciousness" or of knowing objects disappears. The so-called "sensation" signifies simply a perception of a *discriminated* quality; the limit of perceptual discrimination by means of a given organ, Red, is not *a* sensation; it is a quality which we perceive, differing only from the perception of sunset in its relative simplicity and isolation, a difference which is not in any sense original and primitive, but which is the product of discerning analysis purposefully undertaken, as much so as the chemical determination of hydrogen as simple and different from water the compound. As a matter of fact (though facts have come to have little to do with discussion of these matters), a child recognizes its dresses long before it identifies colors; and it learns to distinguish colors as *marks,* that is as *means* of more effective discrimination between different dresses—or toys or other objects. When the homogeneity of perceptual qualities and objects is acknowledged and firmly held to, one important phase of the so-called epistemological problem of perception assumes the proper form of a familiar logical situation—the relation of a sign, mark, to that which signified.

Fourthly, the question of the spatial location of qualities perceived by means of the senses is one of physics and not of epistemology. The case of the whereabouts of illusory objects is usually cited as the final clincher to demonstrate the psychical character of the characteristic objects of sense-perception. Where is the ghost that isn't there? Where is the imaged tree which moves when the eye-ball is pushed? Where is the bent stick when the straight stick is plunged in water? It has even been suggested that mental or psychical may be defined as that which physical or public space refuses to accept and assign place to,[1] so conclusive is this type of question felt to be.

The source of this difficulty is failure to make a critical analysis of the conception of "where," of situs. Where, for example, is an explosion? Where is an echo? Where is the "magnetism" that causes a sensitized needle to assume a

[1] *Essays in Critical Realism,* p. 61.

certain directional position? Wherever there is an event, there is interaction, and interaction entails the conception of a *field*. No "field" can be precisely delimited; it extends wherever the energies involved in the interaction operate and as far as any redistributions of energy are effected. The field can be limited *practically,* as can all matters of degree; it can not be existentially located with literal exactness. Thus the place of most *intense* disturbance in an earthquake may be located and, with sufficient variety of seismographic apparatus, the boundaries of its *appreciable* presence may be mapped out. But these boundaries are set practically by capacity to detect and record changes; they are not absolute in any existential sense. One might say that existentially the field of the earthquake is the entire universe since the redistribution of energies extends indefinitely. This would be correct, theoretically, though practically of no significance.

In similar fashion, the bent rays of light in the case of the stick partly in air and partly in water are literally an interaction field determined by (presumably) electro-magnetic disturbances, physiological structures, and a refracting agency. It is not "in" the organism, nor is it "at" a highly delimited spot in the environment. The place where light rays impinge on the refracting thing with its different angles of refraction in two media of different density may form one focus in the field; the point where the refracted rays impinge on the molecular structures forming the optical apparatus may be another focus. But these, like foci of an ellipse, are determinations in a wider field. The sun—or other source of light —is a part of the "where" of the bent rays, just as much as some remote portions of the interior of the earth are a part of the "where" of an earthquake.

Specific location is always a relationship to a *further* event; it is additive in character. We "locate" an explosion *at* a given spot because the act of generating or preventing the explosion, the act of control of occurrence, is directed there. If we knew enough and had the power to occasion and to prevent earthquakes, we should undoubtedly say that an earthquake is *where* the act of control is applied. A disease involves the entire organism and (ultimately) some extra-organic interacting event, but its "seat" is where remedial measures most effectively take place. A man's body may be in Europe, since in certain respects he may be reached there most effectively, while his residence is in Florida and his domicile in New York. The demand to know "where" are the images of the tree that move when the eye-ball is pushed is an ambiguous question. Literally they are wherever a certain interaction of at least three factors is taking place. From the everyday practical standpoint, that of "common-sense," "where" signifies the point at which action should be directed to control the occurrence of the phenomenon.

The fact that "where" in ordinary usage contains a reference to an act, originating in an organic agent, is a commonplace. But unfortunately it is not usual to employ the commonplace in discussing questions of this sort. To "common-sense," a thing is located with respect to that locomotion or other movement of the organism which is required to attain or prevent certain results. That a thing is so many paces away in front, to the right and a little above, signifies that the human body must move so far ahead, swerve to one side and raise some part of itself in order to procure certain consequences. Every psychological book is full of instances of the fact that specific location is not inherent or intrinsic, but has reference to the actual or potential behavior of an organism in effecting a course of events. The location of the stick which is in the air is related to a certain habit of reaching and handling. This habit being adapted to a certain medium does not work correctly when the refraction of light occurs under unusual conditions. A wrong, an inefficient, unadapted, act hence takes place. When the habit is re-made, specific location again takes place correctly. There does not appear to be any further mystery in the cases which are frequently employed to show that some objects of perception are mental in nature. Anyone who learns to use a microscope, or even a mirror, learns that specific location is a practical matter, not a literal existential one, and that unusual conditions of the coördination of acts of seeing and reaching occasion difficulty in locating until a new habit is set up. That certain images of light can not be located in space signifies, then, only that the practical act of reaching and grasping in their case, does not without pains and practice, fit into the established systems of habits which customarily determine the seat, residence, or situs of an affair, the latter being physically and literally a complex interaction, covering a vast field. Indeed, the field is so vast and illimitable that, strictly speaking, the interaction may be said to be "of" nature rather than "in" it, in the practical sense in which we quite properly use the terms "in" and "at." The theory criticized is thus also guilty of the third of the misconceptions we have mentioned. It passes surreptitiously from ordinary perceived spatial relations of perceived things to "physical" space in the sense of space as the object of physical science. If we stick strictly to physical terms, there is no peculiar problem, but only the ordinary scientific problem of determining a field. If we stick to empirical perceptual terms, there is only the problem of correct practical adjustments in reaching, grasping, handling, *etc*.

I do not suppose that the four misconceptions which have been considered exhaust the list of antecedent confusions and mistakes which bring about the conversion of a naturalistic view into an epistemological one. But they are important contributing factors. Until these preliminary ambiguities and shiftings have been got rid of, there seems to be little hope that continued discussion of the problem of perception which proceeds without any reference to them will bring us nearer to agreement and settlement. When they are disposed of, as far as there remain anything more than scientific questions of a familiar type, the residual problems concern metaphysical matters, such as import of the casual relationship and the nature and status of qualities.

Perception and Organic Action

EVERY reader of Bergson—and who to-day is not reading Bergson—is aware of a twofold strain in his doctrine. On the one hand, the defining traits of perception, of common sense knowledge, and science are explained on the ground of their intimate connection with action. On the other hand, the standing unresolved conflicts of philosophic systems, the chief fallacies that are found in them, and the failure to make definite progress in the solution of specific philosophic problems, are attributed to carrying over into metaphysics the results and methods of the knowledge that has been formed with the exigencies of action in view. Legitimate and necessary for useful action, they are mere prejudices as respects metaphysical knowledge. Prejudices, indeed, is too mild a name. Imported into philosophy, they are completely misleading; they distort hopelessly the reality they are supposed to know. Philosophy must, accordingly, turn its back, resolutely and finally, upon all methods and conceptions which are infected by implication in action, in order to strike out upon a different path. It must have recourse to intuition which installs us within the very movement of reality itself, unrefracted by the considerations that adapt it to bodily needs, that is to useful action. As a result, Bergson has the unique distinction of being attacked as a pragmatist on one side, and as a mystic on the other.

There are at least a few readers in sympathy with the first of these strains who find themselves perplexed by the second. They are perplexed, indeed, just in the degree in which the first strain has left them convinced. Surely, they say to themselves, if the irresolvable conflicts and the obscurities of philosophy have arisen because of failure to note the connection of every-day and of scientific knowledge with the purposes of action, public and private, the clarification of philosophic issues will arise by correcting this failure, that is to say, by the thorough development of the implications of the genuine import of knowledge. What an emancipation, they say to themselves, is to come to philosophy when it actively adopts this discovery and applies it to its own undertakings!

Perhaps it is because of unredeemed pragmatic prejudice that I find myself among those who have this feeling of a baffled expectation and a frustrate logic. Nevertheless, the feeling indicates a genuine intellectual possibility, a legitimate intellectual adventure. The hypothesis that the same discovery which has illuminated perception and science will also illuminate philosophic topics is an hypothesis not logically excluded; it has not even been discussed. It may, then, be worth trying. Any notion that this road has been closed in advance arises from confusion in reasoning. Bergson supposes that the unresolved antitheses of philosophic systems and the barriers that arrest its progress can be shown to be due to importing into philosophy, from common life and from science, methods and results that are relevant to action alone. If it had been shown that the evils of philosophy have resulted from *knowingly* carrying over into it considerations whose practical character had all along been *knowingly* acknowledged, then the conclusion would follow, that philosophy must throw overboard these considerations and find a radically different method of procedure. But this is a supposition contrary both to fact and to Bergson's premises. Why not, then, try the other hypothesis: that philosophic evils result from a survival in philosophy of an error which has now been detected in respect to every-day knowledge and science? Why not try avowedly and constructively to carry into philosophy itself the consequences of the recognition that the problems of perception and science are straightened out

[203]

when looked at from the standpoint of action, while they remain obscure and obscuring when we regard them from the standpoint of knowledge defined in antithesis to action?

We are thus carried a step beyond the mere suggestion of a possibly valid adventure in philosophy. If a conception of the nature and office of knowledge that has been discarded for common sense and for science is retained in philosophy, we are forced into a dualism that involves serious consequences. Common sense knowledge and science are set in invidious contrast not merely with philosophy—a contrast that they might easily endure more successfully than philosophy—but with "reality." As long as the notion survives that true knowledge has nothing to do with action, being a purely theoretical vision of the real as it is for itself, insistence upon the operation within perceptual and conceptual "knowledge" of practical factors *ipso facto* deprives such "knowledge" of any genuine knowledge status. It gives us not reality as it is, but reality as it is distorted and refracted from the standpoint of bodily needs. To condemn all other "knowledge" (as *knowledge*) to the realm of fiction and illusion seems a high price to pay for the rescue of philosophy from the ills that it may be suffering from.

Thus we are compelled to go still further. A philosophy which holds that the facts of perception and science are to be explained from the standpoint of their connection with organically useful action, while also holding that philosophy rests upon a radically different basis, is perforce a philosophy of reality that is already afflicted with a dualism so deep as seemingly to be ineradicable. It imports a split into the reality with which philosophy is supposed to deal exclusively and at first hand. We account for perception and science by reference to action, use, and need. Very well; but what about action, use, and need? Are they useful fictions? If not, they must be functions of "reality." Then knowledge that is relevant to action, useful in the play of need, must penetrate into "reality" instead of giving it a twist. With respect to *such* characters of the real, a purely theoretical vision of intuition would be refracting. Suppose that conceptions mark fabrications made in the interest of the organic body. Are the organic needs also fabrications and is their satisfaction fabrication? Either that, or else the conceptual intelligence which effects the development and satisfaction of the needs plays a part in the evolution of reality, and a part that can not be apprehended by a mode of knowing that is antithetical, since merely theoretic, to them. From the standpoint of philosophy, accordingly, the analytic intellect, space, and matter—everything related to useful action—must be irreducible surds, for reality as apprehended in philosophic cognition by definition omits and excludes all such affairs.

Precisely the same order of considerations applies to the theory of knowledge. Were it not for the survival in the court of last resort and of highest jurisdiction of the old idea of the separation of knowledge and action, Bergson's special analyses would point to very different conclusions from those which constitute his official epistemology. The connection with action of the characteristic methods and results of knowledge in daily affairs and in science would give us a theory of the *nature* of reflective intelligence, not a theory of its *limitations*. When theoretic and disinterested knowledge cease to occupy a uniquely privileged position with respect to reality, there also cease to be any motive and ground for denying the existence of theoretic and disinterested knowledge. Such knowledge is a fact exhibited *in* sympathetic and liberal action. Its contrast is not with the limitations of practical knowledge, but with the limitations of the knowledge found in routine and partisan action! Genuine theoretic knowledge penetrates reality more deeply, not because it is opposed to practice, but because a practice that is genuinely free, social, and intelligent touches things at a deeper level than a practice that is capricious, ego-istically centered, sectarian, and bound down to routine. To say the same thing the other way round, if it were not for the assumed monopolistic relation to reality of a knowledge dis-connected from organic life, reference to action would cease to be a distorting, or even a limiting, term with respect to knowledge. The reference would be wholly explanatory and clarifying. Just as complications attaching to the questions of the relation of mind and body, or the self and its stream of mental states, are disentangled, and the elements in question fall into ordered perspective when viewed from the stand-point of intelligently effective action, so with the other questions of philosophy.

It is high time, however, to make a transition from these general considerations to the special problems to which they are relevant. In this paper, I propose to deal with their bear-ing upon the topic of perception. Before directly attacking it, I must, however, introduce some further general considera-tions in order to make clear the bearing of what has been said upon what is to follow. Take the matter purely hypotheti-cally. Imagine a philosophy which is convinced that the pecu-liarities of perception remain opaque, defying genuine analy-sis, as long as perception is regarded as a mode of theoretical cognition, while they become luminous with significance when it is treated as a factor in organic action. Imagine also that this conviction is conjoined with a belief that there is something in the nature of organic action marking it off so definitely from the truly real, that the latter must be known by a radically heterogeneous operation. Imagine that in the further course of the discussion the dualism in reality pre-supposed in this mode of treatment threatens to break out, and to break down the account. What is likely to happen? Are we not likely to find, at first, a sharpening of the antithesis be-tween the special topic under consideration (whether it be perception, space, quantity, matter) and pure knowledge and genuine reality; and then, as the metaphysical consequences of this dualism come to view, a toning down of the antithesis between the two, by means of the introduction into each of reconciling traits that approximate each to the other? And surely this is one of the marked traits of the Bergsonian procedure. Suppose, however, we had commenced, not with the view that is afterwards corrected, but with the corrected view. Would not then the special analysis of the specific topic (perception or whatever) have assumed a very different form from that in which it is actually found? And is it not *a priori* likely that the original account will not be found quite consistent even in its own nominal sense? Is it not likely that there will be already present in it elements that, inconsistent with the notion of the sheer opposition of useful action and reality, point to the correction to be later made?

I have asked the above questions not because I expect the reader to answer them, much less because I expect in advance an affirmative answer, but to put the reader in possession at the outset of the point of view from which the following criticism of Bergson's account of perception is written, and, in outline, of the technic of its method. As has been sufficiently intimated, I shall not question his main thesis: the description of perception as a factor in organic action. Neither shall I be called upon to question the specific terms in and by which he carries on this description: the central nature of indeterminate possibilities and the preoccupation of perception with the physical environment, not with mental states. My point is rather that as far as these traits receive due development we are carried to a conclusion where reference to useful action ceases to mark an invidious contrast with reality, and, accordingly, indicates a standpoint from which the need of any rival mode of knowledge, called philosophical, becomes doubtful.

It is not enough to say that perception is relative to action: one needs to know *how* it is relative, and one needs to know the distinguishing traits of action. And as far as Bergson's account makes perception relative to action, that is, makes knowledge qualified by possibilities (by freedom), and *useful* in affording an efficient development of free action, we are taken where the antithetical dualisms of space and time, matter and spirit, action and intuition have no belonging. Let the reader recall the honorific use of "life" in Bergson and his depreciatory use of "action," and decide whether the following sentence (the most emphatic one that I have found in his writings in the sense just indicated) does not break down the barriers supposed to exist between action and life, and connect perception with an action which is naught but the process of life itself. "Restore, on the contrary, the true character of perception; recognize in pure perception a system of nascent acts which plunges roots deep into the real; and at once perception is seen to be radically distinct from recollection; the reality of things is no more constructed or reconstructed, but touched, penetrated, lived." [1]

Place in contrast with this sentence such statements as the following: "My conscious perception has an entirely practical destination, it simply indicates, in the aggregate of things, that which interests my possible action upon them"; [2] and this: "When we pass from pure perception to memory, we definitely abandon matter for spirit." [3] Must not such a view of perception flow from quite another analysis, or at least from another emphasis, from that which yields the conception that in perception we *live* reality itself? I have finally reached a point where I can state what seems to me to be a specific

---

[1] *Matter and Memory*, English translation, pp. 74–75. The significance of the passage stands out the more if one calls to mind that, from the other standpoint, recollection is the index of the real, of time and spirit, while perception, since connected with action, is tied down to space and matter.

[2] *Ibid.*, p. 306.   [3] *Ibid.*, p. 313.

oscillation between inconsistent views in Bergson's account of perception, while it will also be evident, I hope, that the discussion of this oscillation is not a picayune attempt to convict a great writer of a mere technical inconsistency. It involves the whole question of the validity of the knowledge that is connected with action, and of the need in metaphysics of another kind of knowledge.

I

Perception, according to Bergson, must be approached as a problem of selection and elimination, not as one of enhancement and addition. If there were more in the conscious perception of the object than in its presence, the problem of the passage from the latter to the former would be wrapped in impenetrable mystery. Not so, if its perception means less than presence of the object, since all that is then required is to discover the condition that might lead to the abandoning by the unperceived object of some of its entire being.[1] In the search for this condition, note that since the physical world is always a scene of complete transmitting, by equal and opposite reactions, of energy, it follows that "in one sense we might say that the perception of any unconscious material point whatever, in all its instantaneousness, is infinitely greater and more complete than ours, since this point gathers and transmits the influences of all the points of the material universe."[2] Anything, accordingly, that would eliminate some of the transmitting power of some part of the total physical system would throw the phases of this blocked part into contrast with the rest of the system, and thereby into a kind of relief equivalent to its perception. Introduce a living body, with its special interests, and this is just what happens. The activity of the organism allows all influences, all movements, that have no

[1] *Ibid.*, p. 27.   [2] *Ibid.*, p. 30.

interest for it, to pass immediately through it. With respect to them it is a neutral transmitter like any other part of the total system. But those movements that are of concern to it are singled out, disengaged.[1] They are held up, as it were, as a highwayman holds up his intended victim preparatory to exercising upon him the function of robbery that defines a highwayman. This arrest and detachment throws the traits of the things with which it is concerned into relief: they are then perceived. From this interpretation of perception are derived its main traits. It is concerned directly with physical things, no mental states intervening; the perceived objects are arranged about our body as their center; they vary with changes of the body; the extent of the field perceived increases with growth in the variety and scope of our organic interests. Above all, perception is primarily a fact of action, not of cognition.

In making this summary I have tried to leave out of account considerations which would tell one way or another as respects the double analysis of perception to which I referred above, making my account as neutral as may be. The account must now be complicated by referring to the considerations slurred over. In the first place, the fact must be emphasized that in Bergson's professed view (that which leads in the end to invidious contrast with true knowledge of reality) the change from the total world to the perceived part is merely quantitative; it is *merely* a diminution, a subtraction. The relation is just and only that of part and whole. "There is nothing positive here, nothing added to the image [object], nothing new. The objects merely abandon something of their real action."[2] Perception "creates nothing; its office, on the contrary, is to eliminate from the totality of images [objects] all those on which I can have no hold, and then, from each of those which I can retain, all that does not concern the needs

[1] *Matter and Memory*, pp. 28–29.
[2] *Ibid.*, p. 30. The omitted half of the last sentence will be noted later.

of the image [object] which I call my body." [1] This notion of sheer diminution and elimination of most of the parts and aspects of a whole supplies the official definition of pure perception: "a vision of matter both immediate and instantaneous; [2] an uninterrupted series of instantaneous visions, which would be a part of things rather than of ourselves." [3]

The position that seems inconsistent with this one might be arrived at deductively from the stress laid, in the definition of perception, upon indeterminateness of action: upon the operative presence of genuine possibilities. Consider such a statement as the following: "Is not the growing richness of this perception likely to symbolize the wider range of indetermination left to the choice of the living being in its conduct with things? Let us start, then, from this indetermination as from the true principle, and try whether we can not deduce from it the possibility and even the necessity, of conscious perception. . . . The more immediate the reaction is compelled to be, the more must perception resemble a mere contact; and the complete process of perception and of reaction can then hardly be distinguished from a mechanical impulsion followed by a necessary movement. But in the measure that the reaction becomes more uncertain, and allows more room for suspense, does the distance increase at which the animal is sensible of the action of that which interests it. . . . The degree of independence of which a living being is master, or, as we shall say, the zone of indetermination which surrounds its activity, allows, then, of an *a priori* estimate of the number and distance of the things with which it is in relation. . . . So that we can formulate this law: *perception is master of space in the exact measure in which action is master of*

---

[1] *Ibid.*, p. 304.   [2] *Ibid.*, p. 26.

[3] *Ibid.*, p. 69. The reader familiar with the doctrine of space and time in Bergson does not need to be reminded that perception as an *instantaneous* section (non-temporal, non-durational) in an instantaneously complete field inevitably aligns perception with matter to the exclusion of time, mind, and reality as it would be envisaged from within.

time." [1] The passage is quoted because of its statement of the central position of indeterminate action. The explicit reference (in the last sentence) to time *suggests* what I regard as the true doctrine, but a careful reading shows that this reference can not be taken as an assertion of that conclusion. On the contrary, Bergson evidently means that the indeterminateness only acts as a sort of negative condition, a condition *sine qua non,* to throw into relief those objects which have a possible concern for the indeterminate action. As he says elsewhere, it operates "to filter through us that action of external things which is real, in order to arrest and retain that which is virtual." [2] Again the effect is spoken of as one of disassociation, of disengaging. [3] The objects "detach from themselves that which we have arrested on the way, that which we are capable of influencing." [4] He speaks of indetermination acting as a sort of mirror which brings about an apparent reflection of surrounding objects upon themselves. [5] Again, the body "indicates the parts and aspects of matter on which we can lay hold: our perception which exactly measures our virtual action on things thus limits itself to the objects which actually influence our organs and prepare our movements." [6]

All such statements but emphasize the doctrine of mere subtraction, of diminution, as the essence of the act of perception. And if I now quote some passages which seem to have a contrary sense, it is not because I attach any great importance to what may be casual verbal inconsistencies, but because the passages bring to the front a contrasting notion of the facts themselves. The part of the sentence that was omitted in our earlier quotation after saying that objects merely abandon

[1] *Matter and Memory*, pp. 21, 22, 23. It is perhaps superfluous to multiply references, but see also pages 28, 29, 35, 37, 67, 68.
[2] *Ibid.,* p. 309.   [3] *Ibid.,* p. 41.
[4] *Ibid.,* p. 29   [5] *Ibid.,* pp. 29 and 46.
[6] *Ibid.,* p. 232. Compare "It eliminates from the totality of objects all those on which I can have no hold." *Ibid.,* p. 304.

something of their real action "in order to manifest their virtual action" reads: "that is, in the main *the eventual action of the living being upon them.*" (Italics mine.) To the same effect he says (p. 59) around my body "is grouped the representation, i. e., its [the body's] *eventual* influence upon the others [objects]." So (p. 68) perception is said to "express and measure the power of action in the living being, the indetermination of the movement or of the action *which will follow upon the receipt of the stimulus.*" (Italics mine.) Again, "perception consists in detaching, from the totality of objects, the possible action of my body from them." Most significant of all, perhaps, is the following: "Perception, understood, as we understand it, measures *our possible action upon things, and thereby, inversely, the possible action of things upon us.*" [1]

As I have just said, I shall try not to attach undue importance to the mere wording of these passages. It is easy to substitute for the phrase, "bodies upon which we may act," the other phrase, "our possible action upon bodies," and yet *mean* the same thing, verbally opposed as are the two phrases, especially as the idea that perception "measures" our possible action upon things seems to afford a connecting link. But the verbal opposition may be used to suggest that there follows from Bergson's theory of the dependence of perception upon indeterminateness quite another view of the perceived subject-matter than that of quantitative elimination. If we allow our mind to play freely with the conception that perceived objects present our *eventual* action upon the world, or designate our possible actions upon the environment, we are brought to a notion of complication, of qualitative alteration. For the only way in which objects could conceivably designate our future actions would be by holding up to view the objective effects of those actions; that is to say, presenting the prior environ-

[1] *Ibid.,* p. 57. Italics mine.

ment as it will be when modified by our reactions upon it. Perception would then be anticipatory, prognostic; it would exhibit to us in advance the consequences of our possible actions. It would thereby facilitate a choice as respects them, since the act of appreciating in advance the consequences that are to accrue from incipient activities would surely affect our final action.

So far as the *subject-matter* of perception is concerned, we are led to substitute for a material cut out from an instantaneous field, a material that designates the effects of our possible actions. *What* we perceive, in other words, is not just the material upon which we *may* act, but material which reflects back to us the consequences of our acting upon it this way or that. So far as the *act* of perception is concerned, we are led to substitute an act of choosing for an act of accomplished choice. Perception is not an instantaneous act of carving out a field through suppressing its real influences and permitting its virtual ones to show, but is a process of determining the indeterminate.

So far we have, however, simply two contrasting positions placed side by side. What are the grounds for preferring one view to the other? I shall first take up the formal or dialectic analysis of the elements of the situation as Bergson describes them, and then consider his account of perception as choice, closing with his account of the place of the brain in the act of perception.

II

I think it can be shown that the idea of perception as bare instantaneous outstanding of part of an instantaneous larger world is supported only by a rapid alternation between the two conceptions of real and of possible action; and that the moment we hold these two conceptions together in a way that will meet the requirements of the situation we are bound to pass over to the other idea of perception, the one involving a qualitative change of antecedents in the direction of their possible consequences.

The difficulty in Bergson's professed account may perhaps be suggested by the following passage: "If living beings are just centers of indetermination . . . we can conceive that their *mere presence* is equivalent to the suppression of all those parts of objects in which their functions find no interest." [1] But can we conceive anything of the kind, even if we allow our imagination the most generous leeway? We seem to be caught in a dilemma. Either the living bodies are engaged in *no* action, are *merely* present; or else they are really acting. If the former is the case, then no influence is exercised upon the environment, not even a suppressive or relinquishing one. If the latter, the action must modify the bodies upon which it is exercised. We get either less or more than "suppression." Does it not seem *a priori* probable that the idea of perception as the outcome of a sort of purely negative action is but a half-way station between the notion of no perception at all and of perception as an environment modified through a characteristic response of the living body? For we *can* conceive that some act of the organism in accord with its peculiar interests, some gesture, or active attitude, might *accentuate* the parts of the world upon which the organism is interested to act, and that this stress might be equivalent to their perception.

Perhaps, however, our hard and fast dilemma is due to our ignoring just the points upon which Bergson insists: indeterminateness and possibilities. But the dilemma appears to repeat itself. Are the possible actions of the organism *merely* possible? Even if we admit (what seems to me inadmissible) that *mere* potentiality is an intelligible conception, we are still far from seeing how it could exercise even a suppressive influ-

[1] *Matter and Memory*, p. 28. Italics mine.

ence. But if possible activities mean (as it seems to me they must mean to have a meaning) a peculiar quality of actual doing, then we get real influence indeed, but something more and other than sheer elimination and suppression. If we look at it from the side of indetermination, the logic is not changed. Either indetermination and uncertainty mean a qualitatively new type of action, or they mean the total absence of action.

Perhaps I can now make clearer what I meant by Bergson's alternation between real and possible action. The act of carving out a portion of the entire field must be a real act. It is complete at one stroke, all at once. This by itself gives a sheer quantitative limitation. But this act of eliminative selection is still to be accounted for. So we have recourse to the presence of possible actions. What is let go is that upon which the organism can not possibly act; what is held to is that upon which it can act. Bergson thus strings the two conceptions one after the other in this way: *Logically,* possibility antecedes (that is, implies and requires) an act of selection; *really,* the act of selection precedes the actualization of possible actions, furnishing the field upon which they are to operate. Bergson seems to vibrate between the real action of possibilities, and the possible action of real (but future) actualities. The former designates an act that is, however, more than instantaneous, one that is a process; and that does more than cut out, one that qualifies the material upon which it operates, so as to prepare the way for a subsequent action. The latter expresses something that will be instantaneous when it comes and that may be conceived (perhaps) as having only an effect of diminution, but that, unfortunately, is not present to have any effect at all, save as, to meet the requirements of the situation, it suddenly changes to a present real action of possibilities, that is, to a distinctive *quality* of selective action. The same dialectic operates (as we shall shortly see) upon the side of the environment. On the one hand, the perceived subject-matter indicates *possible* action upon the organism, something which has been acquired in the act of perception. But on the other hand, as the perceived subject-matter is an instantaneous section out of a homogeneous totality, any possibilities which the subject-matter can present must have been already in its possession. But as this contradicts the notion of complete presence, we are again forced to the conception of possibility as something conferred by the organism.

Bergson seems to recognize that the bare inoperative presence of potentialities (the conception which seems to provide a middle term between possible future real actions and present real action of possibilities) will not, after all, suffice to account even for a diminution of the physical environment. We somehow *arrest* the influences proceeding from those bodies that we are capable of acting upon. This act of arrest receives some positive characterization in the following passage. After stating that physical bodies act and react mutually by all their elements, he goes on to say: "Suppose, on the contrary, that they encounter somewhere a certain spontaneity of reaction: their action is so far diminished, and this diminution of their action is just the representation which we have of them." [1] Here we have the most explicit statement that I have been able to find of the *modus operandi* of the act of suppression. It is treated as a real act, and in so far meets the necessities of the case, while at the same time spontaneity is suggestive of possibilities. We will admit, without caviling, that spontaneity of action describes a peculiar type of action, one which, instead of following the physical principle of equal and opposite reaction, merely diminishes the real efficacy of the influences that it encounters. But even so, we have only a *real* action, of a peculiar unusual sort, in this reduction of the efficacy of the objects. If, however, spontaneity means that the organic act is already charged with potentiality, its manifesta-

[1] *Matter and Memory*, p. 29.

tion might *convert* the energy of the environment into a form that would involve the inhibition, for the time being, of its usual physical mode of efficacy. But suppression *through conversion into a different form* is a radically different thing from suppression by mere diminution. This latter might, by lowering the resistance that it would otherwise encounter, give a better chance for some subsequent organic activity to express itself, but this would be the limit of its significance. Such a state of affairs would involve no indetermination, and there is no sense in calling the subsequent action a possible action. It is simply a postponed action, bound to occur if the spontaneous action intervenes. It is simply the real future action of which we have spoken. In short, it does not fulfill the conditions for the emergence of the unperceived into the perceived.

Upon occasion, however, Bergson states the situation differently. As stated in a passage already quoted, we allow "to filter through us that action of external things which is real, in order to arrest and retain that which is virtual: this virtual action of things upon our body and of our body is our perception itself.[1] I pass over the question of how this view is to be reconciled with the statements to the effect that perception "limits itself to the objects which *actually influence our organs* and prepare our movements." The point to notice is that virtual or potential action is transferred from our body and made a property of the objects, the peculiarity of our action now being that it isolates this property of the objects. This point of view is even more explicit in such a statement as the following: "Representation is there (that is, in the universe), but always virtual—being neutralized at the very moment when it might become actual, by the obligation to continue itself and to lose itself in something else. To obtain the conversion from the virtual to the actual it would be necessary, not to throw more light upon the object, but on the contrary

[1] *Matter and Memory*, p. 309.

to obscure some of its aspects, to diminish it by the greater part of itself, so that the remainder, instead of being encased in its surroundings as a *thing,* should detach itself from them as a *picture.*" [1] The extraordinary nature of this passage stands out if we recall that the express definition of the physical is complete actuality, total lack of virtuality. Even more significant, however, than this contradiction is, for our present problem, the complete shift of the point of view. Potentiality to begin with was wholly on the side of the living being, just as actuality was the essence of the world. But since any act of elimination, of diminution, affected by the living being would obviously be a real act of a certain kind, the exigencies of the logic require that potentiality be attributed to the object, the real action of the organic being now treated merely as an occasion for the display of this potentiality. But whenever the exigencies of the argument require reference to the indeterminateness of the action of *living* beings, to mark them off from non-living things, potentiality retires from the object to take up again its exclusive residence in the living being. [2]

[1] *Ibid.,* p. 28.

[2] It is worth considering whether this dialetic does not throw light upon Bergson's pan-psychic idealism. It seems as if his final attribution of pan-psychic quality to matter were simply a generalization, once for all, of the circular logic we have just noticed. If (*a*) we define perception as a conscious representation on the basis of potentiality, and then (*b*) fall back on the inherent potentiality of the universe to account for the diminution of the field characteristic of the conscious representation, it follows as matter of course that the universe itself is already consciousness of some sort (*cf.* p. 313). "No doubt also the material universe itself, defined as the totality of images, is a kind of consciousness, a consciousness in which everything compensates and neutralizes everything else, a consciousness of which all the potential parts, balancing each other by a reaction which is always equal to the action, reciprocally hinder each other from standing out." Here we have, I think, the key to his total treatment. Let anything throw the whole out of balance, and a piece of this total consciousness stands out. The cut-out portion is a *conscious* representation just because the whole from which it is cut is conscious. But why is the whole called consciousness? Simply because the whole is conscious and perception is a part cut out from a homogeneous whole. But there must be something to effect the cutting out; the whole does not cut itself up. Hence the need of referring to the differential presence of the organism as a center of indeterminate possibilities. But to stay by this standpoint would connect all the eulogistic traits that are employed in designating philosophic intuition with crises of organic activity. Hence potentiality and freedom are

Quite likely the reader has been brought to a feeling that we are not any longer considering perception at all, but are engaged simply in performing dialectic variations on the themes of actuality and possibility, indeterminateness and determinateness. Let us then attempt to translate the conceptions over into their factual equivalents. I think that the essential of Bergson's view may be correctly stated about as follows: The indeterminateness of the action of a living being serves to delay its motor responses. This delay gives room for deliberation and choice. It supplies the opportunity for the conscious selection of a determinate choice—for freedom of action. But the delay of motor response also signifies something from the standpoint of the world: namely, a division within it. Certain of its movements are still continued through and beyond the organism; with respect to them, there is no delaying response. Consequently those other movements of the world to which response is postponed are sundered; they are thrown into relief, cut out. Moreover, it will be noted that the material that thus stands out presents just those movements upon which the possible, or postponed, responses of the organism may take effect. Material thus cut out and having such reference to subsequent organic actions constitutes pure perception.

The ingenuity of this account is indubitable. For my own part, I think it gives the elements of a true account. But it is possible to arrange these elements quite differently and thereby reach quite a different result. The revised account reads somewhat like this. External movements are involved in the activities of an organism. If and in so far as these activities are indeterminate, there is neither a total, or adequate stimulus in the movements, nor an adequate total response by the organism. Adequate stimulation and adequate response are both delayed (the delay is an effect, not a cause or condition,

transferred back to the whole, which accordingly makes matter into consciousness once more.

as it seems to be in Bergson's account). The partial responses, however, are neither merely dispersed miscellaneously upon the environment, nor are they merely possible. They are directed upon the partial stimuli so as to *convert* them into a single co-ordinated stimulus. Then a total response of the organism follows. This functional transformation of the environment under conditions of uncertain action into conditions for determining an appropriate organic response constitutes perception.

What is the difference between the two views? According to the first, perception *is* a stimulus, ready-made and complete. According to the second, it operates to *constitute* a stimulus. According to the first, the object or given stimulus merely sets a problem, a question, and the process of finding its appropriate answer or response resides wholly with the organism. According to the second, the stimulus or perceived object is a part of the process of determining the response; nay, in its growing completeness, it is the determining of the response. As soon as an integral and clear-cut object stands out, then the response is decided, and the only intelligent way of choosing the response is by forming its stimulus. Meantime organic responses have not been postponed; a variety of them are going on, by means of which the environing conditions are given the status of a stimulus. The change effected in the environment by the final total organic act is just a consummation of the partial changes effected all through the process of perception by the partial reactions that finally determine a clear-cut object of perception. This means that the perceived subject-matter at every point indicates a response that *has* taken effect with reference to its character in determining *further* response. It exhibits what the organism *has* done, but exhibits it with the qualities that attach to it as part of the process of determining what the organism is *to do*. If at any point we let go of the thread of the process of the

organism's determining its own eventual total response
through determining the stimulus to that response by a series
of partial responses, we are lost.

III

We have now to consider the same situation, but this time
from the standpoint of the act of choice concerned in it. Our
previous discussion prepares us for the points at issue. We may
anticipate an alternation between two conceptions, introducing into a choice alleged to be complete in an instantaneous
act, traits which belong to a choice among future possible acts.
The circular reasoning will disappear, we may also anticipate, as soon as substituted for the alternation between a
present choice and a future choice, each of which owes its
character to the other, a temporal act of choice, that is, a
choosing.

Bergson's nominal theory is that the selective elimination
is itself a choice. "Our consciousness only attains to certain
parts and certain aspects of those parts. Consciousness—in
regard to external perception—consists in just this choice." [1]
Such a choice seems, however, exactly like a "choice" exhibited in the selective or differential reaction of a metal to
an acid. The metal also "picks out" the form of energy upon
which it can act and which can act upon it.[2] Permit, however,

[1] *Matter and Memory,* p. 31 (*cf.* p. 304): "Perception appears as only a choice."
[2] Considerations of space compel me to omit many matters of interest which are
relevant to the topic. But I can not forbear here a word of reference to Bergson's
earlier mode of statement of the point at issue between idealism and realism. The
reader will recall that he sets out from a statement of the two ways in which objects
—called, for convenience, "images"—may vary. In one system each varies according
to all the influences brought to bear upon it; in the other, all vary according to the
action of *one privileged* object, the organic body. The former system describes the
physical world; the latter, the perceived world. But *some* of his descriptions of the
peculiarities of the latter surely refer as well to the traits of the former. Thus "I note
that the size, shape, even the color of external objects is modified according as my body
approaches or recedes from them; that the strength of an odor, the intensity of a sound,
increases or decreases with distance" (page 6). Surely, however, the intensity of
an influence exercised by any physical body upon another physical body varies with

the phrase to pass as a metaphor; or permit, if you will, the metaphor to pass as a fact. There is then no indetermination of any kind; nothing undecided and no need of any subsequent choosing. The choice being complete, the reaction of the organism follows at once, or as soon as its time comes. But now there enters upon the scene a present effect attributed to future possible actions. There are many possible acts lying in wait. Otherwise the choice, the relinquishing and the standing out, would not have occurred. Somehow, therefore, the perceived object sketches and measures the many possible acts among which a choice has to be made before a determinate response can occur. The circle is before us. The present complete choice makes possible a presentation of future possibilities; the future possible acts operate to define the peculiar nature of the present act.

The two sides are brought together in the consideration that the perceived object reflects or mirrors our state of suspense, of hesitation, the conditions with respect to which we have to choose. It is unnecessary to go over the ground already traversed; if I have not succeeded in laying bare the circular reason nothing I can add now will be of any avail. But we may note two consequences applicable to the situation as it takes form with respect to choice. Since the unperceived world is, by definition, one that is completely actual in itself—since, in other words, the world as physical already has its mind all made up—this view implies the introduction into the perceived world of a quality contradictory to the conception of a

---

distance. Shape and size, regarded as the angular portion of the total field subtended, vary with distance in the same physical way; so does color with the change in intensity of light effected by distance. Thus choice, as here defined, is only a name for the *specific* action one body exercises upon others. But in his final formula is stated the *peculiar* kind of a change in the physical system effected by the organic body in perception: things not merely change with its changes, but change so as to reflect its *"eventual"* action (p. 13). Here, indeed, is a genuine criterion of distinction; and our further discussion of choice is simply a development of the consequences of introducing reference to *eventual* action into its nature.

mere quantitative selection. Choice, even though instantaneously complete choice, has done something positive after all. But of greater moment is the fact that a subject-matter of perception that merely mirrors our own hesitation is of no use in resolving that hesitation. If we insist upon looking at it as marking a choice, the choice is simply to be undecided as to making a choice. The perceived object just gives back to us, indifferently, sullenly, uninstructively, our own need of a choice. Such a perception could never participate in the "office of *ensuring our effective action* on the object present." [1] Our later choice among possible actions will then be as blind and random as if perception had never intervened. What is the likelihood of an act so chosen being effective, appropriate? Better had it been to have remained in the frying-pan of complete mechanism than to have jumped into the fire of purely random action. [2]

---

[1] *Matter and Memory*, p. 84. Italics mine. In its context the quotation refers to the rôle of the cerebral mechanism in perception, but, by hypothesis, it must be capable of transfer, without injustice to the logic, to the perception as the chosen object.

[2] It may be objected that we have here ignored the distinction between pure and concrete perception and the need of memory to effect the change of the former into the latter, and thereby have treated the essence of the account of pure perception as if it were a difficulty in the account. Pure perception, we may be told, does present us with exactly the indeterminateness which reflects our own hesitation. It gives the field with respect to which choice has to be made. It sets a question to which the motor response has to find a reply (see, for example, p. 41). What guides the motor response in finding the reply is not perception but memory. "Though the function of living bodies is to receive stimulations in order to elaborate them into unforseen reactions, still the choice of the reaction can not be the work of chance. This choice is likely to be inspired by *past experience*, and the reaction does not take place without an appeal to the *memories* which analogous situations may have left behind them. The indetermination of acts to be accomplished requires, then, if it is not to be confounded with pure caprice, the *preservation* of the images perceived" (page 69, italics mine; see also pages 103 and 114). I have no doubt that this quotation represents Bergson's view; perception puts the question, and only puts the question; memory helps the motor response to find the effective and appropriate answer. Even though my whole argument seems left hanging in the air with its underpinning knocked out, I must postpone consideration of this point of view till an explicit discussion of memory is undertaken. But certain indications may be suggested at this point. The assumption leaves totally unexplained the sudden transformation of a physical world totally devoid of virtuality (see pages 80 and 81 for the statement that if the physical world had virtuality it might be the cause of consciousness) into a world that as perceived is nothing but potentialities. Matter as

Note how the difficulties disappear if we regard the act of perceiving as a temporal act, as *choosing*. Follow out literally the idea that our reactions *are uncertain,* not merely "allowing room for suspense," but *involving* suspense.[1]

Since any reactions that we actually make must, no matter how charged they are with uncertainty, modify the environment upon which they exercised,[2] we shall have as the counterpart of the act a field undergoing determination. So far as reactions are dominantly uncertain we shall expect, indeed, to find the subject-matter vague and confused—and we do so find it. But an indefinite reaction may have a certain focus that will further define its subject-matter so that it will afford the stimulus to a more effective subsequent response, and so on till the perceived matter gets outline and clearness. If, however, the reactions continue wholly and only indeterminate, the confusion of the subject-matter will remain, and, correspondingly, the indeterminateness of response will persist. The only perception that can be a useful part of the act of choosing a useful response will be one that exhibits the effects of responses already performed in such a way as to provide continuously improving stimuli for subsequent responses. The only way in which a living being with indeterminate possibilities of action can be intelligently helped to their determina-

---

perceived is now pure freedom; mind as memory is pure determination. But more significant to the present problem is the recognition that action based on pure perception is a matter of "chance," of "pure caprice." If such be the case, how can the object of pure perception provide any clew to the recall of the proper memory? Why is not that a work of chance, of caprice? But most significant of all is the pre-established harmony set up between perception and memory, space and time, matter and mind, by this view that perception sets the problem to which an alleged radically different power unique supplies the answer. For like all pre-established harmonies it testifies to the probability of a prior artificial separation.

[1] *Ibid.,* page 22.

[2] It will be interesting to watch the logic of those neo-realists who connect the act of perception with the organism instead of with "consciousness" when they develop their views in detail. Professor Montague's theory of potential energy as the physical side of consciousness seems to avoid the snares, but if I mistake not, potential energy which is all located at one spot instead of marking a stress in a larger field alleges an unprecedented physical fact.

tion by perceived objects is by having perceived objects serve as anticipations of the consequences of the realization of this or that possibility. And only through a presentation in anticipation of the objective consequences of a possible action could an organism be guided to a choice of actions that would be anything except either mechanical or purely arbitrary. Perception can prepare our further movements effectively and appropriately in the degree in which it continuously provides the stimuli for them. In words of Bergson's own which can not be bettered: "That which constitutes our pure perception is our dawning action, in so far as it is prefigured in those images [namely, objects]. The *actuality* of our perception thus lies in its *activity*, in the movements which prolong it."[1] Take this passage seriously and literally, and you have the precise view of perception here contended for. It is not a choice accomplished all at once, but is a process of choosing. The possible responses involved are not merely postponed, but are operative in the quality of present sensori-motor responses. The perceived subject-matter is not simply a manifestation of conditions antecedent to the organic responses, but is their transformation in the direction of further action.

IV

. In the references which we have made in this discussion to sensori-motor responses we have already implicitly trenched upon our last topic: the body, as implicated in perception. Just what part does the brain have, in the act of perception? The reader need not be reminded how central is this aspect of the matter for Bergson. From one standpoint, his entire discussion of perception is intended as a demonstration that the brain is not the cause of conscious representations, but is, and is solely, the organ of a certain kind of action. The undoubted correspondence between the *facts* of the subject-matter of per-

[1] *Matter and Memory*, p. 84. Italics in the original.

ception (the conscious representations) and brain events is to be explained, not by invoking materialism or psycho-physical parallelism (both of which depend upon regarding perception as a case of knowledge instead of action), but by showing that both the conscious representations and the brain states are functions of nascent or potential action. The "representations" designate action on the side of its material, the environing conditions; the brain movements designate it on the side of the organs intimately involved in it.[1] The correspondence is that of material and tool of action, like that of soil and plow with reference to the act of sowing seed.

The reader is invited to traverse the field for a third and last time. We have, once more, to see how Bergson provides all the factors of an adequate statement; how he places them in temporal alternation to each other and thereby renders them incapable of performing the office attributed to them; and how the account stands when it is corrected by making the factors of actuality and indeterminateness contemporaneous instead of successive.

The nervous system, being a physical structure, is a medium of the transmission of movements, and is only that. Consequently any correspondence or correlation that can be made out between the brain processes and the object of conscious perception (the so-called conscious content or representation) must be in terms of correspondence of modes of movement. The nervous process concerned in the act of perception must be describable, in other words, in a way analogous to the peculiar type of action that is exhibited in the perceived object. The marks that distinguish cortical action from the so-called reflex action of the lower structures furnish the clew. In the latter, the incoming movement is shunted at once into a return movement. In the former the paths of communication are immensely multiplied and the nature of transmission corre-

[1] *Ibid.*, pp. 35, 309.

spondingly complicated. The same incoming stimulus has many outgoing paths open to it. Thus the brain has a double office. On the one hand, it provides a mechanism by which peripheral disturbance, upon reaching the spinal cord instead of being deflected into its immediate reflex track, may be put in flexible connection with other motor mechanisms of the cord. The cortical cells termed sensory "allow the stimulation received to reach *at will* this or that motor mechanism of the spinal cord, and *so to choose* its effect." "On the other hand, as a great multitude of motor tracks can open simultaneously in this substance to one and the same excitation from the periphery, this disturbance may subdivide to any extent, and consequently dissipate itself in innumerable motor reactions which are merely nascent. Hence the office of the brain is sometimes to conduct the movement received to a *chosen* organ of reaction, and sometimes to open to this movement the totality of the motor tracks, so that it may manifest there all the potential reactions with which it is charged, and may divide and so disperse. . . . The nervous elements . . . do but indicate a number of possible actions at once, or organize one of them." [1]

With respect to the matter under discussion, the significant element is the statement that *sometimes* the brain has one office —allowing a *chosen* reaction to proceed; and *sometimes* another office—to permit its dispersal into a number of channels. The same duality is repeated in the statement that the brain indicates a number of possible reactions *or* organizes one of them. The alternation already considered here presents itself overtly and externally. And the dilemma is presented in an equally definite way. So far as there is choice, organization of a fixed path, there is just a single actual response. So far as there is dispersal in many paths, there are many actual responses. In neither case does possibility, or choice among

[1] *Matter and Memory*, p. 20.

possibilities, show its face. At the same time, there is indicated the true state of affairs: the brain expresses the operation of organizing one mode of total response *out of* a number of conflicting and partial responses.

We can of course imagine that the dispersal of energy among many paths is so extensive as to be equivalent to a practical inhibition, for the time being, of any definite action upon the environment. For the time being, the expenditure of energy (barring what leaks through) is intra-organic, or even, anticipating the dispersion into sensori-motor tracks to be mentioned shortly, intracerebral. We might identify this temporary inhibition of overt response with the gap in the instantaneously completed transmission which throws part of the material world into relief. But this identification proves too much. If the dispersal is into *motor* tracks, these discharges are just so *many* overt and disconnected acts in an incipient or nascent condition.[1] They are not the incipiency of one *appropriate* act. No provision is made, none is suggested, for recalling them so that in place of the multitude of dispersive tendencies there may be one concentrated act. With reference to the performance of this one act—that alone could meet any need of life—these dispersive activities are just so much waste energy. They sketch, not what we are going to do, but what we *are* doing futilely.

The single path opened may, however, be said to represent a choice of the effect to be attained if it is regarded as a process of co-ordinating, for greater efficiency, a number of competing partial tendencies. Similarly, these tendencies may be said to represent possible incipient acts (possible paths of choice) if they are brought into contemporary, not alternating, connection with seeking and finding the single most effective line of discharge. Completely real and really complete just as they are when their dispersive character is isolated,

[1] Compare what was said earlier about the reality of future acts, p. 217, above.

they are incipient acts with reference to a unity of organic attitude which they take part in establishing.

The method of realization of the contemporary relation of discovering a unified response to a multitude of dispersive tendencies is incidentally mentioned in Bergson's allusion to the intervention of the "cortical cells termed sensory." All direct motor shunting, whether unified or dispersive, is of the reflex type. Only because of the complication of a situation by the continuation of an incoming stimulus to *sensori*-motor areas in intricate interconnection with one another, can there be that suspension and choosing which constitute the act of perception. This act is as genuinely motor as eating, walking, driving a nail, or firing combustibles, and involves a like change in the environment upon which it takes effect.[1] But its motor peculiarity is that it takes effect not in such acts as eating, walking, driving, firing, but in such acts as tasting, seeing, touching. The motor response, as long as the act of perception is continued, is directed to *moving* the sense-organs so as to secure and perfect a stimulus for a complete organic readjustment—an attitude of the organism as a whole. This is made possible precisely in so far as the incoming disturbance is "dispersed" not into motor tracks, but into *sensori*-motor areas.[2] In the reciprocal interactions of these sensori-motor areas (their reciprocal stimulation of one another) is found the mechanism of co-ordinating a number of present but ineffectual motor tendencies into an effective but future response.

Let us suppose the disturbance reaches the brain by way of the visual organ. If it is directly discharged back to the motor

[1] Not, of course, that the act is, as such, a change of the *perception* (that would involve us in the *regressus ad infinitum* of which the neo-realists have rightly made so much), but that perception *is* the change in the environment effected by the motor phase.

[2] It is doubly significant that Bergson alludes to the sensory elements involved without in any way amplifying the allusion. The allusion is necessary in order to supply the basis for the uncertain character of the situation in which perception

apparatus of the eyes there results not a perception, but an eye-movement. But simultaneously with this reaction there is also a dispersal into the areas connected with tasting, handling and touching. Each of these structures also initiates an incidental reflex discharge. But this is not all; there is also a cross-discharge between these cortical centers. No one of these partial motor discharges can become complete, and so dictate, as it were, the total direction of organic activity until it has been co-ordinated with the others. The fulfillment of, say, eating, depends upon a prior act of handling, this upon one of reaching, and this upon one of seeing; while the act of seeing necessary to stimulate the others to appropriate execution can not occur save as it, in turn, is duly stimulated by the other tendencies to action. Here is a state of inhibition. The various tendencies wait upon one another and they also get in one another's way. The sensori-motor apparatus provides not only the conditions of this circle, but also the way out of it.

How can this be? It is clear that if, under the condition supposed, the act of seeing were overtly complete it would *then* furnish the needed stimulus of reaching, this to handling and so on. The *sensory* aspect of the apparatus is, in its nature, a supplying of this condition. The excitation of the optical area introduces the *quality* of seeing connected (through the simultaneous excitation of the areas of reaching, tasting, and handling) with the specific *qualities* of the other acts. The *quality* of movement, or action, supplied by the sensory aspect, is, in effect, an anticipation of the result of the act when overtly performed. With respect to determining the needed stimulus, it is *as if* the overt responses in question had been actually executed.[1]

occurs, and for explanation of its inherent future reference. It is not amplified because the whole explanation of sensory features in Bergson's scheme is found in memory. "Memory" is thus again found implicated in the very heart of pure perception.

[1] Here we find the *modus operandi* presupposed in our account of perception as

The reader may regard this account as speculative to any degree which he pleases. Personally I think it outlines the main features of the act of perceiving. But that is neither here nor there. The question is whether or no it furnishes the terms of an account which shall avoid the dilemma in which Bergson's account is held captive, while remaining true to the three requirements of his method of definition: namely, that the brain be treated as an organ for receiving and communicating motion; that indeterminateness be introduced as a specifying feature; that brain processes correspond to subject-matter perceived, as an organ of action corresponds to the material of its action.

Our analysis of Bergson's account is now completed. The reader will decide for himself how far we have been successful in showing that his professed account of perception depends upon alternation between two factors which, if they are involved at all, must operate contemporaneously, not alternately. He will judge for himself of the value of the account of perception obtained when these factors are treated as contemporaneously operative. I may however be pardoned for reminding him that if the argument has been successful in its two purposes, the traits that are alleged to demarcate perception and the objective material with which it deals from a reality marked by genuine presence of temporal considerations have disappeared. Perception is a temporal process: not merely in the sense that an act of perception takes time, but in the profounder sense that temporal considerations are implicated in it whether it be taken as an act or as subject-matter. If such be the case, Bergson's whole theory of time, of memory, of mind and of life as things inherently sundered from organic action needs revision. With *this* revision, follows also that of "intuition" severed from practical knowledge.

---

a process of obtaining, by partial reactions to partial stimuli, the determinate stimulus which will evoke a determinate response. See *ante*, p. 659.

The Unit of Behavior

THAT the greater demand for a unifying principle and controlling working hypothesis in psychology should come at just the time when all generalizations and classifications are most questioned and questionable is natural enough. It is the very accumulation of discrete facts creating the demand for unification which breaks down previous lines of classification. The material is too great in mass and too varied in style to fit into existing pigeon-holes, and the cabinets of science break of their own dead weight. The idea of the reflex arc has upon the whole come nearer to meeting this demand for a general working hypothesis than has any other single concept. It being admitted that the sensori-motor apparatus represents both the unit of nerve structure and the type of nerve function, the image of this relationship passed over into psychology, and became an organizing principle to hold together the multiplicity of fact.

In criticizing this conception it is not intended to make a plea for the principles of explanation and classification which the reflex arc idea has replaced; but, on the contrary, to show that they are not sufficiently displaced, and that in the idea of the sensori-motor circuit, conceptions of the nature of sensation and of action derived from the nominally displaced psychology are still in control.

The older dualism between sensation and idea is repeated in the current dualism of peripheral and central structures and functions; the older dualism of body and soul finds a distinct echo in the current dualism of stimulus and response. Instead of interpreting the character of sensation, idea, and action from their place and function in the sensori-motor circuit, we still incline to interpret the latter from our preconceived and preformulated ideas of rigid distinctions between sensations, thoughts and acts. The sensory stimulus is one thing, the central activity, standing for the idea, is another thing, and the motor discharge, standing for the act proper, is a third. As a result, the reflex arc is not a comprehensive, or organic unity, but a patchwork of disjointed parts, a mechanical conjunction of unallied processes. What is needed is that the principle underlying the idea of the reflex arc as the fundamental unit shall be consistently employed to determine the values of its constructive factors. More specifically, what is wanted is that sensory stimulus, central connections, and motor responses shall not be viewed as separate and complete entities in themselves, but as divisions of labor, functioning factors, within the single concrete whole, now designated the reflex arc.

But what can we properly *term* that which is not sensation-followed-by-idea-followed-by-movement, but which is, as it were, the mental organism of which sensation, idea, and movement are the chief organs? Stated on the physiological side, this more inclusive process may most conveniently be termed co-ordination. This is the essence of the facts held together by and subsumed under the reflex arc concept. Let us take, for our example, the familiar child-candle instance. (James, "Psychology," Vol. I, p. 25.) The ordinary interpretation would say the sensation of light is a stimulus to the grasping as a response, the burn resulting is a stimulus to withdrawing the hand as response and so on. No doubt this is a rough, practical way of representing the seeming course of events. But when we ask for its psychological adequacy, the case is quite different. Upon analysis, we find that we *begin*, not with a sensory stimulus, but with a sensori-motor co-ordination, the optical-ocular, and that in a certain sense it is the movement which is primary, and the sensation which is secondary, the movement of body, head, and eye muscles determining the quality of what is experienced. In other words, the real beginning is with the *act* of seeing; it is looking, and not a sensation of light. The sensory quale gives the value of the act, just as the movement furnishes its mechanism and control, but both sensation and movement lie inside, not outside the act.

Now if this act, the seeing, stimulates another act, the reaching, it is because both of these acts fall within a larger co-ordination; because seeing and grasping have been so often bound together to reinforce each other, to help each other out, that each may be considered practically a subordinate member of a bigger co-ordination. More specifically, the ability of the hand to do its work will depend, either directly or indirectly, upon its control, as well as its stimulation, by the act of vision. If the light did not inhibit as well as excite the reaching, the latter would be purely indeterminate, it would 'be for anything or nothing, not for the particular object seen. The reaching, in turn, must both stimulate and control the seeing. The eye must be kept upon the candle if the arm is to do its work; let it wander, and the arm takes up another task. In other words, we now have an enlarged and transformed co-ordination; the act is seeing no less than before, but it is now seeing-for-reaching purposes. There is still a sensori-motor circuit—one with more content or value, not a substitution of a motor response for a sensory stimulus.[1]

Now take the affair at its next stage, that in which the child gets burned. It is hardly necessary to point out again that this is also a sensori-motor co-ordination and not a mere sensation. It is worth while, however, to note especially the fact that it is simply the completion, or fulfillment, of the previous eye-arm-hand co-ordination and not an entirely new occurrence. Only because the heat-pain quale enters into the

---

[1] See *The Psychological Review* for May, 1896, p. 253, for an excellent statement and illustration, by Messrs. Angell and Moore, of this mutuality of stimulation.

same circuit of experience with the optical-ocular and muscular quales, does the child learn from the experience and get the ability to avoid the experience in the future.

More technically stated, the so-called response is not merely to the stimulus; it is, so to speak, *into* it. The burn is the original seeing, the original optical-ocular experience, enlarged and transformed in its value. It is no longer mere seeing; it is seeing-of-a-light-that-means-pain-when-contact-occurs. The ordinary reflex arc theory proceeds upon the more or less tacit assumption that the outcome of the response is a totally new experience; that it is, say, the substitution of a burn sensation for a light sensation through the intervention of motion. The fact is that the sole meaning of the intervening movement is to maintain, reinforce or transform (as the case may be) the original quale; we do not have the replacing of one sort of experience by another, but the development or, as it seems convenient to term it, the mediation of an experience. The seeing, in a word, remains to control the reaching, and is, in turn, interpreted by the burning.[1]

The discussion up to this point may be summarized by saying that the reflex arc idea, as commonly employed, is defective, first, in that it assumes sensory stimulus and motor response as distinct mental existences, while in reality they are always inside a co-ordination and have their significance purely from the part played in maintaining or reconstructing the co-ordination; and secondly, in assuming that the quale of experience which precedes the "motor" phase and that which succeeds it are two different states, instead of the last being always the first reconstituted, the motor phase coming in only for the sake of such mediation. The result is that the reflex arc idea leaves us with a disjointed psychology, whether viewed from the standpoint of development in the individual or the race, or from that of the analysis of the mature con-

[1] See, for a further statement of mediation, my *Syllabus of Ethics*, p. 15.

sciousness. As to the former, in its failure to see that the "arc" of which it talks is actually a *circuit,* a continual reconstitution, it breaks continuity and leaves us nothing but a series of jerks, the origin of each jerk to be sought outside the process of experience itself in either an external pressure of "environment," or else in an unaccountable spontaneous variation from within the "soul" or the "organism."[1] As to the latter, failing to see the unity of activity, no matter how much it may prate of unity, still leaves us with sensation or peripheral stimulus; idea, or central process (the equivalent of attention); and motor response, or act, as three disconnected existences, having to be somehow adjusted to each other, whether through the intervention of an extra-experimental soul, or by mechanical push and pull.

Before proceeding to a consideration of the general meaning for psychology of the summary, it may be well to give another descriptive analysis, as the value of the statement depends entirely upon the universality of its range of application. For such an instance we may conveniently take Baldwin's analysis of the reactive consciousness. In this there are, he says (*Feeling and Will,* p. 60), "three elements corresponding to the three elements of the nervous arc. First, the receiving consciousness, the stimulus—say a loud, unexpected noise; second, the attention involuntarily drawn, the registering element; and, third, the muscular reaction following upon the sound— say flight from fancied danger." Now, in the first place, such an analysis is incomplete; it ignores the status prior to hearing the sound. Of course, if this status is irrelevant to what happens afterwards, such ignoring is quite legitimate. But is it

---

[1] It is not too much to say that the whole controversy in biology regarding the source of variation, represented by Weismann and Spencer respectively, arises from beginning with stimulus or response instead of with the co-ordination with reference to which stimulus and response are functional divisions of labor. The same may be said, on the psychological side, of the controversy between the Wundtian "apperceptionists" and their opponents. Each has a *disjectum membrum* of the same organic whole, whichever is selected being an arbitrary matter of personal taste.

irrelevant either to the quantity or to the quality of the stimulus?

If one is reading a book, if one is hunting, if one is watching in a dark place on a lonely night, if one is performing a chemical experiment, in each case, the noise has a very different mental value; it is a different experience. In any case, what precedes the "stimulus" is a whole act, a sensori-motor co-ordination. What is more to the point, the "stimulus" emerges out of this co-ordination; it is born from it as its matrix; it represents as it were an escape from it. I might here fall back upon authority, and refer to the widely accepted sensation continuum theory, according to which the sound cannot be absolutely *ex abrupto* from the outside, but is simply a shifting of focus of emphasis, a redistribution of tensions within a former act; and declare that unless the hearing activity had been present to some extent in the prior co-ordination, it would be impossible for it now to come to prominence in consciousness. And such a reference would be only an amplification of what has already been said concerning the way in which the prior activity influences the value of the sound sensation. Or, we might point to cases of hypnotism, monoidealism and absent-mindedness, like that of Archimedes, as evidences that if the previous co-ordination is such as rigidly to lock the door, the auditory disturbance will knock in vain for admission, so that the auditory activity must already have one foot over the threshold if it is ever to gain admittance.

But it will be more satisfactory, probably, to refer to the biological side of the case, and point out that as the ear activity has been evolved on account of the advantage gained by the whole organism, it must stand in the strictest histological and physiological connection with the eye, or hand, or leg, or whatever other organ has been the overt center of action. It is absolutely impossible to think of the eye center as monopolizing consciousness and the ear apparatus as wholly quiescent.

What happens is a certain relative prominence and subsidence as between the various organs which maintain the organic equilibrium.

Furthermore, the sound is not a mere stimulus, or mere sensation; it again is an act, that of hearing. Muscular response as well as sensory stimulus is involved; that is, there is a certain definite motor apparatus involved in hearing just as much as there is in subsequent running away. The movement and posture of the head, the tension of the ear muscles, are required for the "reception" of the sound. It is just as true to say that the sensation of sound arises from a motor response as that the running away is a response to the sound. This may be brought out by reference to the fact that Professor Baldwin, in the passage quoted, has inverted the real order as between his first and second elements. We do not have first a sound and then activity of attention, unless sound is taken as mere nervous shock or physical event, not as conscious quality. The conscious sensation of sound depends upon the motor response having already taken place; or, in terms of the previous statement (if stimulus is used as a conscious fact, and not as a mere physical event), it is the motor response or attention which develops the original nervous shock into the stimulus to another act. Once more, the final "element," the running away, is not merely motor, but is sensori-motor, having its sensory value and its muscular mechanism. It is also a co-ordination. And, finally, this sensori-motor co-ordination is not a new act, supervening upon what preceded. Just as the "response" is necessary to constitute the stimulus, to determine it as sound and as *this* kind of sound—of wildbeast or robber—so the sound experience must persist as a value in the running, to keep it up, to control it. No one thinks that the motor reaction involved in the running is a separate, disconnected event, but neither is it to be regarded as merely reaction to the sound. It occurs to change the sound, or more exactly, to develop the suggested experiences which make the sound really significant. The movement, whatever it may be, has its meaning wholly determined by reference to the hearing of the sound. It *is* that experience mediated.[1] What we have is a circuit, not an arc or broken segment of a circle. This circuit is more truly termed organic than reflex, because the motor response determines the stimulus, just as truly as sensory stimulus determines movement. Indeed, the movement is only for the sake of determining the stimulus, of fixing what kind of a stimulus it is, of interpreting it.

I hope it will not appear that I am introducing needless refinements and distinctions into what, it may be urged, is after all an undoubted fact, that movement as response follows sensation as stimulus. It is not a question of making the account of the process more complicated, though it is always wise to beware of that false simplicity which is attained by leaving out of account a large part of the problem. It is a question of finding out what stimulus or sensation, what movement and response mean; a question of seeing that they mean distinctions of flexible function only, not of fixed existence; that one and the same occurrence plays either or both parts, according to the shift of interest; and that because of this functional distinction and relationship, the supposed problem of the adjustment of one to the other, whether by superior force in the stimulus or an agency *ad hoc* in the center or the soul, is a purely self-created problem.

We may see the disjointed character of the present theory by calling to mind that it is impossible to apply the phrase

[1] In other words, every reaction is of the same type as that which Professor Baldwin ascribes to imitation alone, viz., circular. Imitation is simply that particular form of the circuit in which the "response" lends itself to comparatively unchanged maintenance of the prior experience. I say comparatively unchanged, for so far as this maintenance means additional control over the experience, it is being psychically changed, becoming more distinct. It is safe to suppose, moreover, that "repetition" is kept up only so long as this growth or mediation goes on. There is a new-in-the-old, if it is only the new sense of power.

"sensori-motor" to the occurrence as a simple phrase of description; it has validity only as a term of interpretation, only, that is, as defining various functions exercised. In terms of description, the whole process may be sensory or it may be motor, but it cannot be sensori-motor. The "stimulus," the excitation of the nerve ending and of the sensory nerve, the central change, are just as much, or just as little, motion as are the events taking place in the motor nerve and the muscles. It is one uninterrupted, continuous redistribution of mass in motion. And there is nothing in the process, from the standpoint of description, which entitles us to call this reflex. It is redistribution pure and simple; as much so as the burning of a log, or the falling of a house or the movement of the wind. In the physical process, as physical, there is nothing which can be set off as stimulus, nothing which reacts, nothing which is response. There is just a change in the system of tensions.

The same sort of thing is true when we describe the process purely from the psychical side. It is now all sensation, all sensory quale; the motion, as psychically described, is just as much sensation as is sound or light or burn. Take the withdrawing of the hand from the candle flame as example. What we have is a certain visual-heat-pain-muscular quale, transformed into another visual-touch-muscular quale—the flame now being visible only at a distance, or not at all, the touch sensation being altered, etc. If we symbolize the original visual quale by v, the temperature by h, the accompanying muscular sensation by m, the whole experience may be stated as vhm-vh$m$-vhm'; m being the quale of withdrawing, m' the sense of the status after the withdrawal. The motion is now not a certain kind of existence; it is a sort of sensory experience interpreted, just as is candle flame, or burn from candle flame. All are on a par.

But, in spite of all this, it will be urged, there is a distinction between stimulus and response, between sensation and motion. Precisely, but we ought now to be in a condition to ask of what nature is the distinction, instead of taking it for granted as a distinction somehow lying in the existence of the facts themselves.

If the previous descriptive analysis has made obvious the need of reconsideration of the reflex arc idea, and the nest of difficulties and assumptions in the apparently simple statement, it is now time to undertake an explanatory analysis. The fact is that stimulus and response are not distinctions of existence, but teleological distinctions, that is, distinctions of function, or part played, with reference to reaching or maintaining an end. With respect to this teleological process, two stages should be discriminated, as their confusion is one cause of the confusion attending the whole matter. In one stage, the relation represents an organization of means with reference to a comprehensive end. It represents an accomplished adaptation. Such is the case in all well developed instincts, as when we say that the contact of eggs is a stimulus to the hen to set; or the sight of corn a stimulus to peck; such also is the case with all thoroughly formed habits, as when the contact with the floor stimulates walking. In these instances there is no question of consciousness of stimulus *as* stimulus, of response *as* response. There is simply a continuously ordered sequence of acts, all adapted in themselves and in the order of their sequence, to reach a certain objective end, the reproduction of the species, the preservation of life, locomotion to a certain place. The end has got thoroughly organized into the means. In calling one stimulus, another response we mean nothing more than that an orderly sequence of acts is taking place. The same sort of statement might be made equally well with reference to the succession of changes in a plant, so far as these are considered with reference to their adaptation to, say, producing seed. It is equally applicable to the series of events in the circulation of the blood, or the sequence of acts occurring in a self-binding reaper.[1]

Cases of organization which already attained, we may say, positively, that it is only the assumed common reference to an inclusive end which marks either member off as stimulus or response, that apart from such reference we have only antecedent and consequent;[2] in other words, the distinction is one of interpretation. Negatively, it must be pointed out that it is not legitimate to carry over, without change, exactly the same order of considerations to cases where it is a question of *conscious* stimulation and response. We may, in this stage, regard, if we please, stimulus and response each as an entire act, having an individuality of its own, subject even here to the qualification that individuality means not an entirely independent whole, but a division of labor as regards maintaining or reaching an end. But in any case, it is an *act,* a sensori-motor co-ordination, which stimulates the response, itself in turn sensori-motor, not a sensation which stimulates a movement. Hence the illegitimacy of identifying, as is so often done, cases of organized instincts or habits with the so-called reflex arc, or of transferring, without modification, considerations valid of this serial co-ordination of acts to the sensation-movement case.

The fallacy that arises when this is done is virtually the psychological or historical fallacy. A set of considerations which hold good only because of a completed process, is read into the content of the process which conditions this completed result. A state of things characterizing an outcome is regarded as a true description of the events which led up to

[1] To avoid misapprehension, I would say that I am not raising the question as to how far this teleology is real in any one of these cases; real or unreal, my point holds equally well. It is only when we regard the sequence of acts *as if* they were adapted to reach some end that it occurs to us to speak of one as stimulus and the other as response. Otherwise, we look at them as a *mere* succession.

[2] Whether, even in such a determination, there is still not a reference to a more latent kind of an end is, of course, left open.

this outcome; when, as a matter of fact, if this outcome had already been in existence, there would have been no necessity for the process. Or, to make the application to the case in hand, considerations valid of an attained organization or co-ordination, the orderly sequence of minor acts in a comprehensive co-ordination, are used to describe a process, viz., the distinction of mere sensation as stimulus and of mere movement as response, which takes place only because such an attained organization is no longer at hand, but is in process of constitution. Neither mere sensation, nor mere movement, can ever be either stimulus or response; only an act can be that; the *sensation* as stimulus means the lack of and search for such an objective stimulus, or orderly placing of an act; just as mere movement as response means the lack of and search for the right act to complete a desired co-ordination.

A recurrence to our example will make these formulæ clearer. As long as the seeing is an unbroken act, which is as experienced no more mere sensation than it is mere motion (though the onlooker or psychological observer can interpret it into sensation and movement), it is in no sense the sensation which stimulates the reaching; we have, as already sufficiently indicated, only the serial steps in a co-ordination of *acts*. But now take a child who, upon reaching for bright light (that is, exercising the seeing-reaching co-ordination) has sometimes had a delightful exercise, sometimes found something good to eat, and sometimes burned himself. *Now the response is not only uncertain, but the stimulus is equally uncertain; one is uncertain only in so far as the other is.* The real problem may be equally well stated as either to discover the right stimulus, to constitute the stimulus, or to discover, to constitute, the response. The question of whether to reach or to abstain from reaching is the question what sort of bright light have we here? Is it the one which means playing with one's hands, eating milk, or burning one's fingers? The stimulus must be constituted for the response to occur. Now it is at precisely this juncture and because of it that the distinction of sensation as stimulus and motion as response arises.

The conscious sensation of a stimulus is not a thing or existence by itself; it is that phase of a co-ordination requiring attention because, by reason of the conflict within the co-ordination, it is uncertain how to complete it. Uncertainty as to the next act, whether to reach or not, gives the motive to examining the act. The end to follow is, in this sense, the stimulus. It furnishes the motivation to attend to what has just taken place; to define it more carefully. From this point of view the discovery of the stimulus is the "response" to possible movement as "stimulus." We must have an anticipatory sensation, an image, of the movements that may occur, together with their respective values, before attention will go to the seeing to break it up as a sensation of light, and of light of this particular kind. It is the initiated activities of reaching, which, inhibited by the conflict in the co-ordination, turn round, as it were, upon the seeing, and hold it from passing over into further act until its quality is determined. Just here the act as objective stimulus becomes transformed into sensation as *possible,* or conscious, stimulus. Just here, also, motion as conscious response emerges.

In other words, sensation as stimulus does not mean any particular psychical *existence*. It means simply a function, and it will have its value shift according to the special work requiring to be done. At one moment the various activities of reaching and withdrawing will be the sensation, because they are that phase of activity which sets the problem, or creates the demand for the next act. At the next moment the previous act of seeing will furnish the sensation, being, in turn, that phase of activity which sets the pace upon which depends further action. Generalized, sensation as stimulus is always that phase of activity requiring to be defined in order that a co-ordination may be completed. What the sensation will be in particular at a given time, therefore, will depend entirely upon the way in which an activity is being directed. It has no fixed quality of its own. The search for the stimulus is the search for exact conditions of action; that is, for the state of things which decides how a beginning co-ordination should be completed.

Similarly, motion, as response, has only a functional value. It is whatever will serve to complete the disintegrating co-ordination. Just as the discovery of the sensation marks the establishing of the problem, so the constitution of the response marks the solution of this problem. At one time, holding the eye fixed upon the seeing and thus bringing out a certain quale of light is the response, because that is the particular act called for just then; at another time, the movement of the arm away from the light is response. There is nothing in itself which may be labeled response. That one certain set of sensory qualities should be marked off by themselves as "motion" and put in antithesis to such sensory qualities as those of color, sound and contact, as legitimate claimants to the title of sensation, is wholly inexplicable unless we keep the difference of function in view. It is the eye and ear sensations which fix for us the problem; which report to us the conditions which have to be met if the co-ordination is to be successfully completed; and just the moment we need to know about our movements to get an adequate report, just that moment, motion miraculously (from the ordinary standpoint) ceases to be motion and becomes "muscular sensation." On the other hand, take the change in values of experience, the transformation of sensory quales. Whether this change will or will not be interpreted as movement, whether or not any consciousness of movement will arise, will depend upon whether this change is satisfactory, whether or not it is regarded as a harmonious development of a co-ordination, or whether the change is regarded simply as a means in solving a problem, an instrument in reaching a more satisfactory co-ordination. So long as our experience runs smoothly we are no more conscious of motion as motion than we are of this or that color or sound by itself.

To sum up: the distinction of sensation and movement as stimulus and response respectively is not a distinction which can be regarded as descriptive of anything which holds of psychical events or physical existences as such. The only events to which the terms stimulus and response can be descriptively applied are minor acts serving by their respective positions the maintenance of some organized co-ordination. The conscious stimulus or sensation, and the conscious response or motion, have a special genesis or motivation, and a special end or function. The reflex arc theory, by neglecting, by abstracting from, this genesis and this function gives us one disjointed part of a process as if it were the whole. It gives us literally an arc, instead of the circuit; and not giving us the circuit of which it is an arc, does not enable us to place, to center, the arc. This arc, again, falls apart into two separate existences having to be either mechanically, or externally, adjusted to each other.

The circuit is a co-ordination, some of whose members have come into conflict with each other. It is the temporary disintegration and need of reconstruction which occasions, which affords the genesis of, the conscious distinction into sensory stimulus on one side and motor response on the other. The stimulus is that phase of the forming co-ordination which represents the conditions which have to be met in bringing it to a successful issue; the response is that phase of one and the same forming co-ordination which gives the key to meeting these conditions, which serves as instrument in effecting the successful co-ordination. They are therefore strictly correlative and contemporaneous. The stimulus is something to be discovered; to be made out; if the activity affords its own adequate stimulation, there is no stimulus save in the objective sense already referred to. As soon as it is adequately determined, then and only then is the response also complete. Attainment of either, means that the co-ordination has completed itself. Moreover, it is the motor response which assists in discovering and constituting the stimulus. It is the holding of the movement at a certain stage which creates the sensation, which throws it into relief.

It is the co-ordination which unifies that which the reflex arc concept gives us only in disjointed fragments. It is the circuit within which fall distinctions of stimulus and response as functional phases of its own mediation or completion. The point of this story is in its application; but the application of it to the question of the nature of mental development, to the distinction between sensational and rational consciousness, and to the nature of judgment must be deferred to a more favorable opportunity.

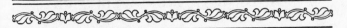

Conduct and Experience

"CONDUCT," as it appears in the title, obviously links itself with the position taken by behaviorists; "experience," with that of the introspectionists. If the result of the analysis herein undertaken turns out to involve a revision of the meaning of both concepts, it will probably signify that my conclusions will not be satisfactory to either school; they may be regarded by members of both as a sterile hybrid rather than a useful mediation. However, there are many subdivisions in each school, and there are competent psychologists who decline to enroll in either, while the very existence of controversy is an invitation to reconsideration of fundamental terms, even if the outcome is not wholly satisfactory.

Before we enter upon the theme, an introductory remark should be made. One is that the subject is so highly complex and has so many ramifications that it is impossible to deal with it adequately. The difficulty is increased by the fact that these ramifications extend to a historical, intellectual background in which large issues of philosophy and epistemology are involved, a background so pervasive that even those who have no interest in, or use for, philosophy would find, if they took the trouble to investigate, that the words they use—the words we all must use—are deeply saturated with the results of these earlier discussions. These have escaped from philosophy and made their way into common thought and speech.

The problem for psychology is connected with the controversy, so active about thirty years ago, between structuralists and functionalists. The introspectionists are more lineal descendants of the structuralists than are the behaviorists of the functionalists, and I do not mean to equate the terms. The basic error of the structuralists was, it seems to me, the assumption that the phenomena they dealt with had a structure which direct inspection could disclose. Admitting, for the moment, that there are such things as conscious processes which constitute "experience" and which are capable of direct inspection, it still involves an immense leap of logic to infer that direct inspection can disclose their structures. One might go so far as to say that, supposing that there are such things, they are just the sort of things that are, in their immediate occurrence, structureless. Or, to put it in a more exact way, if they have any structure, this is not carried in their immediate presence but in facts that are external to them and which cannot be disclosed by the method of direct inspection.

Take, for example, the classification of some immediate qualities as sensations, others as perceptions, and the sub-classification of sensations into auditory, visual, tactile, etc. As a classification, it involves an interpretation, and every interpretation goes outside of what is directly observed. I can attach no meaning to the statement that any immediately present quality announces, "I am sensory, and of the visual mode." It is called visual because it is referred to the optical apparatus, and this reference depends upon facts that are wholly external to the quality's own presence: upon observation of the eyes and anatomical dissection of bodily organs. The distinction between qualities to which the names "sensation" and "perception" are given involves a still more extensive operation of analytic interpretation, depending upon further considerations extraneous to what is immediately present and inspected.

The difficulty cannot be met by saying that a "sensory" quality is immediately given as simple, while a perceptual one is a complex of simples, for this distinction is itself precisely the result of an analytic interpretation and not an immediately given datum. Many "percepts" present themselves originally as total and undifferentiated, or immediately simple, and the least discriminable simple quality termed a sensation is itself arrived at as the end-term of a prolonged research, and is known as an end-term and as simple only because of extraneous reference to bodily organs, which is itself made possible by physical apparatus.

A simple example is found in the fact that sensori-motor schematism of some sort is now a commonplace in most psychological literature. If it could be detected by direct inspection of immediate qualities, it would always have been a commonplace. In fact, it is a product of an independent investigation of the morphology and physiology of the nervous system. If we generalize from such an instance, we shall be led to say that the structure of so-called mental process or conscious process, namely, of those immediate qualities to which the name "experience" was given, is furnished by the human organism, especially its nervous system. This object is known just as any other natural object is known, and not by any immediate act called introspection.

We cannot stop at this point, however. No organism is so isolated that it can be understood apart from the environment in which it lives. Sensory receptors and muscular effectors, the eye and the hand, have their existence as well as their meaning because of connections with an outer environment. The moment the acts made possible by organic structure cease to have relevancy to the milieu, the organism no longer exists; it perishes. The organisms that manifest a minimum of structure within themselves must have enough structure to enable them to prehend and assimilate food from their surroundings. The *structure* of the immediate qualities that have sometimes been called "consciousness," or "experience" as a synonym for consciousness, is so external to them that it must be ascertained by non-introspective methods.

If the implication of the last two paragraphs were made explicit, it would read: The structure of whatever is had by

way of immediate qualitative presences is found in the recurrent modes of interaction taking place between what we
term organism, on one side, and environment, on the other.
This interaction is the primary fact, and it constitutes a *trans-
action*. Only by analysis and selective abstraction can we
differentiate the actual occurrence into two factors, one called
organism and the other, environment. This fact militates
strongly against any form of behaviorism that defines behavior
in terms of the nervous system or body alone. For present purposes, we are concerned with the fact as indicating that the
structure of consciousness lies in a highly complex field outside of "consciousness'" itself, one that requires the help of
objective science and apparatus to determine.

We have not finished with the topic of the extent of this
objective structure. It includes within itself a temporal spread.
The interactions of which we have just spoken are not isolated but form a temporal continuity. One kind of behaviorism is simply a generalized inference from what takes place
in laboratory experimentation plus a virtual denial of the fact
that laboratory data have meaning only with reference to behavior having a before and after—a from which and an into
which. In the laboratory a situation is arranged. Instructions
being given to the subject, he reacts to them and to some, say,
visual stimulus. He accompanies this response with a language
response or record of some sort. This is all which is immediately relevant to the laboratory procedure. Why, then, speak
of sensations and perceptions as conscious processes? Why not
stick to what actually happens, and speak of behavioristic
response to stimuli? It is no derogation to the originality of
those who began the behaviorist movement to say that a behavioristic theory was bound, logically, to emerge from laboratory procedure. Conscious processes drop out as irrelevant
accretions.

There is something in the *context* of the experiment which

goes beyond the stimuli and responses directly found within it. There is, for example, the *problem* which the experimenter has set and his *deliberate* arrangement of apparatus and selection of conditions with a view to disclosure of facts that bear upon it. There is also an *intent* on the part of the subject. Now I am not making this reference to "problem," "selective arrangement," and "intent" or purpose in order to drag in by the heels something mental over and beyond the behavior. The object is rather to call attention to a definite characteristic of behavior, namely, that it is not exhausted in the immediate stimuli-response features of the experimentation. From the standpoint of behavior itself, the traits in question take us beyond the isolated act of the subject into a content that has a temporal spread. The acts in question came out of something and move into something else. Their whole scientific point is lost unless they are placed as one phase of this contextual behavior.

It is hardly possible, I think, to exaggerate the significance of this fact for the concept of behavior. Behavior is serial, not mere succession. It can be resolved—it must be—into discrete acts, but no act can be understood apart from the series to which it belongs. Although the word "behavior" implies comportment, as well as de-portment, the word "conduct" brings out the aspect of seriality better than does "behavior," for it clearly involves the facts both of direction (or a vector property) and of conveying or conducing. It includes the fact of passing through and passing along.

I do not mean to suggest that behaviorists of the type that treats behavior as a succession rather than as serial exclude the influence of temporal factors. The contrary is the case.[1]

[1] For example, Hunter says: "Has not the behaviorist always appealed to the results of heredity and previous training as factors which co-operate with present stimuli in determining behavior? Was there ever a behaviorist who explained maze training without calling upon the retained effects of previous training for a part of his explanation, or a behaviorist who ignored childhood peculiarities in accounting for adult behavior?" (2, p. 103).

But I am concerned to point out the difference made in the concept of behavior according as one merely appeals to the *effects* of prior acts in order to account for some trait of a present act, or as one realizes that *behavior* itself is serial in nature. The first position is consistent regarding behavior as consisting of acts which merely succeed one another so that each can be understood in terms of what is actually found in every one act taken by itself, provided one includes the *effects* of prior acts as part of the conditions involved in it. The second position, while, of course, it recognizes this factor, goes further. In introducing into behavior the concept of series, the idea of ordinal position connected with a principle which binds the successive acts together is emphasized.[2]

The import of the formulation just made may be more definitely gathered from a consideration of the stimulus-response concept. That every portion of behavior may be stated as an instance of stimulus-response, I do not doubt, any more than that any physical occurrence may be stated as an instance of the cause-effect relation. I am very skeptical about the value of the result reached until that which serves as stimulus and as response in a given case has been carefully analyzed. It may be that, when the concept of cause-effect first dawned, some persons got satisfaction by stringing gross phenomena together as causes and effects. But, as physical science advanced, the general relation was forgotten by being absorbed into a definite analytic statement of the particular conditions to which the terms "cause" and "effect" are assigned. It seems to me that there is considerable behavioristic and semi-behavioristic theory in psychology at present that is content merely to subsume the phenomena in question under the

[2] It is not meant, of course, to carry over in a rigid way the mathematical concept of series, but the idea underlying this concept, namely, that of sequential continuity, is employed. It is meant that even the instances in which abrupt succession is most marked, i.e., jumping at a noise when engaged in deep study, have to be treated as limiting cases of the serial principle and not as typical cases from which to derive the standard notion of behavior-acts.

rubric of *S-R* as if they were ready-made and self-evident things.

When we turn to the consideration of *what* is a stimulus, we obtain a result which is fatal to the idea that isolated acts, typified by a reflex, can be used to determine the meaning of stimulus. That which is, or operates as, a stimulus turns out to be a function, in a mathematical sense, of behavior in its serial character. Something, not yet a stimulus, breaks in upon an activity already going on and *becomes* a stimulus in virtue of the relations it sustains to what is going on in this continuing activity. As Woodworth has said: "Very seldom does a stimulus find the organism in a completely resting, neutral and unpreoccupied status" (4, p. 124). The remark has to be developed, moreover, by making two additions. The first repeats what has just been said. No external change is a stimulus in and of itself. It *becomes* the stimulus in virtue of what the organism is already preoccupied with. To call it, to think of it, as a stimulus without taking into account the behavior that is already going on is so arbitrary as to be nonsensical. Even in the case of abrupt changes, such as a clap of thunder when one is engrossed in reading, the *particular* force of that noise, its property as stimulus, is determined by what the organism is already doing in interaction with a particular environment. One and the same environmental change becomes, under different conditions of ongoing or serial behavior, a thousand different actual stimuli—a consideration which is fatal to the supposition that we can analyze behavior into a succession of independent stimuli and responses.

The difficulty cannot be overcome by merely referring to the operation of a *prior* response in determining what functions as stimulus, for exactly the same thing holds of that situation. Nor can it be overcome by vague reference to the "organism as a whole." While this reference is pertinent and necessary, the *state* of the whole organism is one of *action* which is continuous, so that reference to the organism as a whole merely puts before us the situation just described: that environmental change *becomes* a stimulus in virtue of a continuous course of behavior. These considerations lead us to the second remark. A stimulus is always a *change* in the environment which is connected with a *change* in activity. No stimulus is a stimulus to action as such but only to a change in the *direction* or intensity of action. A response is not action or behavior but marks a change in behavior. It is the new ordinal position in a series, and the series is the behavior. The ordinary *S-R* statement is seductive merely because it takes for granted this fact, while if it were explicitly stated it would transform the meaning of the *S-R* formula.

The discussion thus far has been so general that it may seem to have evaded the concrete questions that alone are important. What has all this to do with the familiar rubrics of analytic psychology, sensation, perception, memory, thinking, etc., or, more generally speaking, with psychology itself? Taking the last question, our conclusion as to the serial character of behavior and the necessity of placing and determining actual stimuli and responses within its course seems to point to a definite subject-matter characteristic of psychology. This subject-matter is the behavior of the organism so far as that is characterized by changes taking place in an activity that is serial and continuous in reference to changes in an environment that persists although changing in detail.

So far, the position taken gives the primacy to conduct and relates psychology to a study of conduct rather than to "experience." It is, however, definitely in opposition to theories of behavior that begin by taking anything like a reflex as the type and standard of a behavior-act, and that suppose it is possible to isolate and describe stimulus and response as ultimates that constitute behavior, since they themselves must be discovered and discriminated as specifiable determinations within the course of behavior. More definitely the position taken points, as it seems to me, to the conception of psychology recently advanced by Dr. Percy Hughes (1), namely, that psychology is concerned with the life-career of individualized activities.[1] Here we have something which marks off a definite field of subject-matter and so calls for a distinctive intellectual method and treatment and thus defines a possible science.

The burning questions, however, remain. What meaning, if any, can be attached to sensation, memory, conceiving, etc., on the basis of conduct or behavior as a developing temporal continuum marked off into specific act-situations? In general, the mode of answer is clear, whatever the difficulties in carrying it out into detail. They designate modes of behavior having their own discernible qualities, meaning by "qualities" traits that enable one to discriminate and identify them as special modes of behavior.

Two considerations are pertinent in this connection, of which the second can best be discussed later along with a discussion of what has been so far passed over; psychology as an account of "experience." The first consideration may be introduced by pointing out that hearing, seeing, perceiving in general, remembering, imagining, thinking, judging, reasoning, are not inventions of the psychologist. Taken as designations of acts performed by every normal human being, they are everyday common-sense distinctions. What some psychologists have done is to shove a soul or consciousness under these acts as their author or locus. It seems to me fair to say that the Wundtian tradition, while it developed in the direction of denying or ignoring the soul and, in many cases, of denying "consciousness" as a unitary power or locus, in its concep-

[1] It is not germane to my subject to go into detail, but I cannot refrain from calling attention to what Dr. Hughes points out, that behaviorism in one of its narrower senses—the behavior of the nervous system—takes its place as a necessary included factor, namely, a study of *conditions* involved in a study of life-careers, while whatever is verifiable in the findings of psychoanalysts, etc., also takes its place in the study of individual life-careers.

tion of least-discriminable qualities as identical with ultimate simple "conscious processes" took a position which did not come from the facts but from an older tradition.

What we are here concerned with is, however, the fact that the ordinary man, apart from any philosophic or scientific interpretation, takes for granted the existence of acts of this type, which are different from acts of locomotion and digestion. Such acts, in a purely denotative way apart from conceptual connotation, constitute the meaning of the word "mental" in distinction from the physical and purely physiological. Is the use of "mental" as a designative term of specifiable modes of behavior found in every human life-career tabu to one who starts from the standpoint of behavior in the sense mentioned above?

The issue turns, of course, about the introduction of the idea of distinctive and discernible qualities that mark off some kinds of behavior and that supply a ground for calling them mental. To many strict behaviorists any reference to qualities seems a reversion to the slough of old introspectionism and an attempt to smuggle its methods in a covert way into behaviorism. Let us see, then, what happens when the position is analyzed. We can hardly do better than to start from the fact that the physicist observes, recalls, thinks. We must note the fact that the things with which he ends, protons-electrons in their complex interrelations of space-time and motions, are things with which he *ends,* conclusions. He reaches them as results of thinking about observed things when his inferences and calculations are confirmed by further observations. What he starts with are things having *qualities,* things qualitatively discriminated from one another and recurrently identifiable in virtue of their qualitative distinctions.

Dr. Hunter, in justifying the use of ordinary objects, whether of the environment or the organism in connection with *S-R* behavior, instead of trying to formulate everything in terms of protons-electrons, remarks: "Even in physics it is still permissible to speak of steel and carbon and to make studies upon these substances without directly involving the question of the nature of the atom" (2, p. 91; cf. p. 104). To this may be added that it is not only permissible but necessary. The physicist must refer to such things to get any point of departure and any point of application for his special findings. That water is H_2O would reduce to the meaningless tautology H_2O is H_2O unless it were identified by means of the thing known to perception and use as water. Now these common-sense things from which science starts and in which it terminates are qualitative things, qualitatively differential from one another.

There can be no more objection, then, to the psychologist's recognizing objects qualitatively marked out than there is for the physicist and chemist. It is simply a question of fact, not of theory, whether there are modes of behavior qualitatively so characterized that they can be discriminated as acts of sensation, perception, recollection, etc., and just what their qualitative traits are. Like other matters of fact, it is to be decided by observation. I share, however, the feeling against the use of the word "introspection." For that reason, I employed earlier the word "inspection." "Introspection" is too heavily charged with meanings derived from the animistic tradition. Otherwise, it might be fitly used to designate the ordinary act of observation when it is directed toward a special kind of subject-matter, that of the behavior of organisms where behavior is what it is because it is a phase of a particular life-career of serial activity.

Of course, these general conceptions remain empty until the acts of sensation, perception, recalling, thinking, etc., with those of fear, love, admiration, etc., are definitely determined as occurring in specified and distinctive junctures or crises of a life-career. Such a task is undoubtedly difficult; but so is any other scientific inquiry. The chief objection, it seems to me, to the narrower forms of behaviorism is that their obsession against the mental, because of previous false theories about it, shuts the door to even entering upon the inquiry. It should even be possible to give the more general term "awareness" or "consciousness" a meaning on this basis, though it would not be that of an underlying substance, cause, or source. It would be discerned as a specifiable quality of some forms of behavior. There is a difference between "consciousness" as a noun, and "conscious" as an adjective of some acts.

Behaviorists have, some of them, at least, implicitly admitted the principle for which I have been arguing. They have said that the psychologist uses perception, thought, consciousness, just as any other scientist does. To admit this and then not go on to say (and act upon the saying) that, while they form no part of the subject-matter of physicist and physiologist, they do form a large part of the subject-matter that sets the problems of the psychologist seems strange to me—so strange as to suggest an emotional complex.

Personally I have no doubt that language in its general sense, or symbols, is connected with all mental operations that are intellectual in import and with the emotions associated with them. But to substitute linguistic behavior for the quality of acts that renders them "mental" is an evasion. A man says, "I feel hot." We are told that the whole affair can be resolved into a sensory process as stimulus and linguistic response. But what *is* the *sensory* process? Is it something *exclusively* capable of visual detection in the nervous system under favorable conditions, or is it something having an immediate quality which is noted without knowing about the sensory physiological process? When a man sees and reports the latter, is there no immediately experienced quality by which he recognizes that he is looking at neuronic structures and not, say, at a balloon? Is it all a matter of another physiological process and linguistic response?

The exposition has brought us to the threshold of the "experience" psychology. Indeed, it will probably seem to some readers that we have crossed the threshold and entered a domain foreign to any legitimate behavioristic psychology. Let me begin, then, by saying that the logic of the above account does not imply that *all* experience is the psychologist's province, to say nothing of its not implying that all experience is psychic in character. "Experience" as James pointed out long ago is a double-barreled word. The psychologist is concerned exclusively with experienc*ing,* with detection, analysis, and description of its different modes. Experienc*ing* has no existence apart from subject-matter experienced; we perceive objects, veridical or illusory, not percepts; we remember events and not memories; we think topics and subjects, not thoughts; we love persons, not loves; and so on, although the person loved may by metonymy be called a "love." Experiencing is not itself an immediate subject-matter; it is not experienced as a complete and self-sufficient event. But everything experienced is in part made what it is because there enters into it a way of experiencing something; not a way of experiencing *it,* which would be self-contradictory, but a way of experiencing something other than itself. No complete account of what is experienced, then, can be given until we know *how* it is experienced, or the mode of experiencing that enters into its formation.

Need of understanding and controlling the things experienced must have called attention very early in the history of man to the way an object is made what it is by the manner in which it is experienced. I heard it, saw it, touched it, are among the first, as they are among the most familiar of these discriminations. "I remember seeing it" would, in most cases at least, be regarded as better evidence for belief than "I remember dreaming it." Such discriminations are not themselves psychology, but, as already stated, they form its raw material just as common-sense determinations of the difference between oil and water, iron and tin, form the original subject-matter of physics and chemistry. There is no more reason for denying the reality of one than of the other, while to deny the reality of either leaves the science in question without any concrete subject-matter.

The discrimination of various modes of experiencing is enormously increased by the need of human beings for instruction and for direction of conduct. It is possible, for example, that a person would never differentiate the fact of getting angry from an experienced obnoxious subject-matter, if others did not call his attention to the rôle of his own attitude in the creation of the particular hateful situation. Control of the conduct of others is a constant function of life, and it can be secured only by singling out various modes of experiencing. Thus, when I say that such selected experiencings or modes of individual behavior supply primary raw material but are not psychological in themselves, I mean that they are primarily treated as having *moral* significance, as matters of a character to be formed or corrected. They are selected and designated not for any scientific reason but in the exigencies, real or supposed, of social intercourse and in the process of social control termed education. The word "moral" hardly conveys in its usual sense the full idea. A child is told to look where he is going and to listen to what he is told, to attend to instructions given him. Indeed, it is rather foolish to cite instances, so much of our contact with others consists in having attention called to attitudes, dispositions, and acts that are referred to selves.

Hence, the statement only raises the question of what takes place when these acts and attitudes, abstracted from the total experience, become definitely psychological subject-matter.

The answer is, in general, that they set problems for investigation, just as other qualitative objects, fire, air, water, stars, set problems to other investigations. What is seeing, hearing, touching, recalling, dreaming, thinking? Now inspection of theses acts to determine their qualities is as necessary as is observation of physical objects and behaviors to determine their qualities. But just as no amount of direct observation of water could ever yield a scientific account of water, so no amount of direct inspection of these individual attitudes and ways of experiencing could yield a science of psychology. Observation helps determine the nature of the subject-matter to be studied and accounted for; it does not carry us beyond suggestions of possible hypotheses when it comes to dealing scientifically with the subject-matter.

It is at this point that the significance of objective material and methods comes in, that derived from physiology, biology, and the other sciences. Identifying modes of individual experiencing with modes of behavior identified objectively and objectively analyzable makes a science of psychology possible. Such a statement cuts two ways. It gives due recognition, or so it seems to me, to the importance of methods that have nothing to do with the immediate quality of the ways of experiencing, as these are revealed in direct inspection, or, if you please, introspection. But it also indicates that the subject-matter which sets the *problems* is found in material exposed to direct observation. This is no different from what happens in the physical sciences, although *what* is observed is different, and the observation is conducted from a different, because personal and social, standpoint.

At a certain period, for example, religionists and moralists were deeply concerned about the nature and fate of human characters. They made many shrewd and penetrating observations on human dispositions and acts on ways of experiencing the world. Or, if this illustration does not appeal, substitute

[263]

modern novelists and dramatists. But aside from an earlier tendency to interpret and classify such observations in terms of the animistic tradition, and later by a logical misconception of Aristotle's potentialities (transformed into "faculties"), these observations did not form a psychology. They do not become truly psychological until they can be attacked by methods and materials drawn from objective sciences. Yet apart from such observations, psychology has no subject-matter with which to deal in any distinctive way in contrast to the physiologist and physicist, on the one hand, and the social student, on the other.

The position here taken differs, then, in two important respects from that of the introspectionist school. The latter assumes that something called "consciousness" is an originally separate and directly given subject-matter and that it is also the organ of its own immediate disclosure of all its own secrets. If the term "experience" be used instead of conscious-ness, it is assumed that the latter, as it concerns the psychologist, is open to direct inspection, provided the proper precautions are taken and proper measures used. A philosopher by pro-fession who does not know much psychology knows the his-toric origin of these ideas in Descartes, Locke, and their suc-cessors in dealing with epistemological problems. He has even better ground than the professed psychologist for sus-pecting that they are not indigenous to psychological subject-matter but have been foisted upon psychology from without.

The special matter in point here, however, is not historical origin, but is the doctrine that direct observation, under the title of introspection, can provide principles of analysis, inter-pretation, and explanation, revealing laws that bind the ob-served phenomena together. Without repeating what was said at the outset to the effect that the structure of immediately ob-served phenomena can be discovered only by going outside of the subject-matter inspected, I refer to it here as indicating one difference between the position here taken and that of the introspectionist. It is a difference between subject-matter that constitutes a *problem* and subject-matter that is supposed to resolve the problem. To discriminate and recognize cases of audition, vision, perception, generally, merely exposes a problem. No persistence in the method which yields them can throw any scientific light upon them.

The other difference is even more fundamental. Psychologists of the school in question have assumed that they are dealing with "experience" instead of with a selected phase of it, here termed experiencing. I do not, for example, see anything psychological at all in the determination of all the least-discriminable qualities of "experience." The result may yield something more or less curious and interesting about the world in which we live; the conclusions may be of some use in æsthetics or in morals for aught I know. But all that is strictly psychological in the endeavor consists in whatever it may incidentally teach about the *act* of sensing and the *act* of discrimination. These are modes of experiencing things or ways of behaving toward things, and as such have psychological relevancy. It may be doubted whether more would have not been found out if they had been approached directly as acts and not under the guise of finding out all the qualities which can enter into experience. It is not, in short, the qualities of things experienced but the qualities that differentiate certain acts of the individual that concern the psychologist. They concern him not as ultimates and as solutions but, as has been said, as supplying him with data for investigation by objective methods.

The fallacy contained in the doctrine that psychology is concerned with experience instead of with experiencing may be brought out by considering a style of vocabulary dear to the heart of the introspectionist. When he speaks of sensation, he does not mean an act but a peculiar content.[1] A color or a sound is to him a sensation; an orange, stone, or table is a percept. Now, from the point of view here taken, a color or sound may be an object of an act termed sensing, and a tree or orange may be an object of the act of perceiving, but *they* are not sensations or perceptions, except by a figure of speech. The act of shooting is sometimes called fowling, because fowl are shot at. Speech even reverses the figure of speech and speaks of the birds killed as so many good shots. But, in the latter case, no one dreams of taking the figure literally, ascribing to the dead birds the properties characterizing the shooting. To call a tree a percept is merely a short way of saying a tree is perceived. It tells us nothing about the tree but something about a new relation into which the tree has entered. Instead of canceling or submerging the tree, it tells of an additive property now taken on by the tree, as much so as if we had said the tree was watered by rain or fertilized.

I hope the aptness of the illustration to the matter of confusion of experiencing with experience is reasonably clear. The tree, when it is perceived, is experienced in one way; when remembered, reflected upon, or admired for its beauty, it is experienced in other ways. By a certain figure of speech we may call it an experience, meaning that it is experienced, but we cannot by any figure of speech call it an experiencing. Nevertheless, the tree *as* experienced lends itself to a different type of analysis than that which is appropriate to the tree as a botanical object. We can first discriminate various ways of experiencing it, namely, perceptually, reflectively, emotionally, practically—as a lumberman might look at it—and then we can attempt to analyze scientifically the structure and mechanism of the various acts involved. No other discipline

[1] I have alluded to Locke as a part author of the introspectionist tradition. He always, however, refers to sensation as an act. Even his "idea" is an *object* of mind in knowledge, not a state or constituent of mind, taking the place of the scholastic species as true object of knowing.

does this. Some study must deal with the problem. Whether the study is called psychology or by some other name is of slight importance compared with that fact that the problem needs scientific study by methods adapted to its solution.

The results of the analysis, if successful, undoubtedly tell us more about the tree as an experienced object. We may be better able to distinguish a veridical tree from an illusory one when we know the conditions of vision. We may be better able to appreciate its æsthetic qualities when we know more about the conditions of an emotional attitude towards it. These are consequences, however, of psychological knowledge rather than a part of psychology. They give no ground for supposing that psychology is a doctrine regarding experience in the sense of things experienced. They are on all fours with the use of the fact of personal equations by an astronomer. The discovery and measurement of personal equation in respect to the time assigned to a perceived event is a psychological matter, because it relates to a way of seeing happenings, but the use of it by an astronomer to correct his time-reading is not a matter of psychology. Much less does it make the star a psychological fact. It concerns not the star but the way the star enters into experience as far as that is connected with the behavior of an experiencing organism.

Returning to the question raised earlier—it now appears that, if the acts of sensing, perceiving, loving, admiring, etc., are termed mental, it is not because they are intrinsically psychic processes but because of something characteristic which they *effect,* something different from that produced by acts of locomotion or digestion. The question whether they do have distinctive consequences is a question of fact, not of theory. An *a priori* theoretical objection to such terms as conscious, mental, etc., should not stand in the way of a fair examination of facts. No amount of careful examination of the nervous system can decide the issue. It is possible that the nervous system and its behavior are *conditions* of acts that have such characteristic effects that we need a name to differentiate them from the behavior of other things, even of the nervous system *taken by itself*.

The above is written schematically with omission of many important points, as well as somewhat over-positively, in order to save time and space. The account may be reviewed by reference to the historical background to which allusion has been made. Modern psychology developed and formed its terminology—always a very important matter because of the rôle of symbols in directing thought—under the influence of certain discussions regarding the possibility and extent of knowledge. In this particular context, *acts* were either ignored or were converted into contents. That is, the function, the peculiar consequences of certain acts, that renders them fit to be called mental was made into a peculiar form of existence called mental or psychic. Then these contents were inserted, under the influence of the theory of knowledge, as intermediaries between the mind and things. Sensations, percepts, treated as mental contents, intervened between the mind and objects and formed the means of knowing the latter. Physics dealt with the things as they were in themselves; psychology, with the things as they were experienced or represented in mental states and processes. In this way, the doctrine arose that psychology is the science of all experience *qua* experience; a view later modified, under the influence of physiological discovery, to the position that it is the science of all experience as far as it is dependent upon the nervous system.

The tendency was reinforced by another historical fact. The special formulations of physics were made in disregard, as far as their own content was concerned, of qualities. Qualities ejected from physics found a home in mind, or consciousness. There was supposed to be the authority of physics for taking them to be mental and psychic in nature. The convergence of these two historic streams created the intellectual background of the beginnings of modern psychology and impregnated its terminology. Behaviorism is a reaction against the confusion created by this mixture. In its reaction it has, in some of its forms, failed to note that some modes of behavior have distinctive qualities which, in virtue of the distinctive properties of the consequences of these acts, are to be termed mental and conscious. Consequently, it assumed that a study of the organic conditions of these acts constitutes all there is to behavior, overlooking in the operation two fundamental considerations. One of these is that the distinctive functions of the nervous system cannot be determined except in reference to directly observable qualities of the acts of sensing, perceiving, remembering, imagining, etc., they serve. The other is precisely the fact that their behavior is the behavior of *organs* of a larger macroscopic behavior and not at all the whole of behavior. If it were not for knowledge of behavior gained by observation of something else than the nervous system, our knowledge of the latter would consist merely of heaping up of details highly curious and intricate but of no significance for any account of behavior.

Since this discussion intends to be for the most part a logical analysis, I can hardly do better than close by citing a recent statement from a distinguishing logician. Speaking of the reflective and analytic method of philosophy, Mr. C. I. Lewis says: "If, for example, the extreme behaviorists in psychology deny the existence of consciousness on the ground that analysis of the 'mental' must always eventually be in terms of bodily behavior, then it is the business of philosophy to correct their error, because it consists simply in a fallacy of logical analysis. The analysis of any immediately presented X must always interpret this X in terms of its relations to other things—to Y and Z. Such end-terms of analysis—Y and Z—will not in general be temporal or spatial constituents of

X but may be anything which bears a constant correlation with it. . . . In general terms, if such analysis concludes by stating X is a certain kind of Y-Z complex, hence X does not exist as a distinct 'reality,' the error consists in overlooking a general characteristic of logical analysis—that it does not discover the 'substance' or cosmic constituents of the phenomenon whose nature is analyzed but only the constant context of experience in which it will be found."

Philosophies of Freedom

A RECENT book on sovereignty concludes a survey of various theories on that subject with the following words: "The career of the notion of sovereignty illustrates the general characteristics of political thinking. The various forms of the notion have been apologies for causes rather than expressions of the disinterested love of knowledge. The notion has meant many things at different times; and the attacks upon it have sprung from widely different sources and been directed toward a multiplicity of goals. The genesis of all political ideas is to be understood in terms of their utility rather than of their truth and falsity."[1] Perhaps the same thing may be said of moral notions; I do not think there is any doubt that freedom is a word applied to many things of varied plumage and that it owes much of its magic to association with a variety of different causes. It has assumed various forms as needs have varied; its "utility" has been its service in helping men deal with many predicaments.

Primary among the needs it has been employed to meet and the interests it has served to promote is the moral. A good deal is assumed in asserting that the center of this moral need and cause is the fact of choice. The desire to dignify choice, to account for its significance in human affairs, to magnify that significance by making it the center of man's moral struggles and achievements has been reflected in the idea of freedom. There is an inexpugnable feeling that choice *is* freedom and that man without choice is a puppet, and that man then has no acts which he can call his very own. Without genuine choice, choice that when expressed in action makes things different from what they otherwise would be, men are but passive

[1] *Sovereignty*, by Paul Ward, p. 167.

[271]

vehicles through which external forces operate. This feeling is neither self-explanatory nor self-justificatory. But at least it contributes an element in the statement of the problem of freedom. Choice is one of the things that demands examination.

The theoretical formulation for the justification of choice as the heart of freedom became, however, involved at an early time with other interests; and they, rather than the unprejudiced examination of the fact of choice, determined the form taken by a widely prevalent philosophy of freedom. Men are given to praise and blame; to reward and punishment. As civilization matured, definite civil agencies were instituted for "trying" men for modes of conduct so that if found guilty they might be punished. The fact of praise and blame, of civil punishment, directed at men on account of their behavior, signifies that they are held liable or are deemed responsible. The fact of punishment called attention, as men became more inquiring, to the ground of liability. Unless men were responsible for their acts, it was unjust to punish them; if they could not help doing what they did, what was the justice in holding them responsible for their acts, and blaming and punishing them? Thus a certain philosophy of the nature of choice as freedom developed as an apologia for an essentially legal interest: liability to punishment. The outcome was the doctrin known as freedom of will: the notion that a power called will lies back of choice as its author, and is the ground of liability and the essence of freedom. This will has the power of indifferent choice; that is, it is equally free to choose one way or another unmoved by any desire or impulse, just because of a causal force residing in will itself. So established did this way of viewing choice become, that it is still commonly supposed that choice and the arbitrary freedom of will are one and the same thing.[1]

[1] Doubt may be felt as to the assertion that this interpretation of freedom developed in connection with the legal motif. The historic connecting link is found in

It is then worth while to pause in our survey while we examine more closely the nature of choice in relation to this alleged connection with free will, free here meaning unmotivated choice. Analysis does not have to probe to the depths to discover two serious faults in the theory. It is a man, a human being in the concrete, who is held responsible. If the act does not proceed from the man, from the human being in his concrete make-up of habits, desires and purposes, why should *he* be held liable and be punished? Will appears as a force outside of the individual person as he actually is, a force which is the real ultimate cause of the act. *Its* freedom to make a choice arbitrarily thus appears no ground for holding the human being as a concrete person responsible for a choice. Whatever else is to be said or left unsaid, choice must have some closer connection with the actual make-up of disposition and character than this philosophy allows.

We may seem then to be in a hopeless dilemma. If the man's nature, original and acquired, makes him do what he does, how does his action differ from that of a stone or tree? Have we not parted with any ground for responsibility? When the question is looked at in the face of facts rather than in a dialectic of concepts it turns out not to have any terrors. Holding men to responsibility may make a decided difference in their *future* behavior; holding a stone or tree to responsibility is a meaningless performance; it has no consequence; it makes no difference. If we locate the ground of liability in future consequences rather than in antecedent causal conditions, we moreover find ourselves in accord with actual practice. Infants, idiots, the insane, those completely upset, are not held to liability; the reason is that it is absurd—meaningless— to do so, for it has no effect on their further actions. A child as

the invasion of moral ideas by legal considerations that grew up in the Roman Empire. The association was perpetuated by the influence of Roman law and modes of moral thought, and even more by the incorporation of the latter in the theology and practices of the Christian Church, the nurse of morals in Europe.

he grows older finds responsibilities thrust upon him. This is surely not because freedom of the will has suddenly been inserted in him, but because his assumption of them is a necessary factor in his *further* growth and movement.

Something has been accomplished, I think, in transferring the issue from the past to the future, from antecedents to consequences. Some animals, dogs and horses, have their future conduct modified by the way they are treated. We can imagine a man whose conduct is changed by the way in which he is treated, so that it becomes different from what it would have been, and yet like the dog or horse, the change may be due to purely external manipulation, as external as the strings that move a puppet. The whole story has not then been told. There must be some practical participation from within to make the change that is effected significant in relation to choice and freedom. From *within*—that fact rules out the appeal, so facilely made, to will as a cause. Just what is signified by that participation by the human being himself in a choice that makes it really a choice?

In answering this question, it is helpful to go, apparently at least, far afield. Preferential action in the sense of selective behavior is a universal trait of all things, atoms and molecules as well as plants, animals and man. Existences, universally as far as we can tell, are cold and indifferent in the presence of some things and react energetically in either a positive or negative way to other things. These "preferences" or differential responses of behavior, are due to their own constitution; they "express" the nature of the things in question. They mark a distinctive contribution to what takes place. In other words, while changes in one thing may be described on the basis of changes that take place in other things, the *existence* of things which make certain changes having a certain quality and direction occur cannot be so explained. Selective behavior is the evidence of at least a rudimentary individuality or uniqueness in things. Such preferential action is not exactly what makes choice in the case of human beings. But unless there is involved in choice at least something continuous with the action of other things in nature, we could impute genuine reality to it only by isolating man from nature and thus treating him as in some sense a supra-natural being in the literal sense. Choice is more than just selectivity in behavior but it is *at least* that.

· What is the more which is involved in choice? Again, we may take a circuitous course. As we ascend in the range of complexity from inanimate things to plants, and from plants to animals and from other animals to man, we find an increasing variety of selective responses, due to the influence of life-history, or experiences already undergone. The manifestation of preferences becomes a "function" of an entire history. To understand the action of a fellow-man we have to know something of the *course* of his life. A man is susceptible, sensitive, to a vast variety of conditions, and undergoes varied and opposed experiences—as lower animals do not. Consequently a man in the measure of the scope and variety of his past experiences carries in his present capacity for selective response a large set of varied possibilities. That life-history of which his present preference is a function is complex. Hence the possibility of continuing diversification of behavior: in short, the distinctive *educability* of men. This factor taken by itself does not cover all that is included within the change of preference into genuine choice, but it has a bearing on that individual participation and individual contribution that is involved in choice as a mode of freedom. It is a large factor in our strong sense that we are not pushed into action from behind as are inanimate things. For that which is "behind" is so diversified in its variety and so intimately a part of the present self that preference becomes hesitant. Alternative preferences simultaneously manifest themselves.

[275]

Choice, in the distinctively human sense, then presents itself as one preference among and out of preferences; not in the sense of one preference already made and stronger than others, but as the formation of a new preference out of a conflict of preferences. If we can say upon what the formation of this new and determinate preference depends, we are close to finding that of which we are in search. Nor does the answer seem far to seek nor hard to find. As observation and foresight develop, there is ability to form signs and symbols that stand for the interaction and movement of things, without involving us in their actual flux. Hence the new preference may reflect this operation of mind, especially the forecast of the consequences of acting upon the various competing preferences. If we sum up, pending such qualification or such confirmation as further inquiry may supply, we may say that a stone has its preferential selections set by a relatively fixed, a rigidly set, structure and that no anticipation of the results of acting one way or another enters into the matter. The reverse is true of human action. In so far as a variable life-history and intelligent insight and foresight enter into it, choice signifies a capacity for deliberately changing preferences. The hypothesis that is suggested is that in these two traits we have before us the essential constituents of choice as freedom: the factor of individual participation.

Before that idea is further examined, it is, however, desirable to turn to another philosophy of freedom. For the discussion thus far has turned about the fact of choice alone. And such an exclusive emphasis may well render some readers impatient. It may seem to set forth an idea of freedom which is too individual, too "subjective." What has this affair to do with the freedom for which men have fought, bled and died: freedom from oppression and despotism, freedom of institutions and laws? This question at once brings to mind a philosophy of freedom which shifts the issue from choice to action,

action in an overt and public sense. This philosophy is sufficiently well presented for our purposes in the idea of John Locke, the author, one may say, of the philosophy of Liberalism in its classic sense. Freedom is *power to act* in accordance with choice. It is actual ability to carry desire and purpose into operation, to *execute* choices when they are made. Experience shows that certain laws and institutions prevent such operation and execution. This obstruction and interference constitutes what we call oppression, enslavement. Freedom, in fact, the freedom worth fighting for, is secured by abolition of these oppressive measures, tyrannical laws and modes of government. It is liberation, emancipation; the possession and active manifestation of *rights,* the right to self-determination in action. To many minds, the emphasis which has been put upon the formation of choice in connection with freedom will appear an evasion, a trifling with metaphysical futilities, in comparison with this form of freedom, a desire for which has caused revolutions, overthrown dynasties, and which as it is attained supplies the measure of human progress in freedom.

Before, however, we examine further into this notion in its relation to the idea of choice already set forth, it will be well to consider another factor which blended with the political *motif* just mentioned in forming the classic philosophy of Liberalism. This other factor is the economic. Even in Locke the development of property, industry and trade played a large part in creating the sense that existing institutions were oppressive, and that they should be altered to give men power to express their choices in action. About a century after Locke wrote this implicit factor became explicit and dominant. In the later eighteenth century, attention shifted from power to execute choice to power to carry *wants* into effect, by means of free—that is, unimpeded—labor and exchange. The test of free institutions was the relation they bore to the unobstructed play of wants in industry and commerce and to the enjoyment of the fruits of labor. This notion blended with the earlier political idea to form the philosophy of Liberalism so influential in a large part of the nineteenth century. It led to the notion that all positive action of government is oppressive; that its maxim should be Hands Off; and that its action should be limited as far as possible to securing the freedom of behavior of one individual against interference proceeding from the exercise of similar freedom on the part of others; the theory of *laissez-faire* and the limitation of government to legal and police functions.

In the popular mind, the same idea has grown up in a non-economic form, and with the substitution of instincts or impulses for wants. This phase has the same psychological roots as the economic philosophy of freedom, and is a large part of the popular philosophy of "self-expression." In view of this community of intellectual basis and origin, there is irony in the fact that the most ardent adherents of the idea of "self-expression" as freedom in personal and domestic relations are quite often equally ardent opponents of the idea of a like freedom in the region of industry and commerce. In the latter realm, they are quite aware of the extent in which the "self-expression" of a few may impede, although manifested in strict accordance with law, the self-expression of others. The popular idea of personal freedom as consisting in "free" expression of impulses and desire—free in the sense of unrestricted by law, custom and the inhibitions of social disapprovals—suggests the fallacy inhering in the wider economic concept, suggests it in a more direct way than can readily be derived from the more technical economic concept.

Instincts and impulses, however they may be defined, are part of the "natural" constitution of man; a statement in which "natural" signifies "native," original. The theory assigns a certain intrinsic rightness in this original structure, rightness in the sense of conferring upon impulses a title to pass into direct action, except when they directly and evidently interfere with similar self-manifestation in others. The idea thus overlooks the part played by interaction with the surrounding medium, especially the social, in generating impulses and desires. These are supposed to inhere in the "nature" of the individual when that is taken in a primal state, uninfluenced by interaction with an environment. The latter is thus thought of as purely external to an individual, and as irrelevant to freedom except when it interferes with the operation of native instincts and impulses. A study of history would reveal that this notion, like its theoretically formulated congeners in economic and political Liberalism, is a "faint rumor" left on the air of morals and politics by disappearing theological dogmas, which held that "nature" is thoroughly good as it comes from the creative hand of God, and that evil is due to corruption through the artificial interference and oppression exercised by external or "social" conditions.

The point of this statement is that it suggests the essential fallacy in the elaborate political and economic theories of freedom entertained by classic Liberalism. They thought of individuals as endowed with an equipment of fixed and ready-made capacities, the operation of which if unobstructed by external restrictions would be freedom, and a freedom which would almost automatically solve political and economic problems. The difference between the theories is that one thought in terms of natural rights and the other in terms of natural wants as original and fixed. The difference is important with respect to special issues, but it is negligible with respect to the common premise as to the nature of freedom.

The Liberalistic movement in each of its phases accomplished much practically. Each was influential in supplying inspiration and direction to reforming endeavors that modified institutions, laws and arrangements that *had* become oppressive. They effected a great and needed work of liberation. What were taken to be "natural" political rights and "natural" demands of human beings (natural being defined as inherent in an original and native fixed structure, moral or psychological) marked in fact the sense of new potentialities that were possessed only by limited classes because of changes in social life due to a number of causes. On the political side, there was the limited class that found its activities restricted by survivals of feudal institutions; on the economic side, there was the rise of a manufacturing and trading class that found its activities impeded and thwarted by the fact that these same institutions worked to protect property-interests connected with land at the expense of property-interests growing out of business and commerce. Since the members of the two classes were largely identical, and since they represented the new moving forces, while their opponents represented interests vested and instituted in a past that knew nothing of these forces, political and economic liberalism fused as time went on, and in their fusion performed a necessary work of emancipation.

But the course of historic events has sufficiently proved that they emancipated the *classes* whose special interests they represented, rather than human beings impartially. In fact, as the newly emancipated forces gained momentum, they actually imposed new burdens and subjected to new modes of oppression the mass of individuals who did not have a privileged economic status. It is impossible to justify this statement by an adequate assemblage of evidence. Fortunately it is not necessary to attempt the citation of relevant facts. Practically, every one admits that there is a new social problem, one that everywhere affects the issues of politics and laws; and that this problem, whether we call it the relation of capital to labor, or individualism versus socialism, or the emancipation of wage-earners, has an economic basis. The facts here are sufficient evidence that the ideals and hopes of the earlier liberal school have been frustrated by events; the universal emancipation and the universal harmony of interests they assumed are flagrantly contradicted by the course of events. The common criticism is that the liberal school was too "individualistic"; it would be equally pertinent to say that it was not "individualistic" enough. Its philosophy was such that it assisted the emancipation of individuals having a privileged antecedent status, but promoted no general liberation of all individuals.

The real objection to classic Liberalism does not then hinge upon concepts of "individual" and "society."

The real fallacy lies in the notion that individuals have such a native or original endowment of rights, powers and wants that all that is required on the side of institutions and laws is to eliminate the obstructions they offer to the "free" play of the natural equipment of individuals. The removal of obstructions did have a liberating effect upon such individuals as were antecedently possessed of the means, intellectual and economic, to take advantage of the changed social conditions. But it left all others at the mercy of the new social conditions brought about by the freed powers of those advantageously situated. The notion that men are equally free to act if only the same legal arrangements apply equally to all— irrespective of differences in education, in command of capital, and the control of the social environment which is furnished by the institution of property—is a pure absurdity, as facts have demonstrated. Since actual, that is, effective, rights and demands are products of interactions, and are not found in the original and isolated constitution of human nature, whether moral or psychological, mere elimination of obstructions is not enough. The latter merely liberates force and ability as that happens to be distributed by past accidents of history. This "free" action operates disastrously as far as the many are concerned. The only possible conclusion, both intellectually and practically, is that the attainment of freedom conceived as power to act in accord with choice depends upon positive and constructive changes in social arrangements.

We now have two seemingly independent philosophies, one finding freedom in choice itself, and the other in power to *act* in accord with choice. Before we inquire whether the two philosophies must be left in a position of mutual independence, or whether they link together in a single conception, it will be well to consider another track followed by another school of thinkers, who also in effect identify freedom with operative power in action. This other school had a clear consciousness of the dependence of this power to act upon social conditions, and attempted to avoid and correct the mistakes of the philosophy of classic Liberalism. It substituted a philosophy of institutions for a philosophy of an original moral or psychological structure of individuals. This course was first charted by Spinoza, the great thinker of the seventeenth century. Although the philosophy of Liberalism had not as yet taken form, his ideas afford in anticipation an extraordinarily effective means of criticizing it. To Spinoza freedom was power. The "natural" rights of an individual consist simply in freedom to do whatever he *can* do—an idea probably suggested by Hobbes. But what *can* he do? The answer to that question is evidently a matter of the amount of the power he actually possesses. The whole discussion turns on this point. The answer in effect is that man in his original estate possesses a very limited amount of power. Men as "natural," that is, as native beings are but parts, almost infinitesimally small fractions, of the whole of Nature to which they belong. In Spinoza's phraseology, they are "modes" not substances. As merely a part, the action of any part is limited on every hand by the action and counteraction of other parts. Even if there is power to initiate an act—a power inhering in any natural thing, inanimate as well as human—there is no power to carry it through; an action is immediately caught in an infinite and intricate net-work of *inter*actions. If a man acts upon his private impulse, appetite or want and upon his private judgment about the aims and measures of conduct, he is just as much a subjected part of an infinitely complex whole as is a stock or stone. What he actually does is conditioned by equally blind and partial action of other parts of nature. Slavery, weakness, dependence, is the outcome, not freedom, power and independence.

There is no freedom to be reached by this road. Man has however intellect, capacity of thought. He is a mode not only of physical existence but of mind. Man is free only as he has power, and he can possess power only as he acts in accord with the whole, being reinforced by its structure and momentum. But in being a mode of mind he has a capacity for understanding the order of the whole to which he belongs, so that through development and use of intellect he may become cognizant of the order and laws of the whole, and in so far align his action with it. In so far he shares the power of the whole and is free. Certain definite political implications follow from this identification of freedom with reason in operation. No individual can overcome his tendencies to act as a mere part in isolation. Theoretic insight into the constitution of the whole is neither complete nor firm; it gives way under the pressure of immediate circumstances. Nothing is of as much importance to a reasonable creature in sustaining effectively his actual—or forceful—reasonableness as another reasonable being. We are bound together as parts of a whole, and only as others are free, through enlightenment as to the nature of the whole and its included parts, can any one be free. Law, government, institutions, all social arrangements must be informed with a rationality that corresponds to the order of the whole, which is true Nature or God, to the end that power of unimpeded action can be found anywhere. It would be difficult to imagine a more complete challenge to the philosophy of Locke and the Liberalistic school. Not power but impotency, not independence but dependence, not freedom but subjection, is the natural estate of man—in the sense in which this school conceived "the natural." Law, however imperfect and poor, is at least a recognition of the universal, of the interconnection of parts, and hence operates as a schoolmaster to bring men to reason, power and freedom. The worst government is better than none, for some recognition of law, of universal relationship, is an absolute prerequisite. Freedom is not obtained by mere abolition of law and institutions, but by the progressive saturation of all laws and institutions with greater and greater acknowledgment of the necessary laws governing the constitution of things.

It can hardly be said that Spinoza's philosophy either in its general form or in its social aspect had any immediate effect—unless it was to render Spinoza a figure of objurgation. But some two centuries later a phase of reaction against the philosophy of Liberalism and all the ideas and practices associated with it arose in Germany; and Spinoza's ideas were incorporated in deed in a new metaphysical scheme and took on new life and significance. This movement may be called institutional idealism, Hegel being selected as its representative. Hegel substituted a single substance, called Spirit, for the two-faced substance of Spinoza, and restated the order and law of the whole in terms of an evolutionary or unfolding development instead of in terms of relations conceived upon a geometrical pattern. This development is intrinsically timeless or logical, after the manner of dialectic as conceived by Hegel. But externally this inner logical development of a whole is manifested serially or temporally in history. Absolute spirit embodies itself, by a series of piecemeal steps, in law and institutions; they are objective reason, and an individual becomes rational and free by virtue of participation in the life of these institutions, since in that participation he absorbs their spirit and meaning. The institutions of property, criminal and civil law, the family and above all the national state are the instrumentalities of rationality in outward action and hence of freedom. History is the record of the development of freedom through development of institutions. The philosophy of history is the understanding of this record in terms of the progressive manifestation of the objective form of absolute mind. Here we have instead of an anticipatory criticism and challenge of the classic liberal notion of freedom, a deliberate reflective and reactionary one. Freedom is a growth, an attainment, not an original possession, and it is attained by idealization of institutions and law and the active participation of individuals in their loyal maintenance, not by their abolition or reduction in the interests of personal judgments and wants.

We now face what is admittedly the crucial difficulty in framing a philosophy of freedom: What is the connection or lack of connection between freedom defined in terms of choice and freedom defined in terms of power in action? Do the two ways of conceiving freedom have anything but the name in common? The difficulty is the greater because we have so little material to guide us in dealing with it. Each type of philosophy has been upon the whole developed with little consideration of the point of view of the other. Yet it would seem that there must be some connection. Choice would hardly be significant if it did not take effect in outward action, and if it did not, when expressed in deeds, make a difference in things. Action as power would hardly be prized if it were power like that of an avalanche or an earthquake. The power, the ability to command issues and consequences, that forms freedom must, it should seem, have some connection with that something in personality that is expressed in choice. At all events, the essential problem of freedom, it seems to me, is the problem of the relation of choice and unimpeded effective action to each other.

I shall first give the solution to this problem that commends itself to me, and then trust to the further discussion not indeed to prove it but to indicate the reasons for holding it. There is an intrinsic connection between choice as freedom and power of action as freedom. A choice which intelligently manifests individuality enlarges the range of action, and this enlargement in turn confers upon our desires greater insight and foresight, and makes choice more intelligent. There is a circle, but an enlarging circle, or, if you please, a widening spiral. This statement is of course only a formula. We may perhaps supply it with meaning by first considering the matter negatively. Take for example an act following from a blind preference, from an impulse not reflected upon. It will be a matter of luck if the resulting action does not get the one who acts into conflict with surrounding conditions. Conditions go against the realization of his preference; they cut across it, obstruct it, deflect its course, get him into new and perhaps more serious entanglements. Luck may be on his side. Circumstances may happen to be propitious or he may be endowed with native force that enables him to brush aside obstructions and sweep away resistances. He thus gets a certain freedom, judged from the side of power-to-do. But this result is a matter of favor, of grace, of luck; it is not due to anything in himself. Sooner or later he is likely to find his deeds at odds with conditions; an accidental success may only reinforce a foolhardy impulsiveness that renders a man's future subjection the more probable. Enduringly lucky persons are exceptions.

Suppose, on the other hand, our hero's act exhibits a choice expressing a preference formed after consideration of consequences, an intelligent preference. Consequences depend upon an interaction of what he starts to perform with his environment, so he must take the latter into account. No one can foresee all consequences because no one can be aware of all the conditions that enter into their production. Every person builds better or worse than he knows. Good fortune or the favorable co-operation of environment is still necessary. Even with his best thought, a man's proposed course of action may be defeated. But in as far as his act is truly a manifestation of intelligent choice, he learns something: as in a scientific experiment an inquirer may learn through his experimentation, his intelligently directed action, quite as much or even more from a failure than from a success. He finds out at least a little as to what was the matter with his prior choice. He can choose better and *do* better next time; "better choice" meaning a more reflective one, and "better doing" meaning one better co-ordinated with the conditions that are involved in realizing purpose. Such control or power is never complete; luck or fortune, the propitious support of circumstances not foreseeable is always involved. But at least such a person forms the habit of choosing and acting with conscious regard to the grain of circumstance, the run of affairs. And what is more to the point, such a man becomes able to turn frustration and failure to account in his further choices and purposes. Everything in so far serves his purpose—to be an intelligent human being. This gain in power or freedom can be nullified by no amount of external defeats.

In a phrase just used, it was implied that intelligent choice may operate on different levels or in different areas. A man may, so to speak, specialize in intelligent choices in the region of economic or political affairs; he may be shrewd, politic, within the limit of these conditions, and in so far attain power in action or be free. Moralists have always held that such success is not success, such power not power, such freedom not freedom, in the ultimate sense.

One does not need to enter upon hortatory moralization in order to employ this contention of the great moral teachers for the sake of eliciting two points. The first is that there are various areas of freedom, because there is a plural diversity of conditions in our environment; and choice, intelligent choice, may select the special area formed by one special set of conditions—familial and domestic, industrial, pecuniary, political, charitable, scientific, ecclesiastic, artistic, etc. I do not mean, of course, that these areas are sharply delimited or that there is not something artificial in their segregation. But within limits, conditions are such that specialized types of choice and kinds of power or freedom develop. The second (and this is the one emphasized by moral teachers in drawing a line between true and false power and freedom), is that there *may* be—these moral idealists insist there *is*—one area in which freedom and power are always attainable by any one, no matter how much he may be blocked in other fields. This of course is the area they call *moral* in a distinctive sense. To put it roughly but more concretely: Any one can be kind, helpful to others, just and temperate in his choices, and in so far be sure of achievement and power in action. It would take more rashness than I possess to assert that there is not an observation of reality in this insight of the great teachers of the race. But without taking up that point, one may venture with confidence upon a hypothetical statement. If and in as far as this idea is correct, there is one way in which the force of fortunate circumstance and lucky original endowment is reduced in comparison with the force of the factor supplied by personal individuality itself. Success, power, freedom in *special* fields is in a maximum degree relatively at the mercy of external conditions. But against kindness and justice there is no law: that is, no counteracting grain of things nor run of affairs. With respect to such choices, there may be freedom and power, no matter what the frustrations and failures in other modes of action. Such is the virtual claim of moral prophets.

An illustration drawn from the denial of the idea that there is an intimate connection of the two modes of freedom, namely, intelligent choice and power in action, may aid in clearing up the idea. The attitude and acts of other persons is of course one of the most important parts of the conditions involved in bringing the manifestation of preference to impotency or to power in action. Take the case of a child in a family where the environment formed by others is such as to humor all his choices. It is made easy for him to do what he pleases. He meets a minimum of resistance; upon the whole others co-operate with him in bringing his preferences to fulfilment. Within this region he seems to have free power of action. By description he is unimpeded, even aided. But it is obvious that as far as he is concerned, this is a matter of luck. He is "free" merely because his surrounding conditions happen to be of the kind they are, a mere happening or accident as far as his make-up and his preferences are concerned. It is evident in such a case that there is *no growth* in the intelligent exercise of preferences. There is rather a conversion of blind impulse into regular habits. Hence his attained freedom is such only in appearance: it disappears as he moves into other social conditions.

Now consider the opposite case. A child is balked, inhibited, interfered with and nagged pretty continuously in the manifestation of his spontaneous preferences. He is constantly "disciplined" by circumstances adverse to his preferences—as discipline is not infrequently conceived. Does it follow then that he develops in "inner" freedom, in thoughtful preference and purpose? The question answers itself. Rather is some pathological condition the outcome. "Discipline" is indeed necessary as a preliminary to any freedom that is more than unrestrained outward power. But our dominant conception of discipline is a travesty; there is only one genuine discipline, namely, that which takes effect in producing habits of observation and judgment that insure intelligent desires. In short, while men do not think about and gain freedom in conduct unless they run during action against conditions that resist their original impulses, the secret of education consists in having that blend of check and favor which influences thought and foresight, and that takes effect in outward action through this modification of disposition and outlook.

I have borrowed the illustration from the life of a child at home or in school, because the problem is familiar and easily recognizable in those settings. But there is no difference when we consider the adult in industrial, political and ecclesiastic life. When social conditions are such as to prepare a prosperous career for a man's spontaneous preferences in advance, when things are made easy by institutions and by habits of admiration and approval, there is precisely the same kind of outward freedom, of relatively unimpeded action, as in the case of the spoiled child. But there is hardly more of freedom on the side of varied and flexible capacity of choice; preferences are restricted to the one line laid down, and in the end the individual becomes the slave of his successes. Others, vastly more in number, are in the state of the "disciplined" child. There is hard sledding for their spontaneous preferences; the grain of the environment, especially of existing economic arrangements, runs against them. But the check, the inhibition, to the immediate operation of their native preferences no more confers on them the quality of intelligent choice than it does with the child who never gets a fair chance to try himself out. There is only a crushing that results in apathy and indifference; a deflection into evasion and deceit; a compensatory over-responsiveness to such occasions as permit untrained preferences to run riot—and all the other consequences which the literature of mental and moral pathology has made familiar.

I hope these illustrations may at least have rendered reasonably clear what is intended by our formula; by the idea that freedom consists in a trend of conduct that causes choices to be more diversified and flexible, more plastic and more cognizant of their own meaning, while it enlarges their range of unimpeded operation. There is an important implication in this idea of freedom. The orthodox theory of freedom of the will and the classic theory of Liberalism both define freedom on the basis of something antecedently given, something already possessed. Unlike in contents as are the imputation of unmotivated liberty of choice and of natural rights and native wants, the two ideas have an important element in common. They both seek for freedom in something already there, given in advance. Our idea compels us on the other hand to seek for freedom in something which comes to be, in a certain kind of growth; in consequences, rather than in antecedents. We are free not because of what we statically are, but in as far as we are becoming different from what we have been. Reference to another philosophy of freedom, that of Immanuel Kant, who is placed chronologically in the generation preceding that of Hegel and institutional idealism, may aid in developing this idea. If we ignore the cumbrous technicalities of Kant, we may take him as one who was impressed by the rise of natural science and the role played in science by the idea of causation, this being defined as a necessary, universal or invariant connection of phenomena. Kant saw that in all consistency this principle applies to human phenomena as well as to physical; it is a law of all phenomena. Such a chain of linked phenomena left no room for freedom. But Kant believed in duty, and duty postulates freedom. Hence in his moral being, man is not a phenomenon but a member of a realm of noumena to which as things-in-themselves free causality may be ascribed. It is with the problem rather than the solution we are concerned. How one and the same act can be, naturalistically speaking, causally determined while transcendentally speaking it is free from any such determination is so high a mystery that I shall pass it by.

But the *problem* as Kant stated it has the form in which it weighs most heavily on contemporary consciousness. The idea of a reign of law, of the inclusion of all events under law, has become almost omnipresent. No freedom seems to be left save by alleging that man is somehow supra-natural in his make-up—an idea of which Kant's noumenal and transcendental man is hardly more than a translation into a more impressive phraseology.

This way of stating the problem of freedom makes overt, explicit, the assumption that either freedom is something antecedently possessed or else it is nothing at all. The idea is so current that it seems hopeless to question its value. But suppose that the origin of every thought I have had and every word I have uttered is in some sense causally determined, so that if anybody knew enough he could explain the origin of each thought and each word just as the scientific inquirer ideally hopes to explain what happens physically. Suppose also—the argument is hypothetical and so imagination may be permitted to run riot—that my words had the effect of rendering the future choices of some one of my hearers more thoughtful; more cognizant of possible alternatives, and thereby rendering his future choices more varied, flexible and apt. Would the fact of antecedent causality deprive those future preferences of their actual quality? Would it take away their reality and that of their operation in producing their distinctive effects? There is no superstition more benumbing, I think, than the current notion that things are not what they are, and do not do what they are seen to do, because these things have themselves come into being in a causal way. Water is what it *does* rather than what it is caused by. The same is true of the fact of intelligent choice. A philosophy which looks for freedom in antecedents and one which looks for it in consequences, in a developing course of action, in becoming rather than in static being, will have very different notions about it.

Yet we cannot separate power to become from consideration of what already and antecedently is. Capacity to become different, even though we define freedom by it, must be a present capacity, something in some sense present. At this point of the inquiry, the fact that all existences whatever possess selectivity in action recurs with new import. It may sound absurd to speak of electrons and atoms exhibiting preference, still more perhaps to attribute bias to them. But the absurdity is wholly a matter of the words used. The essential point is that they have a certain opaque and irreducible individuality which shows itself in what they do; in the fact that they behave in certain ways and not in others. In the description of causal sequences, we still have to start with and from existences, things that are individually and uniquely just what they are. The fact that we can state changes which occur by certain uniformities and regularities does not eliminate this original element of individuality, of preference and bias. On the contrary, the statement of laws presupposes just this capacity. We cannot escape this fact by an attempt to treat each thing as an effect of other things. That merely pushes individuality back into those other things. Since we have to admit individuality no matter how far we carry the chase, we might as well forego the labor and start with the unescapable fact.

In short, anything that is has something unique in itself, and this unique something enters into what it does. Science does not concern itself with the individualities of things. It is concerned with their *relations*. A law or statement of uniformity like that of the so-called causal sequence tells us nothing about a thing inherently; it tells us only about an invariant relation sustained in behavior of that thing with that of other things. That this fact implies contingency as an ultimate and irreducible trait of existence is something too complicated to go into here. But evidence could be stated from many contemporary philosophers of science, not writing with any thought of freedom in mind, but simply as interpreters of the methods and conclusions of science, to the effect that the laws leave out of account the inner being of things, and deal only with their relations with other things. Indeed, if this were the place and if I only knew enough, it could be shown, I think, that the great change now going on in the physical sciences, is connected with this idea. Older formulas were in effect guilty of confusion. They took knowledge of the relations that things bear to one another as if it were knowledge of the things themselves. Many of the corrections that are now being introduced into physical theories are due to recognition of this confusion.

The point needs an elaboration that cannot here be given if its full import for the idea and fact of freedom is to be clearly perceived. But the connection is there and its general nature may be seen. The fact that all things show bias, preference or selectivity of reaction, while not itself freedom, is an indispensable condition of any human freedom. The present tendency among scientific men is to think of laws as statistical in nature—that is, as statements of an "average" found in the behavior of an enormous number of things, no two of which are exactly alike. If this line of thought be followed out, it implies that the existence of laws or uniformities and regularities among natural phenomena, human acts included, does not in the least exclude the item of choice as a distinctive fact having its own distinctive consequences. No law does away with individuality of existence, having its own particular way of operating; for a law is concerned with relations and hence presupposes the being and operation of individuals. If choice is found to be a distinctive act, having distinctive consequences, then no appeal to the authority of scientific law can militate in any way against its reality. The problem reduces itself to one of fact. Just what *is* intelligent choice and just what does it effect in human life? I cannot ask you to re-traverse the ground already gone over. But I do claim that the considerations already adduced reveal that what men actually cherish under the name of freedom is that power of varied and flexible growth, of change of disposition and character, that springs from intelligent choice, so there is a sound basis for the common-sense practical belief in freedom, although theories in justification of this belief have often taken an erroneous and even absurd form.

We may indeed go further than we have gone. Not only is the presence of uniform relations of change no bar to the reality of freedom, but these are, *when known,* aids to the development of that freedom. Take the suppositions case already mentioned. That my ideas have causes signifies that their *rise,* their *origin* (not their nature), is a change connected with other changes. If I only knew the connection, my power over obtaining the ideas I want would be that much increased. The same thing holds good of any effect my idea may have upon the ideas and choices of some one else. Knowledge of the conditions under which a choice *arises* is the same as potential ability to guide the formation of choices intelligently. This does not eliminate the distinctive quality of choice; choice is still choice. But it is now an intelligent choice instead of a dumb and stupid one, and thereby the probability of its leading to freedom in unimpeded action is increased.

This fact explains the strategic position occupied in our social and political life by the issue of freedom of thought and freedom of speech. It is unnecessary to dwell by way of either laudation or exhortation upon the importance of this freedom. If the position already taken—namely, that freedom resides in the development of preferences into intelligent choices—is sound, there is an explanation of the central character of this particular sort of freedom. It has been assumed, in accord with the whole theory of Liberalism, that all that is necessary to secure freedom of thought and expression is removal of external impediments: take away artificial obstructions and thought will operate. This notion involves all the errors of individualistic psychology. Thought is taken to be a native capacity or faculty; all it needs to operate is an outer chance. Thinking, however, is the most difficult occupation in which man engages. If the other arts have to be acquired through ordered apprenticeship, the power to think requires even more conscious and consecutive attention. No more than any other art is it developed internally. It requires favorable objective conditions, just as the art of painting requires paint, brushes and canvas. The most important problem in freedom of thinking is whether social conditions obstruct the development of judgment and insight or effectively promote it. We take for granted the necessity of special opportunity and prolonged education to secure ability to think in a special calling, like mathematics. But we appear to assume that ability to think effectively in social, political and moral matters is a gift of God, and that the gift operates by a kind of spontaneous combustion. Few would perhaps defend this doctrine thus boldly stated; but upon the whole we act as if that were true. Even our deliberate education, our schools, are conducted so as to indoctrinate certain beliefs rather than to promote habits of thought. If that is true of them, what is not true of the other social institutions as to their effect upon thought?

This state of things accounts, to my mind, for the current indifference to what is the very heart of actual freedom: freedom of thought. It is considered to be enough to have certain legal guarantees of its possibility. Encroachment upon even the nominal legal guarantees appears to arouse less and less resentment. Indeed, since the mere absence of legal restrictions may take effect only in stimulating the expression of half-baked and foolish ideas, and since the effect of their expression may be idle or harmful, popular sentiment seems to be growing less and less adverse to the exercise of even overt censorships. A genuine energetic interest in the cause of human freedom will manifest itself in a jealous and unremitting care for the influence of social institutions upon the attitudes of curiosity, inquiry, weighing and testing of evidence. I shall begin to believe that we care more for freedom than we do for imposing our own beliefs upon others in order to subject them to our will, when I see that the main purpose of our schools and other institutions is to develop powers of unremitting and discriminating observation and judgment.

The other point is similar. It has often been assumed that freedom of speech, oral and written, is independent of freedom of thought, and that you cannot take the latter away in any case, since it goes on inside of minds where it cannot be got at. No idea could be more mistaken. Expression of ideas in communication is one of the indispensable conditions of the awakening of thought not only in others, but in ourselves. If ideas when aroused cannot be communicated they either fade away or become warped and morbid. The open air of public discussion and communication is an indispensable condition of the birth of ideas and knowledge and of other growth into health and vigor.

I sum up by saying that the possibility of freedom is deeply grounded in our very beings. It is one with our individuality, our being uniquely what we are and not imitators and parasites of others. But like all other possibilities, this possibility has to be actualized; and, like all others, it can only be actualized through interaction with objective conditions. The question of political and economic freedom is not an addendum or afterthought, much less a deviation or excrescence, in the problem of personal freedom. For the conditions that form political and economic liberty are required in order to realize the potentiality of freedom each of us carries with him in his very structure. Constant and uniform relations in change and a knowledge of them in "laws," are not a hindrance to freedom, but a necessary factor in coming to be effectively that which we have the capacity to grow into. Social conditions interact with the preferences of an individual (that *are* his individuality) in a way favorable to actualizing freedom only when they develop intelligence, not abstract knowledge and abstract thought, but power of vision and reflection. For these take effect in making preference, desire and purpose more flexible, alert, and resolute. Freedom has too long been thought of as an indeterminate power operating in a closed and ended world. In its reality, freedom is a resolute will operating in a world in some respects indeterminate, because open and moving toward a new future.

Body and Mind

THERE was a time when philosophy, science and the arts, medicine included, were much closer together than they have been since. For both philosophy and the sciences were conceived and begotten of the arts. It was once their aspiration to find their issue in arts; the sciences in arts of the special branches of life and philosophy in the comprehensive art of the wise conduct of life as a whole.

There is a contemporary philosophic movement, popularly known as pragmatism, which, discontented with the current separation of theory and practice, knowledge and action, regards thought and the beliefs which proceed from it as themselves modes of action and strives to envisage them in their directive office in conduct. This movement is often regarded as a heresy, indeed as a novel and peculiarly American heresy indicative of an insensate love of keeping busy, no matter how. But in truth it marks a return to the idea of philosophy which prevailed when reflective thought was young and lusty, eager to engage in combat in the public arena, instead of living a sheltered and protected life. In those days science and philosophy had not parted ways because neither of them was cut loose from the arts. One word designated both science and art: technē. The desire was to command practices that were rational and a reason embodied in practice. During the almost countless ages of prior human history men had pursued the arts thoughtlessly, relying upon the bare accumulation of accidental successes, without paying heed to causes and reasons. In consequence, the arts were routines, devoted to separate ends and meeting only in a common medium of magic and supernatural belief.

The Greeks define an epoch in the history of civilization

[299]

because they turned back to examine these routines and accidents, and made it their business to discover the principles which underlay them in order that they might reincarnate them in a more intelligent pursuit of ends. In liberating the arts from routine and blind accumulation, they gave birth to science; in view of this achievement there arose the idea of an art of life based upon the most comprehensive insight into the relationships between conditions and ends. Medicine was one of the first-fruits of the scientific emancipation, and, since the Greeks recognized the necessity of a sound mind in a sound body for the conduct of life in its wholesomeness, medicine and philosophy were in close alliance.

The relevant facts are exhibited in the history of the school of Hippocrates. Philosophy appears in it as search for a whole which shall bind together a mass of otherwise disconnected details; while the spirit of science was operative in a loving, patient and prolonged search for facts and their significance, and the medical art was the use of the knowledge and insight thus attained. The union of these three things is seen in the school's glorification of technē; in its criticism of other schools of physicians for studying symptoms in isolation and multiplying diseases and remedies; in its emphasis upon prognosis by which was meant not just a prediction of outcome but a reconstruction of the entire course of a disease; in study of health and disease in relation to environment, climate, seasons and seasonal variations, air, water and soil, while the oath of Hippocrates endures as evidence that human and social ties were included in the wide and searching vision. What at first sight may seem to be an attack upon mingling philosophy and medicine turns out upon closer inspection to be an attack upon basing medicine upon a narrow philosophical foundation. For the school, borrowing from Heracleitus, Empedocles and Pythagoras, insisted upon the measured harmony of all elements as the conditions of maintaining

and restoring health. As Hippocrates said: "We cannot understand the body without a knowledge of the whole of things."
And again, speaking of epilepsy and other disorders regarded
as sacred and hence treated by means of magical incantations,
he said: "These maladies, like all other things, are divine,
and yet no one thing is any more divine than another. For all
things alike are divine and yet each one of them has its own
natural being and proceeds from a natural cause."

We may indeed now smile at the crudeness of their philosophy and science and in view of this crudeness be led to
deplore the connection of philosophy, science and medical
art. The disparagement of the union may readily become
more pronounced when we consider the later development
of various medical schools, the dogmatic, empirical, method-
istic and pneumatistic, each allied with a particular school
of philosophic thought. But objection is really directed
against the crude state of knowledge and culture at the time,
a state of which both philosophy and medicine were victims.
The philosophic spirit at least kept alive the sense of need
for general principles and aided in preventing relapse into
the earlier crude empiricism.

This introduction is overlong, and may indeed not seem
to be at all an introduction to the special topic of the evening,
the relations of body and mind. But it was in the course of
such reflections that I was led to this topic as a fitting theme.
For the conspicuous trait of the period in which science,
philosophy and the arts were closely connected was the sense
of wholeness, while the very problem of mind and body suggests the disastrous effect of the divisions that have since
grown up. I do not know of anything so disastrously affected
by the tradition of separation and isolation as is this particular
theme of body-mind. In its discussion are reflected the splitting off from each other of religion, morals and science; the
divorce of philosophy from science and of both from the arts

of conduct. The evils which we suffer in education, in religion —for example the fundamentalist attack about the evolution of men rests upon the idea of complete separation of mind and body—in the materialism of business and the aloofness of "intellectuals" from life, the whole separation of knowledge and practice—all testify to the necessity of seeing mind-body as an integral whole.

The division in question is so deep-seated that it has affected even our language. We have no word by which to name mind-body in a unified wholeness of operation. For if we said "human life" few would recognize that it is precisely the unity of mind and body in action to which we were referring. Consequently when we discuss the matter, when we talk of the relations of mind *and* body and endeavor to establish their unity in human conduct, we still speak of body *and* mind and thus unconsciously perpetuate the very division we are striving to deny. I shall make no attempt to consider all the various theories which have developed in discussing their relation: panpsychism, epiphenomenalism, pre-established harmony, interactionism, parallelism, etc. I shall not even try to prove the unity. I shall beg that question and devote the time to stating the nature of the unity and considering some of the causes which work against recognition of it.

I have used, in passing, the phrases "wholeness of operation," "unity in action." What is implied in them gives the key to the discussion. In just the degree in which action, behavior, is made central, the traditional barriers between mind and body break down and dissolve. Were this the fit time and place, it could be shown, I think, that the habit of regarding the mental and physical as separate things has its roots in regarding them as substances or processes instead of as functions and qualities of action. In contrast to such a notion, it is asserted that when we take the standpoint of human action, of life in operation, body presents itself as the

BODY AND MIND

mechanism, the instrumentality of behavior, and mind as its
function, its fruit and consummation. To the interpretation
of this statement our further remarks are given.

When we take the standpoint of action we may still treat
some functions as primarily physical and others as primarily
mental. Thus we think of, say, digestion, reproduction and
locomotion as conspicuously physical, while thinking, desiring, hoping, loving, fearing are distinctively mental. Yet if
we are wise we shall not regard the difference as other than
one of degree and emphasis. If we go beyond this and draw
a sharp line between them, consigning one set to body exclusively and the other to mind exclusively we are at once confronted by undeniable facts. The being who eats and digests
is also the one who at the same time is sorrowing and rejoic-
ing; it is a commonplace that he eats and digests in one way
to one effect when glad, and to another when he is sad. Eating
is also a social act and the emotional temper of the·festal
board enters into the alleged merely physical function of
digestion. Eating of bread and drinking of wine have indeed
become so integrated with the mental attitudes of multitudes
of persons that they have assumed a sacramental spiritual
aspect. There is no need to pursue this line of thought to
other functions which are sometimes termed exclusively physical. The case of taking and assimilating food is typical. It
is an act in which means employed are physical, while the
quality of the act determined by its consequences is also
mental. The trouble is that instead of taking the act in its
entirety we cite the multitude of relevant facts only as evidence of influence of mind on body and of body on mind,
thus starting from and perpetuating the idea of their independence and separation even when dealing with their connection. What the facts testify to is not an influence exercised
across and between two separate things, but to behavior so
integrated that it is artificial to split it up into two things.

[303]

The more human mankind becomes, the more civilized it is, the less is there some behavior which is purely physical and some other purely mental. So true is this statement that we may use the amount of distance which separates them in our society as a test of the lack of human development in that community. There exists in present society, especially in industry, a large amount of activity that is almost exclusively mechanical; it is carried on with a minimum of thought and of accompanying emotion. There is a large amount of activity especially in "intellectual" and "religious" groups in which the physical factor is at a minimum and what little there is, is regretted as a deplorable necessity. But either sort of behavior in the degree of its one-sidedness marks a degradation, an acquired habit whose formation is due to undesirable conditions; each marks an approximation to the pathological, a departure from that wholeness which is health. When behavior is reduced to a purely physical level and a person becomes like a part of the machine he operates, there is proof of social maladjustment. This is reflected into disordered and defective habits of the persons who act on the merely physical plane.

Action does not cease to be abnormal because it is said to be spiritual and concerned with ideal matters too refined to be infected with the gross matter. Nor is it enough that we should recognize the part played by brain and nervous system in making our highly intellectual and "spiritual" activities possible. It is equally important that we realize that the latter are truncated and tend toward abnormality in the degree that they do not eventuate in employing and directing physical instrumentalities to effect material changes. Otherwise that which is called spiritual is in effect but indulgence in idle phantasy.

Thus the question of the integration of mind-body in action is the most practical of all questions we can ask of our civilization. It is not just a speculative question; it is a demand: a demand that the labor of multitudes now too predominantly physical in character be inspirited by purpose and emotion and informed by knowledge and understanding. It is a demand that what now pass for highly intellectual and spiritual functions shall be integrated with the ultimate conditions and means of all achievement, namely the physical, and thereby accomplish something beyond themselves. Until this integration is effected in the only place where it can be carried out, in action itself, we shall continue to live in a society in which a soulless and heartless materialism is compensated for by soulful but futile and unnatural idealism and spiritualism. For materialism is not a theory, but a condition of action; that in which material and mechanical means are severed from the consequences which give them meaning and value. And spiritualistic idealism is not a theory but a state of action; that in which ends are privately enjoyed in isolation from means of execution and consequent public betterment.

In insisting upon the need of viewing action in its integrated wholeness, the need of discriminating between different qualities of behavior due to the mode of integration is emphasized, not slurred. We need to distinguish between action that is routine and action alive with purpose and desire; between that which is cold, and as we significantly say inhuman, and that which is warm and sympathetic; between that which marks a withdrawal from the conditions of the present and a retrogression to split off conditions of the past and that which faces actualities; between that which is expansive and developing because including what is new and varying and that which applies only to the uniform and repetitious; between that which is bestial and that which is godlike in its humanity; between that which is spasmodic and centrifugal, dispersive and dissipating, and that which is centred and consecutive. Until we can make such distinctions and make them in a multitude of shades and degrees, we shall not be able to understand the conduct of individuals, and not understanding, shall not be able to help them in the management of their lives. Because of this lack, education will be a guess in the dark; business a gamble in shifting about and circulating material commodities, and politics an intrigue in manipulation. What most stands in the way of our achieving a working technique for making such discriminations and employing them in the guidance of the actions of those who stand in need of assistance is our habitual splitting up the qualities of action into two disjoined things.

It is necessary, however, to be explicit about what is meant in saying that within the unity of behavior "body" stands for the means and agencies of conduct, and "mind" for its incorporated fruits and consequences. The bodily phase of action may be approached and studied in two ways. We may take it in its connection with processes which are going on outside the body, the processes which it shares with inanimate things. Or we may take it in connection with what it actually does and effects in the distinctively human medium. The first mode of approach views action in all its modes as a variegated complex of physico-chemical interactions. This kind of study is more than legitimate; it is indispensable. If organic changes are regarded as something unique, cut off from and unlike in kind to those occurring in inanimate nature, we cannot understand them, and therefore cannot direct and modify the manner of their taking place. Only when we identify them with events in inanimate nature does our knowledge in physics and chemistry become available for knowing them; only then do the appliances and techniques that we have developed for control of affairs outside the body become adaptable for use in dealing with what goes on within the body. As long as organic processes and changes are connected with any unique, non-physical force or principle, our knowledge of them is rudimentary and accidental. When they are seen to be shared with processes going on in inanimate nature, all that is discovered about the latter becomes an intellectual tool for systematic knowledge of vital process and the apparatus and technics for directing physical nature are capable of utilization in hygienic, medical and surgical treatment of bodily changes.

If this were the whole of the story, bodily action would be wholly assimilated to inorganic action, and the inclusion of the body in behavior that has mental quality would be impossible. The remainder of the story is that chemico-physical processes go on in ways and by interactions which have reference to the needs of the organism as a whole and thus take on psychical quality, and in human beings at least are in such connection with the social environment as confers upon them intellectual quality. Any notion that human action is identical with that of non-living things or with that of the "lower" animals is silly. It is contradicted by the fact that behavior is so *organized* in human beings as to have for its consequence all that we call civilization, culture, law, arts—fine and industrial, language, morals, institutions, science itself. And by its fruits we know it. Organic processes are thus seen to be the constituent means of a behavior which is endued with purpose and meaning, animate with affection, and informed by recollection and foresight. In the end, the bodily is but a name for the fact that wherever we have consequences, no matter how ideal, there are conditions and means. Materialism does not consist in a full and frank recognition of this fact, but in the isolation of means and conditions from what they actually do.

We have spoken so much of action and behavior that it is needful that we should be explicitly aware of what these words signify. In particular it is indispensable to note that when we are dealing with human behavior, the word designates a kind of behavior in which outcomes of the past and outlook on the future are incorporated; with something longitudinal and not something cross-sectionally lateral. We may isolate a particular organic structure or process for study. In as far as we do so, we regard it as similar to arrangements and processes which are shared with inanimate things. But we cannot understand the organism until we have taken its history into account. We have to know whether we are studying an embryonic, an infantile, a mature, or a senescent form. We have to place the particular affair studied in a career of development. In dealing with a special chemical reaction, say that of hydrogen and oxygen in bringing water into existence, we may neglect past history. We select a brief segment for study because we are not concerned with the individuality of the molecules involved; it is enough that what happens is a specimen of something which recurs and is repeated in other situations independently of the individuality of just these molecules. This is precisely the omission we cannot make in studying phenomena of human behavior. A human being carries his past in his habitudes and habituations, and we can rightly observe and understand the latter only as we are aware of the history which is included within them. That the practitioner, physician, psychiatrist and educator, is capable of dealing intelligently with the phenomena which confront him only when he knows something of their life history is a commonplace. And it is not just the life history of the particular symptom of disorder he needs to know, but the life history of the individual in whom it appears. It is equally a commonplace that the need of such knowledge of life history as a whole increases in the degree in which the mental phase of disturbance is prominent.

Such facts point to what is signified when it is said that human behavior is longitudinal, not just cross-sectional. It forms a history, an autobiography, not indeed written but enacted. The import of this fact in relation to the mental phase of action should be evident. When it is neglected, any item of behavior is regarded as an immediate lateral cross-section, and thus becomes purely mechanical, and without intellectual and emotional quality. This is precisely what happens when a reflex or specific reaction to a specific stimulus is treated as the unit of behavior, and all other behavior is treated as a compound of such units. Since the simple reflex is devoid of emotional and intellectual quality, it then logically follows that mind is not a property of any behavior. It is a fiction or a meaningless by-product accompaniment like the beauty of a rainbow with reference to a purely physical account of the refraction of light by vapor. To assert, then, that *conscious* behavior is a fiction is to draw a logical deduction from a premise, not to observe a fact. And since the fact of conscious behavior, of observing, analyzing, noting, reasoning, is involved in the whole undertaking, the absurdity of the conclusion shows the falsity of the premise. We know that the structures involved in reflexes are not as matter of fact primitive and original. The converse is true as both phylogeny and ontogeny prove. The beginning is with action in which the entire organism is involved, and the mechanism of reflexes is evolved as a specialized differentiation within an inclusive whole of behavior. The assumption that the nature of behavior is exemplified in a simple reflex is a typical case of the fallacy of neglecting development, historical career. In consequence an account of the mechanism of a particular account of behavior is converted into an account of behavior in its entirety. Only in this fashion is the role of the mental in action relegated to the realm of fiction.

The criticism may be broadened to take in the whole reduction of mental phenomena to the stimulus-response type, as that reduction obtains in current psychological theory, even among those who do not call themselves behaviorists. There

is no doubt that any item of behavior can be stated in terms
of a response to a stimulus—just as it may be stated in terms
of cause-effect. But as the doctrine is usually employed it
omits to consider the one question which is scientifically and
practically important: namely, how did an object or situation
acquire the capacity to *be* a stimulus? For to be a stimulus in
evoking a response is an additive property of physical things.
The organism is constantly surrounded by indefinitely numerous conditions which affect it. If we regard them all as
stimuli because they enter into casual interaction with the
living creature we say in effect that the whole universe is
stimulus and also response. Such a view clearly makes the
theory worthless for purposes of *analysis*. It is the occurrence
of a particular mode of action we are trying to describe and
account for, an attempt which implies that some special feature of the environment is so weighted as to operate as stimulus. Now what makes some physical thing or trait a stimulus
is the condition of the whole organism at the time, its needs
and the kind of behavior in which it is already engaged. And
both of these things are longitudinal, historical; they include
factors formed in previous life history. Any particular thing
at any particular time is a stimulus, evoking an adaptive
response and use, only in virtue of the enacted biography of
the organism.

There is an attempt to recognize the importance of historical development in some forms of the stimulus-response
theory. Present behavior is traced back to original "bonds"
in the nervous system which are innate, or to behavior in the
form of what are usually called instincts. Thus previous
development is nominally taken into account. But such recognition of life history is nominal rather than real. An earlier
cross-section of behavior is postulated back of which development is not traced. Consequently the position of the lateral
segment in the development of action as a whole is left out.

The theory is only a verbal re-statement of the compounding of reflex units theory; the only difference is that an "instinct" or a performed "bond" of stimulus and reaction, is somewhat more extensive and complex than is a reflex. But since it is not sufficiently complex and extensive to take in the needs, demands and disposition of the organism as a whole, the basic fallacy remains the same.

The reference to stimuli proceeding from the environment brings us in effect to the second way in which the account of behavior is rendered so partial and split off that its mental phase has either to be denied as a fiction or else regarded as mysterious and unnatural. For the stimulus-response theory, as usually held, cuts off the environment from behavior. It treats environment simply as an external occasion from which behavior proceeds. Behavior is thus treated exclusively as going on inside the organism, something which is simply set off or initiated by the environment. In reality, the environment is just as much comprised within behavior as are organic processes. Behavior is not just something which goes on *in* a surrounding medium. If it were, behavior could be studied and described as something which goes on in the organism or which goes forth out of it in total neglect of environment, save the reference to some part of the latter as a touch-and-go stimulus. Behavior in fact is a continuous interaction in which environing as well as organic factors are included. This is true even of the functions we often regard as exclusively physiological. We do not just breathe, we breathe air; we do not just digest, we digest foodstuffs. We do not just move the legs and body; we walk on the ground, and from one place to another, so as to obtain a more favorable environment to be incorporated in subsequent behavior.

To describe the structures and processes of the organism in isolation, in their exclusive reference to organic structures, and then call the result an account of behavior, is to omit the most distinctive character of behavior. Sherrington's classic work *The Integrative Action of the Nervous System* marks an epoch in the development of science. What is it which the action of the nervous system integrates? Simply its own self, turning upon itself as a snake is said to swallow its tail? Clearly not, but the behavior of the entire organism of which it is a part. But when and how is the action of the organism integrated? There can be but one answer. It is integrated in the degree that it utilizes and transforms its environment by means of incorporating some element of the latter within behavior. Utilization here signifies that something in the surroundings is rendered a means in the carrying on of some phase of behavior, as assimilation of food and the breathing of air maintains life-behavior itself. Transformation signifies that some part of surrounding conditions is actually changed so that the environment is modified into a form more favorable than before to the maintenance of life-behavior. To describe the action of a part of the nervous system, or of the entire nervous system, or of the entire organism in isolation from the environment included within behavior is like thinking that we can understand a machine, say a loom, if we omit the material, the yarn, upon which it works and the transformation of the material into cloth wrought in the operation. Since the mental, if it can be found anywhere, must be found in behavior which comprises *objects* of desire, thought and affection, to accept the premise which identifies behavior with the action going on inside the organism is to commit ourselves to denial of mental quality as a dialectical conclusion from a premise. Many persons will remain so assured that mental phenomena are actual facts, that they will then prefer to go on believing in them, and will treat them as proofs of a mysterious substance called mind, soul or consciousness. Thus the one-sidedness of the theory about behavior perpetuates the very tradition which a complete account of behavior would eliminate.

The bearing of the one-sided omission of environment in description of behavior upon the truly mental phase of behavior is most evident when we consider the elimination of the human or social environment. For it is the incorporation of this environment in action which is most intimately and extensively connected with the intellectual and emotional quality of behavior. The question of the role of language and other constructed signs in mind gives a crucial test. I do not question the connection of thinking with speech and other signs. Speech and the use of signs is an affair of behavior. What is questionable is the elimination of relations with other human beings from the account given of language habits and of thinking conceived as "exercised implicitly behind the closed doors of the lips"—in other words as something which goes on subcutaneously, wholly inside the organism. Such a description reduces speech to vocalization or making of sounds, and thinking to a silent exercise of the organs of vocalization and other internal structures. Now the making of sounds is not speech. Sounds issuing from vocalization are speech only when they are used to institute a mode of behavior on the part of another human being which will favorably affect the behavior of the one speaking. Sounds issue from phonograph or radio, sounds which imitate articulate speech. The phonograph does not speak, however. For while the sounds that issue may induce action on the part of others, anticipation of such action does not enter as a factor in its putting forth of sounds. Any modification of the behavior of others which is effected by the sounds emitted by the radio is not incorporated as a factor in *its* behavior. Precisely such inclusion of objective social consequences is what transforms sounds into speech or language, as may be seen from taking any simple case of command, request or advice. Speech is primarily a mode of action by which the behavior of one is so influenced by the expected or hoped for behavior of others as to become an integral part of concerted action.

Thinking as implicit speech is made on the same pattern. It represents the social situation carried over into the habits of the organism. One talks to himself as a way of anticipating objective consequences (that is, consequences into which the environment enters) before they happen, and as a means of eventually securing those which are disliked. This renders behavior intelligent, thoughtful. It is all to the good when "consciousness" is thrown overboard as a substance or separate process designated by a noun: for "ness" indicates that the noun is abstract and results from erecting a quality of action into a thing in itself. But the quality of being conscious remains; the difference between behavior that is aware of what it is about and routine or impulse behavior is as marked a factual difference as we can anywhere discover. To deny the reality of meaning in the sense of something mysterious and unnatural, outside of connection with the range of interactions which form behavior, is to the good. But refusal to admit meaning as a quality of behavior is another matter, and one which confutes itself. For the propounders of the doctrine that meaning is non-existent address words on that subject to others; they expect their language to be understood and not be taken as a nonsensical farrago; they anticipate consequences in the way of modified behavior to result from understanding and their language behavior is modified by this expectation of response. They take it for granted that some behavior has meaning; this cannot be granted without implying that some behavior, their own for example, in the observations and analyses whose conclusion they present, is conscious: that is, is aware of what it is about, of what it is doing and trying to do. The conception of behavior in its integrity, as including a history and environment, is the alternative to a theory which eliminates the mental because it considers only the behavior of the mechanism of action as well as the theory which thinks it ennobles the mental by placing it in an isolated realm.

Thus we are reminded of our beginning, the recall of happier days when the divorce of knowledge and action, theory and practice, had not been decreed, and when the arts as action informed by knowledge were not looked down upon in invidious disparagement with contemplation complete in itself; when knowledge and reason were not so "pure" that they were defiled by entering into the wider connections of an action that accomplishes something because it uses physical means. There are signs that we are perforce, because of the extension of knowledge on one side and the demands of practice on the other, about to attempt a similar achievement on our own account. I close with suggesting the imperative need of such an integration in the art of education, an integration which can become real only as the scientific man, the philosopher, the physician and psychiatrist co-operate.

The art of education is one in which every person is compelled whether he will or not to take an interest, because it so intimately concerns his own conduct. A person may begin with a narrow interest, one that cares only about, say, the education of his own children or of members of his own profession. But he does not go far before he is forced to note that he is building on a sandy foundation because of deficiencies due to earlier education. Professional education has its results limited and twisted because of the general state of education. Surveying that, it appears that its improvement cannot be made secure merely by better training of teachers. Parents, school officials, taxpayers have the last word, and the character of that word is dependent upon their education. They may and do block or deflect the best laid plans. That is the circle in which education moves. Those who received education are those who give it; habits already engendered deeply influence its course. It is as if no one could be educated in the full sense until everyone is developed beyond the reach of prejudice, stupidity and apathy.

There is no possibility of complete escape from this circle. Education returns upon itself in such a multitude of ways as to render out of the question any short cut solution. It is a matter of accelerating momentum in the right direction, and of increasing the effective energy of the factors that make for removing obstacles. Chief among these obstacles are the practices which are associated with the traditional separation of mind and body and the consequent neglect of informed and intelligent action as the aim of all educational development. The division has affected every subject of study, every method of instruction and discipline. More than anything else it explains the separation of theory and practice, of thought and action. The result is a so-called cultural education which tends to be academic and pedantic, in any case aloof from the concerns of life, and an industrial and manual education which at best gives command of tools and means without intelligent grasp of purposes and ends. The consequences of this divided education are writ large in the state of our civilization. The physician meets them in a wide range of induced disorders, to say nothing of waste and incapacitation. The walls which mark the separation are beginning to crack, although they are far from crumbling. From all sides the artificiality of isolation from one another of mind and body are commencing to be seen. There is at least the beginning of co-operation between those who are traditionally occupied with the concerns of mind and those busy with the affairs of the body. The planning of any good school building is an illustrative symbol. Architect, engineer, hygienist, teacher and public official may join forces. But there are still many who should have a say, like the psychologist, who are left out, and such co-operation as there is lacks balance. It would be interesting for example to know what physicians would say of the wisdom of the herding together of thousands of children in our gigantic buildings with the enforced need of dealing with children en masse and the institution of lockstep methods—would say if they were consulted and if they thought their voice would be heeded. The growing interest in pre-school education, nursery schools and parental education, the development of medical inspection, the impact of social hygiene, the institution of school visitors and the use of schools as social centres are other evidences that the isolation of schools from life is beginning to give way because of co-operative action. But not even the most optimistic would hold that we have advanced beyond the outer breastworks. The forces are still powerful that make for centrifugal and divisive education. And the chief of these is, let it be repeated, the separation of mind and body which is incarnated in religion, morals and business as well as in science and philosophy. The full realization of the integration of mind and body in action waits upon the reunion of philosophy and science in art, above all in the supreme art, the art of education.

Science and Society

THE significant outward forms of the civilization of the western world are the product of the machine and its technology. Indirectly, they are the product of the scientific revolution which took place in the seventeenth century. In its effect upon men's external habits, dominant interests, the conditions under which they work and associate, whether in the family, the factory, the state, or internationally, science is by far the most potent social factor in the modern world. It operates, however, through its undesigned effects rather than as a transforming influence of men's thoughts and purposes. This contrast between outer and inner operation is the great contradiction in our lives. Habits of thought and desire remain in substance what they were before the rise of science, while the conditions under which they take effect have been radically altered by science.

When we look at the external social consequences of science, we find it impossible to apprehend the extent or gauge the rapidity of their occurrence. Alfred North Whitehead has recently called attention to the progressive shortening of the time-span of social change. That due to basic conditions seems to be of the order of half a million years; that due to lesser physical conditions, like alterations in climate, to be of the order of five thousand years. Until almost our own day the time-span of sporadic technological changes was of the order of five hundred years; according to him, no great technological changes took place between, say, 100 A.D. and 1400 A.D. With the introduction of steam-power, the fifty years from 1780 to 1830 were marked by more changes than are found in any previous thousand years. The advance of chemical techniques and in use of electricity and radio-energy in the last forty years makes even this last change seem slow and awkward.

Domestic life, political institutions, international relations and personal contacts are shifting with kaleidoscopic rapidity before our eyes. We cannot appreciate and weigh the changes; they occur too swiftly. We do not have time to take them in. No sooner do we begin to understand the meaning of one such change than another comes and displaces the former. Our minds are dulled by the sudden and repeated impacts. Externally, science through its applications is manufacturing the conditions of our institutions at such a speed that we are too bewildered to know what sort of civilization is in process of making.

Because of this confusion, we cannot even draw up a ledger account of social gains and losses due to the operation of science. But at least we know that the earlier optimism which thought that the advance of natural science was to dispel superstition, ignorance, and oppression, by placing reason on the throne, was unjustified. Some superstitions have given way, but the mechanical devices due to science have made it possible to spread new kinds of error and delusion among a larger multitude. The fact is that it is foolish to try to draw up a debit and credit account for science. To do so is to mythologize; it is to personify science and impute to it a will and an energy on its own account. In truth science is strictly impersonal; a method and a body of knowledge. It owes its operation and its consequences to the human beings who use it. It adapts itself passively to the purposes and desires which animate these human beings. It lends itself with equal impartiality to the kindly offices of medicine and hygiene and the destructive deeds of war. It elevates some through opening new horizons; it depresses others by making them slaves of machines operated for the pecuniary gain of owners.

The neutrality of science to the uses made of it renders it silly to talk about its bankruptcy, or to worship it as the usherer in of a new age. In the degree in which we realize this fact, we shall devote our attention to the human purposes and motives which control its application. Science is an instrument, a method, a body of technique. While it is an end for those inquirers who are engaged in its pursuit, in the large human sense it is a means, a tool. For what ends shall it be used? Shall it be used deliberately, systematically, for the promotion of social well-being, or shall it be employed primarily for private aggrandizement, leaving its larger social results to chance? Shall the scientific attitude be used to create new mental and moral attitudes, or shall it continue to be subordinated to service of desires, purposes and institutions which were formed before science came into existence? Can the attitudes which control the use of science be themselves so influenced by scientific technique that they will harmonize with its spirit?

The beginning of wisdom is, I repeat, the realization that science itself is an instrument which is indifferent to the external uses to which it is put. Steam and electricity remain natural forces when they operate through mechanisms; the only problem is the purposes for which men set the mechanisms to work. The essential technique of gunpowder is the same whether it be used to blast rocks from the quarry to build better human habitations, or to hurl death upon men at war with one another. The airplane binds men at a distance in closer bonds of intercourse and understanding, or it rains missiles of death upon hapless populations. We are forced to consider the relation of human ideas and ideals to the social consequences which are produced by science as an instrument.

The problem involved is the greatest which civilization has ever had to face. It is, without exaggeration, the most serious issue of contemporary life. Here is the instrumentality, the most powerful, for good and evil, the world has ever known. What are we going to do with it? Shall we leave our underlying aims unaffected by it, treating it merely as a means by which unco-operative individuals may advance their own fortunes? Shall we try to improve the hearts of men without regard to the new methods which science puts at our disposal? There are those, men in high position in church and state, who urge this course. They trust to a transforming influence of a morals and religion which have not been affected by science to change human desire and purpose, so that they will employ science and machine technology for beneficent social ends. The recent Encyclical of the Pope is a classic document in expression of a point of view which would rely wholly upon inner regeneration to protect society from the injurious uses to which science may be put. Quite apart from any ecclesiastical connection, there are many "intellectuals" who appeal to inner "spiritual" concepts, totally divorced from scientific intelligence, to effect the needed work. But there is another alternative: to take the method of science home into our own controlling attitudes and dispositions, to employ the new techniques as means of directing our thoughts and efforts to a planned control of social forces.

Science and machine technology are young from the standpoint of human history. Though vast in stature, they are infants in age. Three hundred years are but a moment in comparison with thousands of centuries man has lived on the earth. In view of the inertia of institutions and of the mental habits they breed, it is not surprising that the new technique of apparatus and calculation, which is the essence of science, has made so little impression on underlying human attitudes. The momentum of traditions and purposes that preceded its rise took possession of the new instrument and turned it to their ends. Moreover, science had to struggle for existence. It had powerful enemies in church and state. It needed friends and it welcomed alliance with the rising capitalism which it so effectively promoted. If it tended to foster secularism and to create predominantly material interests, it could still be argued that it was in essential harmony with traditional morals and religion. But there were lacking the conditions which are indispensable to the serious application of scientific method in reconstruction of fundamental beliefs and attitudes. In addition, the development of the new science was attended with so many internal difficulties that energy had to go to perfecting the instrument just as an instrument. Because of all these circumstances the fact that science was used in behalf of old interests is nothing to be wondered at.

The conditions have now changed, radically so. The claims of natural science in the physical field are undisputed. Indeed, its prestige is so great that an almost superstitious aura gathers about its name and work. Its progress is no longer dependent upon the adventurous inquiry of a few untrammeled souls. Not only are universities organized to promote scientific research and learning, but one may almost imagine the university laboratories abolished and still feel confident of the continued advance of science. The development of industry has compelled the inclusion of scientific inquiry within the processes of production and distribution. We find in the public prints as many demonstrations of the benefits of science from a business point of view as there are proofs of its harmony with religion.

It is not possible that, under such conditions, the subordination of scientific techniques to purposes and institutions that flourished before its rise can indefinitely continue. In all affairs there comes a time when a cycle of growth reaches maturity. When this stage is reached, the period of protective nursing comes to an end. The problem of securing proper use succeeds to that of securing conditions of growth. Now that science has established itself and has created a new social environment, it has (if I may for the moment personify it) to face the issue of its social responsibilities. Speaking without personification, we who have a powerful and perfected instrument in our hands, one which is determining the quality of social changes, must ask what changes we want to see achieved and what we want to see averted. We must, in short, plan its social effects with the same care with which in the past we have planned its physical operation and consequences. Till now we have employed science absent-mindedly as far as its effects upon human beings are concerned. The present situation with its extraordinary control of natural energies and its totally unplanned and haphazard social economy is a dire demonstration of the folly of continuing this course.

The social effects of the application of science have been accidental, even though they are intrinsic to the private and unorganized motives which we have permitted to control that application. It would be hard to find a better proof that such is the fact than the vogue of the theory that such unregulated use of science is in accord with "natural law," and that all effort at planned control of its social effects is an interference with nature. The use which has been made of a peculiar idea of personal liberty to justify the dominion of accident in social affairs is another convincing proof. The doctrine that the most potent instrument of widespread, enduring, and objective social changes must be left at the mercy of purely private desires for purely personal gain is a doctrine of anarchy. Our present insecurity of life is the fruit of the adoption in practice of this anarchic doctrine.

The technologies of industry have flowed from the intrinsic nature of science. For that is itself essentially a technology of apparatus, materials and numbers. But the pecuniary aims which have decided the social results of the use of these technologies have not flowed from the inherent nature of science. They have been derived from institutions and attendant mental and moral habits which were entrenched before there was any such thing as science and the machine. In consequence, science has operated as a means for extending the influence of the institution of private property and connected legal relations far beyond their former limits. It has operated as a device to carry an enormous load of stocks and bonds and to make the reward of investment in the way of profit and power one out of all proportion to that accruing from actual work and service.

Here lies the heart of our present social problem. Science has hardly been used to modify men's fundamental acts and attitudes in social matters. It has been used to extend enormously the scope and power of interests and values which anteceded its rise. Here is the contradiction in our civilization. The potentiality of science as the most powerful instrument of control which has ever existed puts to mankind its one outstanding present challenge.

There is one field in which science has been somewhat systematically employed as an agent of social control. Condorcet, writing during the French Revolution in the prison from which he went to the guillotine, hailed the invention of the calculus of probabilities as the opening of a new era. He saw in this new mathematical technique the promise of methods of insurance which should distribute evenly and widely the impact of the disasters to which humanity is subject. Insurance against death, fire, hurricanes and so on have in a measure confirmed his prediction. Nevertheless, in large and important social areas, we have only made the merest beginning of the method of insurance against the hazards of life and death. Insurance against the risks of maternity, of sickness, old age, unemployment, is still rudimentary; its idea is fought by all reactionary forces. Witness the obstacles against which social insurance with respect to accidents incurred in industrial employment had to contend. The anarchy called natural law and personal liberty still operates with success against a planned social use of the resources of scientific knowledge.

Yet insurance against perils and hazards is the place where the application of science has gone the furthest, not the least, distance in present society. The fact that motor cars kill and maim more persons yearly than all factories, shops, and farms is a fair symbol of how backward we are in that province where we have done most. Here, however, is one field in which at least the idea of planned use of scientific knowledge for social welfare has received recognition. We no longer regard plagues, famine and disease as visitations of necessary "natural law" or of a power beyond nature. By preventive means of medicine and public hygiene as well as by various remedial measures we have in idea, if not in fact, placed technique in the stead of magic and chance and uncontrollable necessity in this one area of life. And yet, as I have said, here is where the socially planned use of science has made the most, not least, progress. Were it not for the youth of science and the historically demonstrated slowness of all basic mental and moral change, we could hardly find language to express astonishment at the situation in which we have an extensive and precise control of physical energies and conditions, and in which we leave the social consequences of their operation to chance, *laissez-faire,* privileged pecuniary status, and the inertia of tradition and old institutions.

Condorcet thought and worked in the Baconian strain. But the Baconian ideal of the systematic organization of all knowledge, the planned control of discovery and invention, for the relief and advancement of the human estate, remains almost as purely an ideal as when Francis Bacon put it forward centuries ago. And this is true in spite of the fact that the physical and mathematical technique upon which a planned control of social results depends has made in the meantime incalculable progress. The conclusion is inevitable. The outer arena of life has been transformed by science. The effectively working mind and character of man have hardly been touched.

Consider that phase of social action where science might theoretically be supposed to have taken effect most rapidly, namely, education. In dealing with the young, it would seem as if scientific methods might at once take effect in transformation of mental attitudes, without meeting the obstacles which have to be overcome in dealing with adults. In higher education, in universities and technical schools, a great amount of research is done and much scientific knowledge is imparted. But it is a principle of modern psychology that the basic attitudes of mind are formed in the earlier years. And I venture the assertion that for the most part the formation of intellectual habits in elementary education, in the home and school, is hardly affected by scientific method. Even in our so-called progressive schools, science is usually treated as a side line, an ornamental extra, not as the chief means of developing the right mental attitudes. It is treated generally as one more body of ready-made information to be acquired by traditional methods, or else as an occasional diversion. That it is the method of all effective mental approach and attack in all subjects has not gained even a foothold. Yet if scientific method is not something esoteric but is a realization of the most effective operation of intelligence, it should be axiomatic that the development of scientific attitudes of thought, observation, and inquiry is the chief business of study and learning.

Two phases of the contradiction inhering in our civilization may be especially mentioned. We have long been committed in theory and words to the principle of democracy. But criticism of democracy, assertions that it is failing to work and even to exist are everywhere rife. In the last few months we have become accustomed to similar assertions regarding our economic and industrial system. Mr. Ivy Lee, for example, in a recent commencement address, entitled *This Hour of Bewilderment,* quoted from a representative clergyman, a railway president, and a publicist, to the effect that our capitalistic system is on trial. And yet the statements had to do with only one feature of that system: the prevalence of unemployment and attendant insecurity. It is not necessary for me to invade the territory of economics and politics. The essential fact is that if both democracy and capitalism are on trial, it is in reality our collective intelligence which is on trial. We have displayed enough intelligence in the physical field to create the new and powerful instrument of science and technology. We have not as yet had enough intelligence to use this instrument deliberately and systematically to control its social operations and consequences.

The first lesson which the use of scientific method teaches is that control is co-ordinate with knowledge and understanding. Where there is technique there is the possibility of administering forces and conditions in the region where the technique applies. Our lack of control in the sphere of human relations, national, domestic, international, requires no emphasis of notice. It is proof that we have not begun to operate scientifically in such matters. The public press is full of discussion of the five-year plan and the ten-year plan in Russia. But the fact that the plan is being tried by a country which has a dictatorship foreign to all our beliefs tends to divert attention from the fundamental consideration. The point for us is not this political setting nor its communistic context. It is that by the use of all available resources of knowledge and experts an attempt is being made at organized social planning and control. Were we to forget for the moment the special Russian political setting, we should see here an effort to use co-ordinated knowledge and technical skill to direct economic resources toward social order and stability.

To hold that such organized planning is possible only in a communistic society is to surrender the case to communism. Upon any other basis, the effort of Russia is a challenge and a warning to those who live under another political and economic regime. It is a call to use our more advanced knowledge and technology in scientific thinking about our own needs, problems, evils, and possibilities so as to achieve some degree of control of the social consequences which the application of science is, willy-nilly, bringing about. What stands in the way is a lot of outworn traditions, moth-eaten slogans and catchwords, that do substitute duty for thought, as well as our entrenched predatory self-interest. We shall only make a real beginning in intelligent thought when we cease mouthing platitudes; stop confining our idea to antitheses of individualism and socialism, capitalism and communism, and realize that the issue is between chaos and order, chance and control: the haphazard use and the planned use of scientific techniques.

Thus the statement with which we began, namely, that we are living in a world of change extraordinary in range and speed, is only half true. It holds of the outward applications of science. It does not hold of our intellectual and moral attitudes. About physical conditions and energies we think scientifically; at least, some men do, and the results of their thinking enter into the experiences of all of us. But the entrenched and stubborn institutions of the past stand in the way of our thinking scientifically about human relations and social issues. Our mental habits in these respects are dominated by institutions of family, state, church, and business that were formed long before men had an effective technique of inquiry and validation. It is this contradiction from which we suffer to-day.

Disaster follows in its wake. It is impossible to overstate the mental confusion and the practical disorder which are bound to result when external and physical effects are planned and regulated, while the attitudes of mind upon which the direction of external results depends are left to the medley of chance, tradition, and dogma. It is a common saying that our physical science has far outrun our social knowledge; that our physical skill has become exact and comprehensive while our humane arts are vague, opinionated, and narrow. The fundamental trouble, however, is not lack of sufficient information about social facts, but unwillingness to adopt the scientific attitude in what we do know. Men floundered in a morass of opinion about physical matters for thousands of years. It was when they began to use their ideas experimentally and to create a technique or direction of experimentation that physical science advanced with system and surety. No amount of mere fact-finding develops science nor the scientific attitude in either physics or social affairs. Facts merely amassed and piled up are dead; a burden which only adds to confusion. When ideas, hypotheses, begin to play upon facts, when they are methods for experimental use in action, then light dawns; then it becomes possible to discriminate significant from trivial facts, and relations take the place of isolated scraps. Just as soon as we begin to use the knowledge and skills we have to control social consequences in the interest of shared abundant and secured life, we shall cease to complain of the backwardness of our social knowledge. We shall take the road which leads to the assured building up of social science just as men built up physical science when they actively used the techniques of tools and numbers in physical experimentation.

In spite, then, of all the record of the past, the great scientific revolution is still to come. It will ensue when men collectively and co-operatively organize their knowledge for application to achieve and make secure social values; when they systematically use scientific procedures for the control of human relationships and the direction of the social effects of our vast technological machinery. Great as have been the social changes of the last century, they are not to be compared with those which will emerge when our faith in scientific method is made manifest in social works. We are living in a period of depression. The intellectual function of trouble is to lead men to think. The depression is a small price to pay if it induces us to think about the cause of the disorder, confusion, and insecurity which are the outstanding traits of our social life. If we do not go back to their cause, namely our half-way and accidental use of science, mankind will pass through depressions, for they are the graphic record of our unplanned social life. The story of the achievement of science in physical control is evidence of the possibility of control in social affairs. It is our human intelligence and human courage which are on trial; it is incredible that men who have brought the technique of physical discovery, invention, and use to such a pitch of perfection will abdicate in the face of the infinitely more important human problem.

INDEX

[331]

INDEX

INDEX

INDEX

St. German, 166
Saleilles, 151 *n.*
Santayana, G., 32
Savage, 173, 179–80, 182–3, 187
Savigny, 163
Schneider, H. W., 152 *n.*
Scholasticism, 131
Science, 10–12, 44, 53, 82–3, 89, 120, 128, 203–4, 291, 293–4, 299–301, 312, 318–24, 326, 328–30
Self-expression, 278
Sense, 188–93, 196–7, 226, 228–31, 233–9, 241, 243–8, 250–1, 258, 260, 265–6
Sentiment, see *Affectivity*
Shakespeare, Wm., 5, 63
Sherrington, 312
Similarity, 111–2, 115
Simples, 79
Situation, 96–102, 108, 110–11
Social, 77, 79–88, 90–2
Society, 80, 86, 304–5, 325
Sociology, 176
Socrates, 112, 132–3
Soul, 257, 312
Sound, 238–9, 240, 313
Sovereignty, 271
Space, 211
Specific location, 198–200
Speech, 313–4
Spencer, H., 29, 168, 173–4, 182, 184 *n.*, 237 *n.*
Spinoza, B., 282, 284
Spirit, 208, 284
State, 157, 160–3, 164, 285
Stimulus, 177, 213, 220–2, 225, 228, 230–1, 233–4, 236–42, 244–8, 252–6, 309–11
Stream of consciousness, 28
Structuralists, 249
Structure, 250–2
Subject, 30, 105, 107
Subjectivity, 146–7
Sun, 59, 63, 75–6
Supernatural, 85

Suppression, 217–8
Supreme Court, 170
Syllogism, 131–4
Symbols, 102, 104, 268

Taboos, 185
Techne, 299–300
Technology, 82, 321–3, 328
Tertullian, 155 *n.*
Theism, 19, 21
Thinking, 17, 90, 114, 116, 119, 135, 140, 296, 313
Thomas, 180 *n.*, 187 *n.*
Thought, 4, 7, 25, 30–1, 68, 86, 89, 91–5, 97–8, 100–2, 107–8, 111, 117
Time, 212, 232
Totemism, 184
Tradition, 6, 7, 10, 33
Transportation, 138
Tree, 266–7
Truth, 4, 5, 8–9, 17–18, 22–4, 49, 53
Tufts, J. H., 91 *n.*
Tugwell, 82 *n.*

Unconscious, 121
Universal, 133
Universe, 19–21, 25, 31
Universes of discourse, 195–6
Universitas, see *Corporate Body*

Volition, 117–8

Wales, 112, 115 *n.*
Ward, P., 271 *n.*
Watson, Dr. J., 27
Weismann, 237 *n.*
Whitehead, A. N., 149 *n.*, 318
Whole, 92
Will, 82, 145–6, 151–2, 164–5, 272–4, 291
Will to believe, 21–2
Women, 181
Woodworth, 255
Wundt, 257

CAPRICORN TITLES

2. *Rilke,* NOTEBOOKS OF MALTE LAURIDS BRIGGE. $1.25.
A semi-autobiographical memoir by the "greatest German poet since the death of Goethe," the *Notebooks* are also a basic text of the Existentialists and a penetrating study of "the lonely crowd" as seen through a mind and sensibility of extreme sensitivity and maturity.

10. *Hough,* THE DARK SUN: A STUDY OF D. H. LAWRENCE, $1.25.
Mr. Hough, an experienced and able English critic and scholar, makes no attempt to divorce the man from his works, but his first emphasis is on Lawrence's literary production. He analyzes Lawrence's novels, poems, short stories and philosophical writings in detail.

12. *Shaw,* ADVENTURES OF THE BLACK GIRL. $.95.
A gem of satire, this late prose work of Shaw illustrates the philosophical penetration of the mature GBS. A modern *Candide,* an innocent and forthright young girl, wanders out into the world to find the God mentioned in her Bible.

15. *Chekhov,* ST. PETER'S DAY. $1.25.
A volume of wonderful Chekhov stories, none of which have ever appeared before in America in book form. These early short stories of Chekhov are masterpieces of rowdy comedy, and they include perhaps the best comic writing he ever did.

16. *Nashe,* THE UNFORTUNATE TRAVELLER. $1.15.
"The first novel in English" is the claim that has been made for this wonderful book. Published in 1594, it displays Nashe's wild imagination, his madly inventive prose style, and his uncanny ability to create marvelously alive personalities. It is of first importance in the history of the Novel.

17. *Weil,* WAITING FOR GOD. $1.25.
Since her death in 1943, Simone Weil has come to seem more and more a special representative of our time, a person whose predicament many have recognized, in fact, as the central predicament of our "Age of Longing." She speaks of the problems of belief in the vocabulary of the unbeliever, of the doctrines of the church in the words of the unchurched.

18. *Coates,* EATER OF DARKNESS. $1.15.
The first surrealist novel in English, *The Eater of Darkness* is a wildly fantastic multiple-murder story; but it is more than that. It is a strangely moving love story, and a science-fiction story of chilling implication.

22. *Wain,* LIVING IN THE PRESENT. $1.25.
The author proves in this, his second novel, in its first appearance in the United States, that he is one of the funniest writers now practicing. His hero is a would-be murderer who pursues his chosen victim through dozens of hilarious complications, as incompetent to effect a death as he is to cope with life.

23. *diPrima,* VARIOUS FABLES FROM VARIOUS PLACES. $1.15.
Selected fables from all over the world, from the East as well as
the West, from ancient literature as well as modern, including such
little-known tales as the fables of the Russian fabulist Krylov and
those of the Scot Robert Henryson. Here is an unusual and enchant-
ing collection. Profusely illustrated by Bernard Krigstein.

26. *White,* THE BESTIARY. $1.45.
Add T. H. White's superb style to the writings of twelfth-century
scholars bent on cataloguing fabulous beasts, and you have a witty,
erudite, unusual volume of enormous appeal and immediate en-
chantment. *With over 130 beautiful illustrations from the original
manuscript.*

27. *Chesterton,* THE MAN WHO WAS THURSDAY. $1.15.
A wild, mad, hilarious and profoundly moving tale. The reader
will soon discover that it is much more than a magnificent tour-de-
force of suspense-writing. He will soon see that he is being carried
into much deeper waters than he had planned on as the investigators finally discover who Sunday is.

35. *Fowlie,* FOUR MODERN FRENCH COMEDIES. $1.25 (Hard-
cover $2.50).
Four great comic dramas which between them illustrate all of the
most important elements of modern French comedy: *Ubi Roi* by
Alfred Jarry; *The Commissioner* by Georges Courteline; *Professor
Taranne* by Arthur Adamov; and *Clérambard* by Marcel Aymé.

39. *White,* MISTRESS MASHAM'S REPOSE. $1.35.
When this story of the Lilliputians in England first appeared, in
1946, its grave charm and superb style immediately drew thousands
of readers to it, and it rapidly acquired the stature of a classic.

45. *Viereck,* METAPOLITICS. $1.75.
The subject of Metapolitics, that is, the roots of the unprecedented
phenomenon known as Nazism, is probably the most important
topic of the twentieth century. The author has located elements
of the Nazi philosophy in German romantic poetry, music, and
social thought.

50. *Dangerfield,* STRANGE DEATH OF LIBERAL ENGLAND:
1910-1914, $1.75.
The author has woven together the three wild strands of Tory
Rebellion (the rebellion in Ulster), the Suffragette Movement and
the Labour Movement and has produced a great work of social
history.

57. NEWGATE CALENDAR. $1.45.
Profusely illustrated, here is a magnificent collection of some of
the most famous crimes and criminals who ever existed, including
Eugene Aram, Dick Turpin, Jack Sheppard, and Elizabeth Brown-
rigg. This book presents a social picture of the 18th century impossible to get from any other source.

58. *Symonds,* LIFE OF MICHELANGELO. $1.75.
Generally acknowledged as one of the greatest biographies ever
written, Symonds' work is a classic on the subject and on the artistic currents of the Italian Renaissance ever since it was written
more than seventy years ago. Illustrated.

59. *Disraeli,* CONINGSBY. $1.75.
The most subtle, witty and significant novel of the astonishing
Disraeli. It is of extreme importance in the history of the novel,
since it was one of the first novels of politics published in England.

61. *Dewey,* INDIVIDUALISM, OLD AND NEW. $1.25.
The subject of individualism, in our age when the individual seems to be threatened by impersonal governmental and social forces, has suddenly become a vital issue, and Dewey is just the man to read on the subject of individual responsibilities and rights.

63. *Conant,* GERMANY AND FREEDOM. $.95.
James Bryant Conant, former President of Harvard and High Commissioner of Germany after World War II, answers important questions about Germany's recovery from Nazism and the chances of its attaining a responsible status among the nations of the world.

64. *Shepherd,* THE AMERICA OF GEORGE ADE. $1.35.
George Ade, one of the greatest comic writers America has yet produced, actually created modern American humor; he marks the transition from the humor of Artemus Ward and Mark Twain to such modern writers as Ring Lardner, S. J. Perelman, James Thurber and Robert Benchley. He was also, however, a great realistic writer, as the stories in this volume reveal.

65. *Trotsky,* LENIN. $1.25.
Only a small number of men have ever been in a position to write the secret and personal history of the Russian revolutionary movement, and of these Trotsky was one of the few still living when it could be written about.

66. *Golding,* PINCHER MARTIN. $1.25.
PINCHER MARTIN is an elemental adventure story, a tale of frightening suspense. It is also, as all great literature must be, a story of man's ultimate struggle—not so much with fate and death as with himself.

67. *Roosevelt,* THE WINNING OF THE WEST. $1.25.
The chronological narrative of THE WINNING OF THE WEST is here given in all the vigor of the original language of the author.

68. *Dowden,* SHAKESPEARE—HIS MIND AND ART. $1.45.
This is one of the most famous books about Shakespeare ever written, and rightly so. Edward Dowden was one of a number of modern critics of Shakespeare who generated the contemporary critical and scholarly examination of Shakespeare.

69. *Jerome,* ASPECTS OF THE STUDY OF ROMAN HISTORY. $1.45.
Jerome's posthumous study, ASPECTS OF THE STUDY OF ROMAN HISTORY, published nine years after his death, has acquired the status of a classic in the field of Roman historiography.

70. *Lewis & Lee,* THE STUFFED OWL—AN ANTHOLOGY OF BAD VERSE. $1.25.
This is the funniest book ever published. Containing as it does the most hilariously awful poems and sections of poems written since the eighteenth century in American and England, it is practically a history of magnificent pratfalls in the noble art of poesy.

71. *Astrov,* AMERICAN INDIAN PROSE AND POETRY. $1.45.
Margot Astrov's THE WINGED SERPENT was the first anthology of American Indian prose and poetry, and reveals that aboriginal American had a body of primitive literature worthy to rank beside those of other continents and races.

72. *Bynner,* THE WAY OF LIFE ACCORDING TO LAOTZU. $.95.
The Way of Life of Laotzu was the way of poise, serenity, and complete assurance. His gentle warnings on the futility of egoistic struggle have made THE WAY OF LIFE the basis for one of the world's great religions, Taoism, and one of the most important books that was ever written.